BURMA SURGEON RETURNS

Hpongyi Sari Ya, Senior Buddhist Abbot of the Namkham Valley, Welcomes
Dr. Seagrave Home to His Old Hospital

BURMA SURGEON RETURNS

GORDON S. SEAGRAVE, M.D.

AUTHOR OF "BURMA SURGEON"

Maps by

PHOA LIENG SING AND LUCAS MANDITCH

W · W · NORTON & COMPANY · INC ·

NEW YORK

TO

THE MEN AND WOMEN

OF THE

SEAGRAVE HOSPITAL UNIT

1942–1946

BOTH

BURMESE AND AMERICAN

CIVILIAN AND MILITARY

who by their unstinted effort

and

unselfish devotion to duty

were a constant source of inspiration

to their

commanding officer

Contents

Illustrations

Maps

Publisher's Foreword

IN THE remote wilds of Northeast Burma, long before world war threatened, Dr. Gordon Seagrave was carrying on his own war against misery, disease, and death. Born in Rangoon, he was the fourth generation of his family to serve as an American missionary —and the first to be a doctor. To the little village of Namkham he brought his young wife, Tiny, and started his medical mission. His hospital was a little frame building, his equipment a wastebasketful of broken-down surgical instruments salvaged from his training at Johns Hopkins. There were plenty of sick people to treat. Malaria, dysentery, plague, blackwater fever, and all manner of bodily disorders challenged the doctor's knowledge and skill. Patients thronged to the little hospital, and a larger hospital was needed. The Seagraves, assisted by some Chinese coolies and their friends and nurses, built it out of cobblestones with their own hands. Simple native girls were trained to be nurses whose abilities astonished all who came to know them. "Seagrave's Burmese nurses," they were called; they were not Burmese but Karen, Shan, Kachin, and a half dozen other races. Different in their nature, they were alike in their devotion to the doctor they called "Daddy" and to the exacting standards of their work. Their charm and gaiety were in striking contrast to their efficiency in every direction—from giving intravenous injections to driving trucks.

The world and the war came nearer. The Burma Road was built, and Dr. Seagrave set up a chain of field hospital stations to give medical aid to the Chinese during its construction. The Japs were fighting in China, and an airplane factory servicing Chennault's A.V.G. was bombed just across the border from

Namkham. When the storm broke over Burma, Dr. Seagrave was commissioned a major in our medical corps, formed a mobile medical unit, organized an emergency ambulance service, and put field hospitals where they were needed. Through days and nights of Japanese bombing, he and his nurses cared for the wounded amid the flames of burning towns, moving back as the Japanese onslaught grew fiercer. Finally the order came—and the Seagrave Unit joined the retreat with Stilwell of American, British, and Chinese Army men and a polyglot mixture of refugees, out of Burma into India—one of the epic stories of the war. On this grueling march, through jungle and over mountains, the little nurses won the admiration of all for their endurance, their unflagging spirits, and their consideration for the welfare of others.

When the refugees reached India, Dr. Seagrave learned that the Japanese high command was quartered in his hospital at Namkham, and later, that the U.S. Air Force had bombed the buildings that had been his home. It was the end of his dreams and hard work, but he had only one thought. "I told General Stilwell," he writes at the end of *Burma Surgeon*, "that we all hoped when new action developed against the Japs he would save out the meanest, nastiest task of all for us. The general turned on me like a flash with a real sparkle in his eye. 'I can certainly promise you that,' he said."

The story that follows tells how that promise was kept.

PART ONE

RAMGARH TO THE NAGA HILLS

IN SEVEN terrible months from December 7, 1941, to June, 1942, Japan conquered an empire in the Pacific. Her armies overran Malaya, Burma, the Netherlands East Indies, and the Philippines. China was isolated and Australia menaced. Then, in the summer and late fall of 1942, the Japanese advance was halted at Midway, Guadalcanal, Port Moresby, and at the gates of India.

With the main military strength of the United Nations then dedicated to the defeat of Nazi Germany, the American commander in the China-Burma-India theater, General Joseph W. Stilwell, saw only one possibility of effective action against the Japanese. With Chinese troops trained and conditioned in India, he would reconquer a route into northern Burma. American engineers and service troops would build a road through some of the worst terrain in the world from Ledo in Assam to the old Burma Road and Kunming. This would relieve China's isolation and make it possible to supply her with weapons and equipment for the war against Japan.

It took a long time to nurse back into health the disease-ridden remnants of the Chinese armies which had retreated from Burma into India. It took even longer to train the Chinese soldiers who were flown into India over the Hump. Early in 1943 General Stilwell was ready to begin an operation which many observers regarded as impossible.

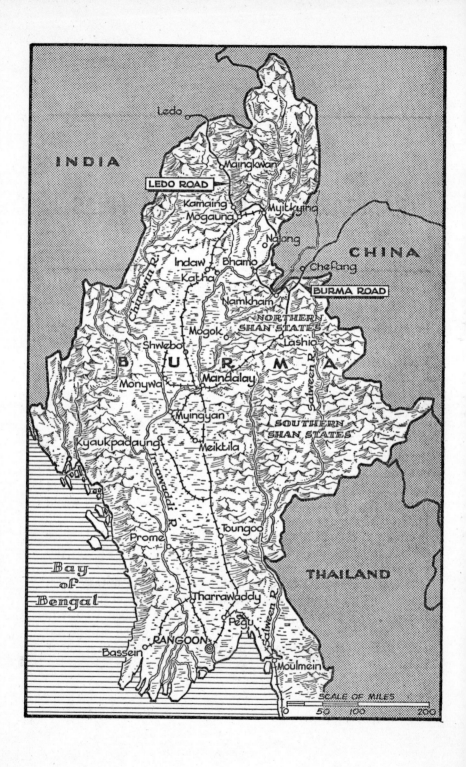

I

The Trail of the Refugees

It was March, 1943, and Burmese refugees were at last on their way back into Burma. At any rate a small group of us were on our way: twelve of the Burmese nurses, Lieutenant Harris of Washington, D.C., and myself. Lieutenant "Bill" Cummings, former charter member of our hospital unit and now on special duty in the wilds of Burma, was our escort.

It had not been easy for us to obtain permission to start back so soon. All of "Uncle Joe" Stilwell's plans for an early return had been given up for lack of support from home. Uncle Joe—"Granddaddy" to our nurses—was XYZ on the priorities list in those days. All the supplies and troops America had were pre-empted for what the world—but not the G.I.'s of China-Burma-India or the Burmese refugees—considered the really important theaters. And that meant every other theater except C.-B.-I. We could get along on a face-saving shoestring to make the Chinese remain in the war until we conquered all enemies but hers. Then we would begin to rescue China in earnest.

General Stilwell couldn't have been very pleased by the meagerness of the resources allotted to him, but distress was never visible in his face or actions. Give him little or give him nothing, he had promised to return the "hell of a licking" the Japs had given him, and he went about his "impossible" task with determination and no complaints. Already his few colored engineers had bulldozed a road from Ledo in Northeast Assam to the Burma border in the Pangsau Pass. Now the road was going down into Burma itself—if you can call the Naga Hills and the Hukawng Valley "Burma." But though the colored boys were working at all hours, with rifles and tommy guns strapped to their backs, Granddaddy knew they would accomplish more if the

Chinese troops he had trained for eight months at Ramgarh were to do their share in opening the Ledo Road to China by throwing a screen in front of the road builders. So the Chinese were on their way and we after them.

It was good luck that had secured the assignment for us. Uncle Joe had been on an inspection trip to Ramgarh where I was post surgeon and asked me, as usual, to tell him what we needed.

"Sir," I said, "since we came to Ramgarh last July we have had no complete set of surgical instruments. The British left in their prisoner of war hospital only a few decrepit instruments, and if Dr. Gurney and I had not brought a lot of our own instruments along with us from Burma we couldn't have done half the surgery the Chinese Army needed. All the new American hospital units that have come to India have had complete sets of surgical instruments allowed in their Table of Basic Allotments in the States. Service of Supply has no bulk stores from which to fill our own requisitions. Now I understand that at Ledo there are large stocks of surgical instruments in China Defense Supplies destined for China. Since our hospital is working for Chinese troops, may I have your permission to go to Ledo and select instruments both for the Ramgarh hospital and for our unit to use when we finally return to Burma?"

"You're not planning a one-man expedition into Burma, are you?" the general asked with a twinkle in his eyes.

"No, sir," I replied with a grin. "I promise not to go beyond the border." Granddaddy was acquainted with my slippery ways.

"My plane starts for Delhi in the morning and then we'll go on to Ledo," the general said. "Be at my headquarters an hour ahead of time."

I was not late for that appointment.

We drove to the airport in Ranchi and took off in "Uncle Joe's Chariot."

One "Cook's Tour" of Delhi is all anyone with a grain of sense ever wants, and I'd had that experience eight years before. So after I got my order from the Theater Medical Supply officer for whatever useful instruments I might find in Ledo, I sat in complete boredom in the hotel.

We had an incredibly beautiful trip straight to Chabua the next day. The atmosphere was delightfully clear and we flew close to the Himalayas all the way. Since it was "winter," the snow on the range was gorgeous. Two brass hats and I had an argument about which of the peaks was Everest. I pointed out Everest's "cocked hat" and beautiful Kinchinjunga as well, but the colonel said, "That isn't Everest. The pilot says we won't see Everest for another hour."

I bit my tongue. Of all lessons I'd learned in the army, the chief was that one does not deny the truth of anything an officer says, no matter how wrong it may be, if that officer happens to be your senior even by a day. I continued to enjoy looking at Everest and Kinchinjunga by myself, recalling the happy days, ten years before, when our whole family had made a four-day march from Darjeeling, opposite the base of Kinchinjunga, to Sandakphu, almost on Kinchinjunga's shoulder, just to have a good look at Everest. One doesn't forget things like that.

The colonel, poor chap, never did see Everest.

We landed at Chabua early in the evening. No transportation was available to Ledo till morning so we spent the night there and I hopped a ride in General Wheeler's car next morning. The portents were good. I knew my travels had really begun when I noticed that I had left my pillow behind in Chabua. I always leave something behind at each stop when I am on a long journey.

At Ledo I found my friend Lieutenant Colonel Victor Haas who once told me in Lashio that no matter how good a teacher I was I would never make a decent nurse out of a Kachin.

Later Haas came to Ramgarh to visit me. "When I was flown out to India," he said on that occasion, "they asked me what famous historical sights I intended to visit and I told them there were only two famous things I wanted to see in India: the Taj Mahal and Seagrave's Burmese nurses. Now let's see them!" At the end of the inspection Haas had to admit that Kachins could be made into wonderful nurses.

Haas was now surgeon of S.O.S. in Ledo. He not only secured my instruments for me but drove me to "Hellgate" in sight of the Pangsau Pass and then back to my assigned quarters at Chih-Hui-Pu. To my delight one of our unit's best friends, Lieutenant Colonel McNally, was in command. Mac was in perfect condition, griping in his best manner at what was going to happen to his Chinese troops when they established their advance screen in the Naga Hills.

"It's ghastly country, littered with the bones of the refugees," he said. "There is malaria everywhere and the streams must be still swarming with the cholera, typhoid, and dysentery that killed the refugees by the thousands. In two weeks I have to send Chinese troops down to Tagap and Punyang and there isn't a medic around to go with them."

"There's me," I said, ungrammatically.

"If I had a chance to see General Stilwell I'd jolly well ask for you. But what would happen to Ramgarh?"

"My executive officer, Major Crew, is a better army officer than I'll ever be," I said. "Besides, there are only about seven hundred patients left in Ramgarh instead of twelve hundred. They could spare a couple of surgical teams from our unit and never miss us, and" I added out of the corner of my mouth, "General Stilwell is in Chabua. I rode up in his plane."

Colonel McNally jumped up and reached for his hat. A few seconds later his jeep vanished around the corner.

Chabua had only one plane out the next day and it was bound for Delhi after one stop in eastern Bengal. I had either to get out at the Bengal field and chance catching a plane for a thirty-six-hour ride to Ramgarh through Calcutta or fly on to Delhi, catch another plane back to Gaya, and thence the short way by train to Ramgarh. I chose the latter as the quickest route.

Back at Ramgarh Lieutenant Harris and Stinky Davis wanted to go along if my Ledo *coup* produced results. It did. General

Stilwell radioed orders for two surgical teams of the Seagrave Unit to report to Ledo for orders.

Major Grindlay and I had a quarrel as to whether he or I should lead the party. At last he agreed that I should go—if I would promise to use all my influence to move him and the rest of the unit out into Burma as soon as possible. I was in a humor to promise him the moon.

Captain Webb headed the smaller group—Stinky, four nurses, and my Lahu boy Aishuri—while Lieutenant Harris and I led the larger group of twelve nurses and Judson, my Burmese supply officer. I discussed the question of Chinese orderlies with General Boatner, and he ordered me to select thirty Chinese sailors and soldiers from our wards and take them along. These sailors had had a hard life. Removed months before from interned ships at Calcutta, they had been a constant headache to the British who gladly dumped them in the lap of the Chinese Army when it reached Ramgarh. The Chinese could think of nothing to do with them except put them in a concentration camp, where they became an American headache. General Boatner cured the headache by turning them over to me to use as orderlies and cooks in the hospital. Having spent their lives on occidental ships, they were the perfect servants.

"But, General," I said, "what if they desert as we pass through Calcutta?"

"You won't be held responsible," he replied.

The thirty men—there were six soldiers among them—were suspiciously eager to go with us.

The railways were, as usual, overloaded. We might have two compartments but no more, so General Boatner ordered me to leave at once with my larger group, while Captain Webb and his group were to follow with the Chinese on the next available train.

On the seventeenth of March, we were at the great jumping-off place for Stilwell's return to Burma—Ledo. We parked the girls at the 20th General Hospital and took up our quarters in a tent at Chih-Hui-Pu. That afternoon some of the girls turned up, their eyes popping.

"You know those American nurses?" they said. "They aren't a bit ashamed of each other. Why, when they bathe they strip to the skin right in the middle of their barracks and even bathe in front of each other!"

In the excitement of moving I was sure the nurses had forgotten my birthday, but at five next morning the entire Chih-Hui-Pu staff, Chinese and American, was astounded to hear "Happy Birthday to You" pour from female throats right in the middle of a male camp. The girls had carried presents for me all the way from Ramgarh. Later I learned that the girls in Ramgarh had also thrown a party in honor of my birthday.

That afternoon, as we were repacking our equipment into forty-pound porter loads, Colonel McNally asked me to take a look at Colonel Rothwell Brown of the tanks who had just returned from a trip to Shingbwiyang in the Hukawng Valley with my former Burmese supply officer Tun Shein. They had been lost for seven days trying to find a road which the maps insisted ran from Taga Sakan to Hkalak. Rothwell Brown is an extremely efficient artist at profanity and he was at his best as he described how their rations had run out and Tun Shein had kept them both alive on roots, leaves, and ferns. "Ferns," he profanely insisted, "are the best three-blank things to eat I ever tasted."

The climax of their trip had come when, at the foot of the incredible climb up to Ngalang, Brown had come down with a terrific chill and a temperature of 106°. But he marched on into Ngalang, 106° and all. Now a shadow of his former self, he was worrying Mac to death insisting that I treat his malaria "on the hoof."

McNally asked Colonel Tate of the colored engineers to get me a hundred porters for our trip. The colonel claimed it couldn't be done, and then promptly went ahead and did it. Stilwell and his men only enjoyed life when they were doing the impossible. So Mac put us all into two Chinese six by six trucks and started us off for Hellgate where the porters would be waiting for us.

How the girls enjoyed the trip! They gurgled with laughter at the signs the colored engineers had stuck up along their "Ledo-Tokyo Road": "DON'T TEAR ME UP, ROLL ME DOWN!" "I'M YOUR BEST FRIEND; DON'T RUIN ME!" "HEADQUARTERS FIRST BATTALION, HAIRY EARS." "TATE DAM. HOT DAMN, WHAT A DAM!" And later, "WELCOME TO BURMA. THIS WAY TO TOKYO!"

Soon we began to pass groups of colored boys at work. One stepped back wearily with his spade, took one look at us, threw his hat in the air, and screamed, "My God! WOMEN!" The girls became a bit scared as they recalled some of the things they had heard about the way American Negroes treat women. They recovered soon enough as they became acquainted at close hand with our colored soldiers. Let me say here, for the record, that though an occasional American white enlisted man or officer and an occasional Chinese soldier or officer had been known to offer insult to our Burmese nurses, not one single colored soldier ever treated them with anything but respect. The girls often recalled with misty eyes the colored soldiers they came to know so well.

When we reached Hellgate—Chinese drivers were not permitted to go farther—we expected to sleep in some of the coolie huts. But Colonel Tate had sent word to the captain of engineers that we were coming, and the captain met us and escorted us to his own camp, where he turned over the newly completed messhall to the nurses and gave me General Wheeler's bed—the only time I ever had the honor to sleep in a major general's bed. I begged the captain to let the girls cook their own Burmese food since they were so fed up with American meals, and much against his sense of hospitality he permitted them to do so. It was the first time the girls had cooked for themselves for many months and the dinner was delicious.

We were a day ahead of schedule so the next day the girls asked to go for a swim. There were Americans, Chinese, and Garos bathing under the Hellgate bridge and the girls refused to bathe there. I led them two miles down the Refugee Trail, where we found a deep hole near a village of aborigines garbed in loincloths. We had a delightful swim, in spite of the fact that we had had to step over a few whitened refugee skulls to get there, and then rushed back to camp to beat the rainstorm that invariably arrived when our unit was about to travel somewhere.

The next morning some colored boys drove us up the mountain until they bogged down in the mud just before reaching the Pangsau Pass. We had been surprised at how good our Chinese drivers had been after their Ramgarh training—we remembered well how they had driven on the Burma Road! But these colored boys could really drive. Even when the fresh earth of the road shoulders slid away they performed miracles getting their trucks back onto solid ground again. We stepped out into the deep mud, when the trucks finally bogged down, and began to march. Almost immediately Sein Bwint's flimsy shoe was sucked off in the mud. We hadn't been able to buy one pair of stout shoes in all India that would fit the girls, and G.I. shoes, three sizes too large, were so ungainly that I never dreamed the girls could use them. Captain Webb, however, thought differently, and the girls clattered around delightedly all day long in their huge oversize G.I. shoes.

As we passed the "WELCOME TO BURMA" sign at the top of the pass the girls began to laugh and sing and trot downhill, though the rain was drenching and cold. They were on their way now, back to Burma and home and parents. That night we slept, still drenched, in three little huts in Nawngyang—the returning refugees' first night in Burma! To our astonishment we were serenaded. "Silent Night," "The Spacious Firmament," "All Hail the Power," and other favorite hymns swelled forth in exquisite harmony from the hundred throats of our Garo porters.

I was proud of the noble work of our Assam colleagues of the American Baptist Mission among these wild Garo tribesmen of southwestern Assam. All our porters were Christian. Garos take their time when portering but they stole none of our goods and

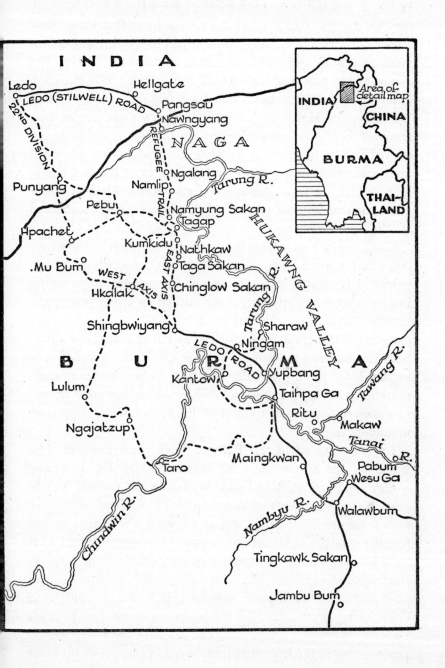

they are the only race I have yet found in India that knows how to give out with a belly laugh. On contract to the British Government and under command of American missionaries, they did almost all the portering for the U.S. Army as far south as Tagap. Later they worked southward as far as Shingbwiyang, the first "town" in the Hukawng Valley. They know their jungle. One group of G.I.'s was astonished to see the Garos suddenly get excited and begin splitting a hollow tree trunk. They were still more astonished to see them start pulling from the tree trunk, foot by foot, an enormous twenty-foot python. Their astonishment knew no bounds when the Garos immediately cooked and ate the huge snake.

Garos will not set out on a journey before seven in the morning. I was worried about how six-foot-two, spindle-legged Lieutenant Harris would stand the trip up the terrible ranges ahead; but we wanted an early start so we pushed on at our best speed, leaving Harris to see the porters off with all our goods. To my amazement Harris caught up with us within an hour. How a man from the most notorious chair-warming city in the world, Washington, D.C., could negotiate these hills on high was a mystery, until he acknowledged that his Washington address was a temporary one and that during most of his life he had been a Tennessee mountaineer.

I was curious about this Refugee Trail which ran from Mogaung on the railway near Myitkyina through the Hukawng Valley and Naga Hills to Ledo. My father had trekked it forty years before when visiting Assam with Dr. Geis of Myitkyina. Geis never saw me without telling me what a fine man he had found my father to be on that journey. No sooner would Geis state his own desires as to where to rest, what to eat, when to start, where to bivouac, when my father would concur with his "extraordinarily intelligent" decisions. It is not difficult for a domineering personality to love someone who lets him have his own way. I suppose Geis's unstinted praise of my father was repeated to me in the hope that I might change my persistent habit of resisting the A.B.M. powers. But I was a hopeless failure at emulating my father.

These Naga Hills were famous for their head-hunting tribes. My father had met many parties of head-hunters on his trip but they showed no interest in his head. The British, however, never entered the Naga Hills along this route unless backed by a small army. I was curious to see these frightful Nagas and compare them with those we met on our retreat with General Stilwell a year before on the Indaw-Imphal trail, much farther south. Would we meet the famous tribe whose women wore nothing before marriage but a tiny apron on their behinds and swung it around to the front after?

Last but not least of the reasons for my interest in the trail was that it was by this trail that "Tiny," my wife, planned to march out of Burma with the two little boys if I had let her remain till the country fell to the Japs.

As we marched along the trail, place names recalled another disastrous expedition of seventy years before when the King of Burma sent his famous General Bandoola with an army to invade and conquer India! From Tingkawk Sakan at the southern entrance of the Hukawng Valley to Namyung Sakan and Namlip Sakan along the Refugee Trail you can trace the line of march of Bandoola's army all the way to the neighborhood of Ledo. *Sakan* is the Burmese word for "bivouac." Other names showed us that all this belt of country was a no man's land rather than a real part of the Naga Hills. Place names like Nawngyang and Namyung were Shan. Names like Tagap Ga and Tanai Hka were Kachin. Hpachet Hi and Shamdak Ku were Naga.

We soon found that the people were no man's people. When we marched around a corner two natives were resting at the entrance to a side road. I could see Kachin blood in the shape of their faces and stopped to pass the time of day with them in Kachin. Thank God we were back in a country where we could converse with people without using several relays of interpreters! I asked them whether they were Kachins or Nagas. "Neither," they said. "We are Chins." People the whites called Nagas called themselves Chins but spoke Kachin. Along the East Axis, as the army called the Refugee Trail, all the Nagas called themselves Chins—which they decidedly were not. They were hybrids. All sorts of conquests and migrations had occurred along the axis through the years. We saw natives with unmistakable Shan, Hkamti, Burmese, Kachin, or Naga physiognomies calling themselves Chin, but there was no pure blood of any of these races. In a few more years people still calling themselves Chin will have American, English, Indian, Negro, Garo, Nepali, Chinese, and Japanese features as well!

We soon found that it was also a no man's land with regard to climate. Assam has the world's heaviest rainfall but at least the rain has sense enough to fall in season. Burma weather is beautifully regular. But that of Hukawng follows no rules whatsoever. It makes all its own climate and every bit of it wrong. July was supposed to be the rainy season, so we had weeks of beautiful weather. We shivered in Tagap in the hot season. As we marched along it was the middle of the dry season, so it poured steadily for a month. This was the country through which Stilwell's engineers had to build their road from Ledo to China, and build it without hard rock with which to surface it—nothing but clay and soft river rock.

Through these torrents of rain the Chinese had marched down the Refugee Trail two days ahead of us and with animal transport. As a result we were continually to our knees in mud even when going up the steepest of hills. At every step you had to yank your leg out of the mud with an angry suck and sink it in to the knee again as you put it down. Stilwell's pace, with a ten-minute rest every hour, had to be abandoned at once. We were lucky when we didn't stop for oxygen every ten minutes. And when the deep mud no longer hampered us we growled inwardly at the lack of mud, for then the path, sloping in every direction at once, was so slippery that we were continually negotiating the road on our behinds. Ground leeches were everywhere. I had always thought people were exaggerating when they claimed that leeches could suck a man to death, but I'm sure that many of the refugees must finally have succumbed to leeches.

Certainly they had succumbed! From the first day on we passed skeletons in ever increasing numbers, yet we could see evidences of camps where, by setting fire to the shacks, hundreds of skeletons had been destroyed en masse. There were skeletons around every water hole, lying sprawled out where the refugees had collapsed. At the foot of every ascent were the bones of those who had died rather than attempt one more climb, and all up the hill were the bones of those who had died trying. Still standing along the road were some extremely crude shacks, each with its ten to twenty skeletons of those who couldn't get up when a new day came. In one shallow stream we were horrified to find that the Chinese had placed a long row of skulls to be used as stepping-stones. Sex and age and even race could be noted, not by such elusive clues as surgeons use but by the rotting clothes. When I saw a skeleton clothed in a delicate English dress I was thankful for Tiny's departure a year before. Looking at the skeletons of little boys in khaki shorts, I realized they might have been John or Sterling. There were men, women, and children of every race and age, their hair white, gray, brown, and black, still lying beside the whitened skulls; there were English, Anglo-Burmese, and Indians—civilian and military.

There were no skeletons of Chinese soldiers. The British had not permitted the Chinese Army to use this trail, the "easier" trail of the East Axis, but had sent the Chinese 22nd Division out on the trail of the West Axis which had much steeper and higher ranges to cross. But the government miscalculated. The rivers that the East Axis crossed were much bigger than those of the West Axis, and while the Chinese were held up at only two or three streams, the Burmese refugees were held up all along the line, dying by the hundreds as they waited for the rivers to go down.

And yet in spite of the hundreds and hundreds of skeletons we saw, we didn't see half of those who had died on the Refugee

Trail, for English and Indian and Chinese burial and cremating squads had been at work. A few months later only a few scattered skulls were left to mark the trail of the refugees. Now we were the first of the refugees to return.

As we reached our second night's camp we began to get a fore-taste of what was to hound us for the entire year to come. There were officers in the area who knew not "Joseph and his daughters" and supposed these girls "couldn't take it." We were told that officers up ahead were horrified at the speed of our advance and were rushing to get proper camps built for the nurses. We were not to proceed until all camps were completed. We halted for Sunday since the coolies were tired and, as Christians, entitled by contract to one day off per week. Then, too, the girls had worn out their first pairs of shoes and were beginning to develop sores on their feet. But by Sunday evening everyone was so restless to get on that we resumed our march the following morning.

On that day we had the worst climb of all—uphill hour after hour, pulling ourselves up out of mud by the roots of trees. On the slippery stretches I stamped my G.I. heels as deeply as possible at each step, hoping the nurses might catch toe holds. Each of us carried a long strong cane to push ourselves along and help us keep erect. But at almost every step one or the other would go down, to the uproarious delight of the rest of the party. Cheers always burst forth when the old man himself went down. And so on, up and up to unbelievable heights, till at last we came onto the air-drop field at Ngalang. There the enlisted men at the radio station made us completely at home in a spare shack, while they prepared for us the kind of meal only our air force units could produce. Unfortunately there was no visibility that afternoon and we missed the magnificent views from Ngalang where to the north on a clear day one can see the snowy range of the Himalayas.

Travel the next day was much easier and brought us to a camp delightfully situated near a rushing stream. The shack was only just building but by night there was a thatched roof over our heads, and what more could returning refugees want?

At no time did we cover more than eight miles in one day, although without a heavy pack sixteen miles a day is quite possible in those hills if it has to be done. We got a big laugh when we read long after an article in a States-side magazine about the Signal Corps man who "taught himself to walk five miles a day" in the head-hunting Naga Hills. We purposely took it easy on this trip because we had no idea how soon the Chinese would begin to have casualties, and the girls had to be ready for them.

On the noon of our sixth day we came to the wide Namyung River at the foot of the enormous mountain on which perched Tagap Ga, the intended base for Chinese operations. We were so anxious to get there that after tanking up on tea we started the last climb at once. The nurses now began to search the jungle for edible plants which they might secure on future forage trips. At last there were wild flowers and a few edible fruits which bravely tried to cover the traces of the refugees.

Nowhere along the road was there a single native village. Even "fierce Naga head-hunters" could not understand the tragedy of the refugees except as the act of one of their mysterious gods, and they had moved away, as far as they could from the haunted and accursed trail. Even at Tagap there was nothing left of the village that formerly housed the tribal chief.

Airplanes were dropping food and ammunition as we reached a knoll in front of Tagap. We watched them free-drop sacks of rice and then parachute down sacks of canned goods and ammunition. It was impossible to cross the field as long as the planes continued to circle and drop. Finally, as colored American Quartermaster boys began to gather in the day's haul, we pushed on to the coolie camp beyond the Chinese troops. We were at Tagap Ga—the base for our work.

The British major in charge was extremely cross because we had come on in spite of his instructions, for he had nothing but a roof and a floor to offer us. I asked him if he had ever heard a nurse complain at having nothing more than a roof and a floor. Quite often they had been happy with a roof and no floor. If there were no roof they could jolly well make one in a hurry.

Major General Wheeler of S.O.S., a day behind us on the trail, reached Tagap in the early morning. His first action was to ask Major Peng, the Chinese commandant, whether he had yet sent forward the company of troops that had been ordered on patrol. Peng had not. Wheeler ordered them off at once. Finally a patrol of one platoon set off and had proceeded only a mile beyond Kumkidu, with a Kachin scout a hundred yards ahead of them, when they bumped smack into a Japanese patrol. Machine-gun bullets tore up the earth around the Kachin scout. The Kachin slipped into the dense jungle and circled back to the Chinese who were frantically deploying to return the Japanese fire. The first engagement of the new Burma campaign was joined within twenty-four hours of our arrival.

The first casualty was, of course, an abdominal case. We had not set up yet. The few available transport planes were bringing in higher priority stuff than tarpaulins. We would have to build thatched bamboo shacks and that would take time. So we borrowed the Signal Corps messhall and did the operation on their dinner table. The intestine had been badly torn and, as in the case of so many Chinese, roundworms were escaping from the various rents and exploring the abdomen on their own. One was actually lying in the abdominal wound, its body cut in two by the bullet. By the light of one gasoline lamp and several flashlights we resected the torn intestine and made an end-to-end anasto-mosis. A respectable number of my abdominal cases had been known to live, but not one where roundworms filled the abdom-inal cavity. This patient lasted twenty-four hours.

While our own Chinese battalion was successfully holding the Japanese, Bill Cummings was ordered to proceed with a Kachin patrol down the Salt Springs Trail that connected the East and West Axes and find out what had happened to the British troops then garrisoning Hkalak at the entrance to the West Axis. The garrison consisted of Indian and Kachin troops officered by former British tea planters of Assam. There was also a radio team of American enlisted men at Hkalak. Bill made a forced march of twenty miles and when he reached the middle trail toward Pebu bumped into the force retreating to Pebu on the double quick. Having been attacked by an "overwhelming force of two hundred Japs," they had barely had time to fire their supplies and run. The American boys, ordered to retreat, had scattered their radio equipment in the jungle. Bill about-faced and marched back over that ghastly trail without rest to report to General Wheeler.

The retreat of the Hkalak garrison, before the arrival of Chinese troops down the center trail, laid Tagap wide open to Japanese encirclement and General Wheeler ordered us to pack up and be ready for immediate evacuation—if the Chinese had to fight their way out of the encirclement. The same old story of the first campaign in Burma: the Japs attack with a party of ten or two hundred, it doesn't matter which; the colonial troops retreat at the drop of a hat, convinced that they will not be able to resist successfully; the Chinese have to retreat or be surrounded; and commanding generals have to start worrying about the safety of American medical units. Was the new campaign to be tainted with the same defeatism? Had no one the guts to make a real stand? What would Stilwell say if we all started running again?

General Wheeler was busy sending out 4-Z radio messages, but twice that day I snared him and pled with him.

"Sir," I said, "the Chinese have so far not discovered much reason to trust the United States fully. They have no proof that we also are not going to run away and leave them holding the bag the minute they come up against danger. During the first campaign General Stilwell kept our unit well out of harm's way and always warned us in time of an imminent Chinese retreat. The general was certainly justified because at that time we were the only surgical unit he had for the entire Chinese Army. That situation has changed. There are all sorts of American medical units now in the theater. If anything happened to us we wouldn't be missed. These nurses are Burmese girls of the country for which we are fighting. They aren't going to gripe if they die for their country."

"Naturally not," interpolated the general.

"Furthermore," I resumed, after the laughter that this outburst provoked had subsided, "nothing would please the Chinese more than to have a high-ranking American officer stick it out with them. If, in addition, that officer is an American officer with a detachment of women nurses who have the guts to stay, their morale will also be enormously improved. As for myself, I had a hard trip here, marching forward over those hills. I know I can't go up them backward!"

The general was noncommittal, so I saluted and left.

Next morning, scouts reported that the Chinese advance patrol at Pebu had thrust south below the entrance of the Salt Springs Trail and had dug in there while the colonials continued to retreat. Colonel Rothwell Brown was with them. Captain Webb and his nurses had arrived at Ledo, minus twenty sailors who had slipped away as they came through Calcutta, and were marching in to Punyang on the West Axis. Judson, whom I had left behind to escort Webb into the jungles, was with them. Our own Chinese were holding at Kumkidu and "had inflicted many casualties on the enemy." General Wheeler, greatly relieved at the stabilizing of the line, permitted us to go ahead with our plans and build the hospital.

Our Garo porters cleared the bamboo jungle and erected wards, a supply shack, an operating room, and, finally, several little bamboo houses with bamboo floors and bamboo beds thatched with bamboo leaves. There was a cottage for every four nurses, one for Harris and any guest who might appear, and one for me. Some Nagas built us a pipeline of bamboos which carried water from a stream nearby right through the hospital grounds to the operating room. As soon as the supply building had been built we moved into it and put up a combined messhall and

Fording Streams along the Refugee Trail through the Naga Hills

Photos by Bill Duncumb

The Bamboo Jungle Furnished Building Materials for the Hospital Unit at Tagap

kitchen. That day there was another casualty whom we placed in the messhall since the wards were not quite ready.

About ten that night there was a tremendous burst of machine-gun and tommy-gun fire and bullets whizzed over us. It was lucky we were in a hollow out of the line of fire. Everyone supposed the Japanese were making a fierce attack and I expected casualties before morning so ordered all the nurses to bed while I went on sentry duty beside our patient.

At midnight the firing reached a new peak of intensity and mortars opened up all around. Suddenly there was a flash of a dozen torches and what in the dark seemed like the entire Japanese Army plunging down the path toward me. I stepped under cover and waited with my automatic. As they drew near, the light from the torches showed me that the Japanese Army was only our Naga coolies.

"Where do you-all think you're going?" I asked in my best Kachin.

"The Japanese have broken through and are coming this way. We're beating it for home."

"If the Japanese were coming they would already be here," I said. I had to talk alternately in Kachin and Burmese now, for my Kachin was fast running out, but the Naga headman knew Burmese. "You guys can run home if you want to but you are not going to run home through this hospital area. I always understood Kachins and Nagas were brave men and made good warriors and yet here you are running away like mad, while girls of your own race are in that shack over there sleeping quite peacefully in spite of all this shooting. Only chickenhearted blank-blanks would start running ahead of women. Back up and run away on some other trail."

The Nagas were armed with rifles and shotguns, but they didn't know what an awful shot I was. My automatic looked very efficient even if I did not, so they milled around for awhile, arguing, and then followed my advice and went back to bed.

In the morning we discovered that the great battle was caused by the appearance not of Japs but of a herd of large monkeys which swarm all over the Naga Hills. I couldn't blame the trigger-happy Chinese for mistaking yellow monkeys for Japs. A few days later a Chinese patrol found that the Japanese had retreated. It was discovered a month later that not more than ten or twenty Japanese troops had caused the rout of the colonials at Hkalak.

The troops in the forward area those first months were the 114th Chinese Regiment under Colonel (now Major General) Lee Hung, and the battalion at Tagap was under the command of Major Peng Ke-Lee, now a full colonel, having taken over command of the 114th when Colonel Lee assumed command of the 38th Chinese Division. I had not known Major Peng before, but Colonel Lee and I had seen quite a bit of each other in Ramgarh. Our relationships with both men were very pleasant. We had to work hard to give them as much co-operation as they gave us. One or the other came every day to the hospital to report information received and enable us to be ready for emergencies. Neither knew English, but they saw to it that interpreters did not last long who tried making speeches for them, instead of actually translating their words. Colonel Lee was young but had the tired eyes of a man who does occasional deep thinking. Major Peng had close-set eyes and a broad mind, a rather unusual combination in my experience. He had an enormous admiration for Nurse Nang Aung whom he called "Miss Wang" and often used her as an interpreter. The relationship between them was interesting to me. There was never any flirtation. Major Peng never came around when off duty. But he never failed to pay his respects to Nang Aung when military affairs brought us together. If he had fresh fish at his table, he would invite us all to enjoy the meal with him or else would send fish over to us. He and Major Hu, who came to Hkalak in October, were our favorite Chinese majors. The most extraordinary characteristic of Colonel Lee, Major Peng, and Major Hu, in my mind, was the fact that not one of them ever came to me with an illegal ax to grind. They never asked me, for example, to use force on American Quartermasters to compel them to issue American rations to Chinese troops. They knew that Chungking had decreed what the Chinese should have and they abode by that decision. If any soldier under their command needed discipline he got it, and quickly. It seemed too good to be true. Another delightful thing about all three was that they wasted no time. They got down to the matter in hand at once without the usual half hour of polite prelude.

We were back in routine work again and now actually in Burma, though none of us was willing to think of the Naga Hills or the Hukawng Valley as Burma. But as the days passed it was forced increasingly on my consciousness that there was something wrong with the nurses. They didn't seem happy, even though they were so very much nearer their own homes. Pouts appeared for no reason at all. There was no cheery singing as they worked and even our Sunday-evening song services went flat. I worked off my own energy studying Japanese surgery, the kind one performs with an ax: I cut loads of firewood. I even took my turn in the kitchen making pies and cakes and delicious curries, hoping to wheedle the nurses out of it—whatever "it" was. Not one would tell me until I was rather mean to Little Bawk one day and then she explained it was because the girls had had to leave their boy friends behind at Ramgarh in order to return to Burma —and what they had returned to was not Burma at all.

Ramgarh certainly had done something to those girls.

2

Ramgarh Training Center

To go back a bit, in July, 1942, we left our work for the sick refugees, military and civilian, at Gauhati, Assam, and went to Ramgarh to open a post hospital. This was the training center Stilwell was organizing to teach the remnants of the Chinese expeditionary force how to use modern weapons to fight an offensive war. Everyone said it couldn't be done, but the general was determined to succeed. The Burmese girls were at their best then, for they were thrilled at the idea of being allowed to help "Granddaddy" with his job.

Colonel Fuller was S.O.S. chief of Ramgarh and he spat in disgust when informed that Burmese nurses were coming in. Why did Stilwell have to send him a bunch of useless civilian nurses? He would probably have to lug the baggage of the helpless fools himself! He was therefore completely astounded when the train pulled to a stop and a group of girls in uniform blue *longyis* jumped out with their own kits and at once fell into columns of threes waiting for further orders. Colonel Fuller drove us to the quarters of the hospital staff, almost getting lost in the maze of prisoner-of-war camps. Ramgarh was one of a system of camps the British had scattered all over India for their German and Italian P.O.W.'s. The British had refused the places Stilwell had first selected for his proposed training center but had finally consented to shift the P.O.W.'s from Ramgarh and let Stilwell set up there.

The P.O.W. hospital at Ramgarh consisted of twenty-two wards, each in a separate building of brick with tile roof and cement floor, surrounded by double barbwire barricades. The five wards, operating room, dental clinic, and orderly room that were nearest to our quarters were again separated from the rest of the hospital by double barricades. This was the Italian hospital. The larger group of buildings was for Germans. Outside the barbwire were three wards for Indian troops, two for "Europeans," and the administration buildings. The central roadway that passed by the office building divided the total area in half. The patients in the P.O.W. hospital had been cared for entirely by medical prisoners of war who had lived in what was now our barracks area; so we, too, were entirely surrounded by barbwire. The hospital had a total of some seven hundred and fifty beds. It was the intention of the theater surgeon, Colonel R. P. Williams, that we take care of all patients till half the hospital was full; then an American station hospital would be sent in to take over the other half. The necessity for using the entire hospital was considered somewhat remote.

The U.S. Army was, no doubt justifiably, skeptical of my ability to run a G.I. institution. An unorthodox arrangement was decided upon. I was to be in complete charge of the professional work of the hospital, while Major Bevil was to be post surgeon and administer the hospital with a Medical Administrative Corps officer and a group of Medical Department enlisted personnel from a casual detachment. The health of the post and the veterinary department would be under Major Bevil. Any extra men from the casuals would be turned over to me for professional work. Major John H. Grindlay and Major Donald M. O'Hara as well as Lieutenant Ray F. Chesley of the Sanitary Corps—the men who had made possible the success of our work in the first Burma campaign—were to return to us as chief of the surgical service, chief of the dental service, and chief of laboratories, respectively. Captains William Webb and H. Myles Johnson of the Medical Corps also joined our staff.

With most casual detachments the units who furnished the cadre took the opportunity to get rid of men for whom they had no further use, and this one was no exception. It contained some of the best and some of the worst. Three of the men, Technical Sergeant Emmet T. (Stinky) Davis, Technical Sergeant Mitchell

(Puss) Opas, and Staff Sergeant Chester Deaton, were so good we held onto them against all odds and they remained with us till September, 1944, when the two-year rotation scheme sent them back to the States. Only Opas was lost to us for a time. I had been ordered to fill a cadre of casuals to work in Chungking, so I took the opportunity to get rid of one who was a thorn in the flesh. He, of course, let me down at once and by the end of a week Chungking had shipped him back to a padded cell in Karachi. Only a few weeks later I was called on to fill another cadre, this time for Stilwell's second training center in China. Determined that all key men should be "tops," I had to send Opas as chief surgical technician. It took me ten months of hard work to get him back.

Providential help was needed by any American unit that took over a hospital from the British. The ways of the two races in conducting a hospital are diametrically opposed. During our first two weeks in Ramgarh the British colonel in charge refused to turn over the hospital to us until a lot of red tape could be cut in New Delhi. He turned over only the empty wards from which furniture and apparatus had been removed to storage. We had to locate the furniture and transportation and get it all back to the wards and at the same time receive trainloads of patients as the 38th Chinese Division arrived. The greatest difficulty was with the pharmacy. British hospital pharmacies wouldn't issue any drug that had not been diluted with water to make a uniform one-ounce dose for all medicines. Our American doctors, however, wanted drugs that could be prescribed by the drop, as, for example, Fowler's solution—liq. arsenic. to the British—to be furnished pure, while mixtures were supplied for a one-dram dose. We had incredible difficulty getting the idea across, and calamity soon overtook us. Forced by British usage to prescribe Fowler's solution by the diluted ounce, the order was so written for fifteen patients on one ward just as the pharmacy caught the American idea and issued pure Fowler's to that ward without

changing the label. There was no difference in color of the solution, so Thelma, one of our nurses, gave each patient three ounces
of pure arsenic. Luckily she noticed that the Chinese didn't react
properly and reported at once. We had a field day washing out
Chinese stomachs. Thelma was in a coma by the time the Chinese
were out of danger.

Finally Delhi red tape was cut and the British colonel announced he would begin the turnover and have it completed by
the end·of three months. Bevil said the turnover must be completed in three days. Fortunately for us, he was supported by the
boards of officers of both the American and British armies, and
the three days sufficed.

The 38th Chinese Division had come out of Burma on the
same road to Imphal that Stilwell had used. Yet they were in an
awful condition when they reached Ramgarh. In addition to all
the diseases the refugees had brought to Gauhati they had picked
up ferocious "Naga sores," ulcers that eat down to and through
bone. Luckily the 22nd Chinese Division was only then beginning to reach Ledo over the West Axis or we would have been
swamped. We had to open two or three new wards every day. It
had been thought we might run slightly over four hundred beds
when both divisions were in, but we were already beyond that
figure with only the 38th Division.

Colonel Fuller was wild. None of the trains ran on schedule.
Frequently he was notified that the train was in, and he would
hurry down to the station only to find it a false alarm. Again and
again trains appeared without warning. Fuller had to find transportation where none existed. He had to see that one of our
medical officers met each train, yet he was determined that our
overworked doctors made no useless visits to the station. And
everywhere he came up against the blank wall of foreign language.
The telephone rang and I answered.

"Hello, hello, hello," said Fuller's voice. "Do you speak
English?"

"A little," I replied. "But I speak American better. I try to improve my English a little every day!"

"Say, who are you?"

"Seagrave."

Thereafter Fuller never met me without asking how my English was getting along.

I had heard of General Sun Li-Jen of the 38th Division in Burma, for it was he who rescued the British from encirclement at Yenangyaung. He had been decorated by both the British and American governments. He came over to us every evening now to check on the physical condition of his men. Sun was a graduate of Virginia Military Institute and spoke superb English. Quite tall and very handsome, he looked much younger than his years.

When General Sun went on rounds in the hospital, he chatted with each patient as if he were one of them, treating the enlisted men much more courteously than their sergeants or lieutenants would have done. As for the soldiers, though they gazed at him with intense respect, they would call to him across the ward to present some gripe or other, more often than not directed against me. Sun always listened patiently, yet usually he did me the honor to recognize the difficulties under which we were trying to give his men adequate attention.

Not all Chinese generals were like General Sun. There was the really big shot who came over with General Stilwell one day, apparently determined to criticize Uncle Joe and all his works. Stilwell brought him over to inspect the hospital and Grindlay and I produced our entire bag of tricks trying to get him interested in the welfare of the soldiers. Finally Stilwell nudged me to one side and growled in an undertone, "Don't waste time on that four-blank. He doesn't give a blankety blank about anything worthwhile. Get him through the hospital and out again as fast as you can." Stilwell seldom broke out in profanity. When he did, it was well deserved. I noticed that Chinese generals who didn't care for their men didn't remain very long in command of the armies under Stilwell.

Soon the 22nd Chinese Division began to arrive. They had had a much more ghastly time getting out of Burma than the 38th. At least three truckloads of men, packed like sardines, were brought to the hospital from each train. During the train ride of one group from Ledo to Ramgarh, fifteen men had died and been buried en route. It was common to have three or four men die within a few hours of arrival. One patient, deathly ill with malaria, refused to wait for our enlisted men to carry him to his bed and stumbled from the truck to the ward by himself. He was dead in three hours. I saw that happen many times among the Chinese. We saw it almost two years later at Maingkwan when the 50th Division was flown in direct from China. In this case the man was sitting up in the truck as it came in beside me. I called to our enlisted men to get him first, that he was dying in his seat. He was dead in a half hour. In Myitkyina I saw it again as the Chinese litter bearers carried in a soldier sitting on the stretcher holding several yards of intestine that had escaped from his shell-torn abdomen. No doctor will ever understand the Chinese. They die when a post-mortem discovers no cause of death, but they live for days, still trying to do their stuff, long after the people of any other race would have died.

Major Grindlay and his surgical technicians, Koi and her surgical nurses, were frantically busy receiving and dressing the new admissions. Every morning hundreds had to be redressed. Grindlay evolved a routine by which these dressings could be done with a minimum loss of time. He commandeered all the towel racks from the bathrooms and fenced off the veranda of the operating theater, so that patients had to come in at one end, get processed by the enlisted technicians, and go out the other end back to their wards. A long production line of two hundred patients with huge Naga sores would be lined up in the yard all morning waiting to be processed.

Naga sores are horribly painful and no matter how gentle the technicians were many of the patients screamed with pain. Yet they all took it in such a brave and cheerful spirit that visitors were astonished. One photographer with a newsreel camera took many shots of these patients being dressed, to show the anguished expression on each face relax into a grin of pure delight as the dressing was finished. At every howl of pain other patients, waiting their turn, let out corresponding howls of laughter.

Many a Naga sore extended from knee to foot. Penetrating to bone the periosteum would be eaten away and nothing but a huge dead sequestrum left. At least three patients had to have the tibia removed completely and there were many more who had to have the entire fibula removed. At that time the service since developed for procuring artificial limbs for Chinese soldiers did not exist. I knew from bitter experience that while a Chinese coolie can eke out a living with a shriveled, crooked leg, he cannot manage without the leg at all. So we never performed amputations except for gangrene. I remember a hopeless-looking foot that I dissuaded Grindlay from amputating and Grindlay's genuine delight when he succeeded in making a very passable foot out of it.

At first we tried wet dressings for the Naga sores of saturated magnesium sulphate solution but there were so many cases that the nurses couldn't keep the dressings wet. Grindlay then discovered a 10 per cent solution of magnesium sulphate in glycerin not only much more effective for the smaller sores but much easier for all hands to take care of. For the enormous sores, nothing was satisfactory except a complete excision, after which the limb was encased in plaster of Paris and "forgotten" for a month or six weeks or until it could no longer be forgotten. Such patients were kept on the verandas of the wards, where they wouldn't remind their comrades of the bodies rotting along the trail out of Burma. After the second change of cast there invariably was a fine bed of granulation tissue which Grindlay and his staff could very successfully graft.

Some of the sores were incredibly full of maggots. Two or three hundred was not an infrequent count. One of these patients was on my ward. After all the maggots had apparently been removed, Grindlay operated on him and put him in a cast, later skin-grafting him successfully. But every time I planned to discharge him, some portion of the area would break down and a long-dead maggot would be extruded from the depths of the wound.

Our wards were crowded long before the bulk of the 22nd Division arrived. We put beds down the aisles of the wards and began to fill the verandas. A British Red Cross unit, on its way to China, was held up by lack of transportation and came in to help us. We gave them five wards, a fair proportion for the number of their personnel. They had English nurses, supposedly much more efficient than our Burmese girls, and most of their personnel spoke Chinese fluently, having previously been missionaries in China. Our receiving office did its best to assign cases evenly, going so far as to send the worst cases to us. But the Red Cross group griped at the number of their admissions, at their quarters, at their food—at everything else. We were relieved when they finally left for China.

The U.S. 98th Station Hospital under Major Warrenburg was ordered to come to help us, but by the time they arrived we were up to 1,200 beds and a few days later topped 1,350. And this in a 750-bed hospital! It was lucky that every ward had verandas on each side running down its length. Aisles and verandas were now packed and there were patients crowding even the decrepit buildings of the P.O.W. isolation camp.

During all this time the nurses were extremely happy, though they put in many a sixteen-hour working day and occasionally even an eighteen-hour day. My malaria gripped me once more just as Colonel Williams was visiting us and he shipped me off to Darjeeling for a month's rest, together with three nurses who were also breaking down. From that day on I never lost half a day's work from illness. But while we were away, Saw Yin, our chief medical nurse, was taken ill and began to develop tuberculosis in the glands of her neck.

Even though their bodies were beginning to give out, the nurses' morale was very high. Our officers treated them with great courtesy and their work was absorbing enough to keep them from being more than normally homesick.

On his first visit to the hospital General Stilwell called our officers together, explained what he was trying to do, and asked us to support him by getting the sick Chinese well as fast as possible by any means, no matter how unorthodox, so that the soldiers could get into the training school and learn how to fight. Grindlay and I were determined to see the general's orders obeyed and with the help of the entire staff set about finding ways to cut short the number of days lost in the hospital. We were handicapped by lack of medicines and supplies and had to adapt ourselves to the drugs in hand. Thus, with malaria, we had at first nothing but Indian quinine which is far from potent, then nothing but the British imitation of atabrine. We were all willing to try anything once.

We classified our wards as far as possible. Webb, Ba Saw, and Johnson had medical wards. Grindlay and Gurney had two wards each for major surgery and I took what the others would not have, an eye-disease ward and a venereal-disease ward among them. So many typhoid cases came in that Webb opened a special typhoid ward. Tuberculosis was rife and Gurney, who was interested to see what he could do with them, segregated seventy particularly severe cases in another building. There was one German P.O.W. still with us, his lungs so full of tuberculous cavities that the British didn't dare move him, assuring me I need not bother about him since he would be dead in a week. I remember my first visits to him. His temperature was extremely erratic, spiking high on the chart several times a day. He was completely helpless and able to eat almost nothing.

Gurney begged me to let him treat these cases with a new

remedy which had been tested out by a few doctors in England before war stopped their researches: an African drug called umckaloabo—a "quack" remedy, if you will. Gurney claimed to have observed some very good results in his own practice in England before setting out for Burma several years before. We could certainly do the German no harm nor, for that matter, the Chinese, since by ordinary methods they would never make soldiers for Stilwell. Furthermore, there was no home for tuberculous Chinese in India and no transportation back to China. I told Gurney to go ahead, and from its own funds our unit purchased two shipments of the drug from Calcutta.

Umckaloabo comes in three forms: a concentrated extract, a dilute extract, and a powder. Gurney gave three doses a day, before meals, diluted in a cup of hot water. Specialists in tuberculosis do not think well of umckaloabo and refuse to give it a trial. It may have been unethical to use a drug not yet passed on favorably by the American or British medical associations, but Gurney obtained such extraordinary results that I was willing to stand court-martial any day for approving of its use. The British had given the German P.O.W. a week to live. With umckaloabo he not only did not die at the end of a week but after six weeks was having no fever or pain. His appetite was greatly improved. At the end of two months I paid him an evening visit. The nurse had propped him up in bed with his guitar, and he was happily strumming away at it, crooning his favorite German love songs. Beside him were two letters that had just reached him from his folks in Germany. The nurse, standing behind him, told me in an amazed whisper that the patient had eaten an entire chicken with trimmings for supper. And so he continued for months, as happy as a sick prisoner could be, until one day, without pain or distress, he suddenly died.

In the Chinese ward Gurney was having just as amazing results. He was working with proved cases, patients with swarms of tubercle bacilli in their sputum. We had all been skeptical but we were so no longer. Gurney proved, first, that the drug had no effect whatever on lung diseases other than tuberculosis, and, second, that in tuberculosis the effect was to improve appetite at once, then reduce the temperature gradually to normal, cause a rapid and very steady increase in weight, and, finally, actually clear the tubercle bacilli from the sputum and cause the disappearance of all physical signs, except in patients with huge cavities. Gurney discharged a great many cured during the months we were there. He had half a dozen deaths—patients who died of malaria, dysentery, or typhoid superimposed on their tuberculosis. Not one died of tuberculosis alone except the German. Gurney set up scales in his ward and each patient was weighed once a week. At first the gains were slight but then there would be an average sustained rise of one pound a week. Twice we ran out of the drug and patients organized committees to complain: they were losing their appetites and putting on less weight. Gurney's results were so undeniable that Colonel Williams authorized the medical supply officer to purchase the drug from government funds.

Typhoid was another worry. The Chinese would not cooperate by staying still in bed or eating the diet we permitted. Friends brought in all sort of indigestible Chinese delicacies which the patients devoured, to their great detriment. Since sulfaguanidine and sulfadiazine were coming in from the States, Webb prescribed sulfaguanidine empirically without much success until he used sulfadiazine simultaneously and then his patients, too, began to stop dying. I will admit, for the sake of argument, that American typhoid patients are not benefited by these drugs; but Chinese certainly are. Webb fortified his cases by giving them two large eggnogs a day, each with an ounce of Scotch. We had no trouble making the Chinese drink those eggnogs. Webb lost no more cases except those complicated with intestinal worms. He asked me whether it was better to leave the worms alone or administer a vermifuge, and I had to reply that I didn't know. Either course seemed fatal. On my advice Webb used vermifuges on alternate cases and found the percentage of death the same. Intestinal parasites were equally obnoxious in cases of dysentery.

American medical officers continually diagnosed primary syphilis as chancroid. They had never seen chancres so enormous, dirty, or painful as those the Chinese had. After wasting weeks in mistaken diagnosis they threw the venereal ward at me. Among the cases they turned over were many that had shown no improvement because the patients needed circumcision. In America it is not considered good practice to operate on the phimosis until the chancre, chancroid, or gonorrhea is cured. With the Chinese it is not good practice not to; and with General Stilwell's order it was imperative that the phimosis be operated at once so that the underlying disease could be brought rapidly to a noninfective stage and the soldier be returned to training. We never had complications from so doing; in fact, the circumcision sometimes removed the lesion, and simultaneous therapy for the disease itself prevented recurrence in the wound.

We used neoarsphenamine or mapharsen with more frequent injections than is customary, until the patient was almost saturated with arsenic, and we usually used bismuth simultaneously. As soon as the primary lesion was healed we sent the patient out to his military training, leaving it up to him whether he would come back weekly for the entire course.

Each staff officer sent a report to the Surgeon, S.O.S., Delhi, on the special phase of our program for which he was responsible. Much to our distress Colonel Tamraz published the reports and distributed copies to all Medical Corps officers in the theater, sharply criticizing my methods with syphilis and instructing a first lieutenant, who happened to be theater venereal disease officer, to inform us how syphilis really should be treated. The lieutenant warned us we were making it almost certain that the syphilis patients would develop locomotor ataxia and general paresis as a result of our therapy.

I shrugged. My reasons were hard boiled: Stilwell needed those boys to be trained for a campaign that might begin at any moment; probably half of them would be killed in that campaign long before they had a chance to develop neurosyphilis; those that were not killed would certainly have repeated attacks of malaria before this campaign, through the worst malaria belt in the world, was completed, and would thereby cure their own syphilis. I happened to know that neurosyphilis never develops in that malaria belt.

Grindlay loved abdominal surgery above all else, but with the Chinese he soon became a rectal specialist. It was amazing how many Chinese soldiers suffered from hemorrhoids and fistula-in-ano. Years previously I had seen specialists in Baltimore and New York have troubles with fistulas, operating repeatedly and having patients return for weeks to the outpatient department. Grindlay developed a type of operation so simple and effective that we could count on discharging the patient within two weeks. With umckaloabo we could even discharge tuberculous fistulas in three or four weeks. There seemed to be no special trick to Grindlay's operation except meticulous care and an effective postoperative routine.

One day, to his utter and complete disgust, Grindlay came down with amoebic dysentery. None of us could understand it, for our water was pure and our diet so good that no one else had developed the disease. I dropped into the operating room soon after he recovered. He was smoking a cigarette between operations with his rubber gloves still on.

"Doc," he said, disgustedly, "I've just discovered how I caught the dysentery."

"How was it?"

"Smoking between fistula operations!"

After all his poisonous remarks about Chinese and their intestinal habits it took Grindlay months to live down our laughter at his direct method of acquiring amoebic dysentery.

That we were able to avoid some serious epidemics during our stay at Ramgarh was entirely due to the brilliance of our laboratory chief, Lieutenant Chesley. When typhoid started he made a complete survey of all the Chinese in town and discovered several carriers in the Chinese restaurants. Their removal stopped the epidemic.. One day, within twenty-four hours of admission, Chesley diagnosed a patient with atypical symptoms as cholera, much to the disgust of the Public Health officer who said such a diagnosis could not be made in less than three days. We had no more cholera. A patient was admitted with epidemic meningitis, in a coma and incontinent. After a fifteen-minute diagnosis by Chesley, the 98th Station Hospital ward officer gave an intravenous injection of sodium sulfathiazole to start his treatment: the following morning incontinence had ceased, by afternoon the patient was conscious, and the next day a nurse had to be on hand continuously to drag him back to isolation when he started to run away. There was no further meningitis.

Napoleon's observation that he would rather fight his allies than other nations was frequently recalled at our officers' mess. Our unit was composed entirely of allies, and we enjoyed ragging each other. Ted Gurney and the Friends Ambulance boys had to take caustic remarks about the frailties of the English. But it wasn't long before one of the Englishmen at the table would take a crack at the frailties of Americans, and then we Americans hadn't a chance, for our frailties were being displayed right under our collective noses. There was an especially heavy silence the day a new medical lieutenant joined the unit: he hadn't taken his bag from the jeep before he demanded that a bearer be secured for him at once. The lieutenant didn't feel happy about joining the unit when I announced that our officers were not allowed to have bearers. Without the excuse of being colonials, the Americans, enlisted men as well as officers, were hiring bearers everywhere. The farther away from the front they were the more bearers they had. The hallways of the Imperial Hotel in New Delhi were crowded with bearers waiting all day just to be on hand to draw "master's" bath, hold his pants for him, or fetch him cigarettes.

Of course, being typical G.I.'s, we griped about our work, and since our work was with the Chinese, we griped about them. Most interracial strife seems to be caused by differences in habits of thinking and acting. In America, men steal. But it is a relatively small per cent who steal and they steal in a big way, wholesale. The Chinese don't steal but they pilfer. It is not stealing to them —if they are not caught. They feel they are salvaging things for their own use. Pilfering is an almost universal Chinese habit, and several good truckloads of stuff could be carried away piecemeal. The Ramgarh hospital was completely surrounded by barbwire, but blankets walked out of the gates even in the daytime.

At our request guards were put on all the gates, but our blankets, mattresses, medicines, and even bedsteads "escaped" in a steady stream. Lieutenant Martin, our M.A.C. officer, discovered that almost four thousand rupees' worth of supplies had "escaped" during the first months. Later Lieutenant Baker, at my command, started several inventories of our stocks and each time had to give up in despair since the inventory became obsolete before he could finish one round of all the wards.

And there was nothing we could do about it. During his first speech to American officers at the post, General Stilwell had made plain the sensitiveness about loss of face which is a national characteristic of the Chinese race, and he warned us it would be an unforgivable offense for any American to lay hands on a Chinese while under his command. No order Stilwell gave caused more griping among the Americans than this one, chiefly because no similar order appeared to have been given to the Chinese, who frequently laid hands and drew guns on us. But Uncle Joe knew what he was doing. If he hadn't given that order there would have been no fighting against Japs in China-Burma-India. There would have been riots with far more casualties than the Japs caused—riots resulting from paltry, trumped-up misunderstanding of each other's customs and language.

General Boatner, then chief of staff of the Chinese Army in India, pretended to be a very ferocious infidel but he knew enough about Christianity to insist on my "giving till it hurt." First he asked me for Bill Cummings, who was then a second lieutenant in the Medical Administrative Corps. He had known Bill in Burma and his liking for him, as well as his respect for his command of the Burmese language, made him determined to acquire Bill for his own staff. Bill felt that more excitement could be found in this work than in a hospital unit, so we reluctantly let him go. A month later Bill and the general drove to the hospital in a jeep and asked to see me. Bill fidgeted around and couldn't look me in the eye. The general just hemmed and hawed.

"All right, all right. I know what you want, sir," I said. "You want Tun Shein."

"Yes, I do," the general admitted. He had all the arguments on his side and I could do nothing but let Tun Shein go too, though he had been invaluable to us as a supply officer. Later the general wheedled me into letting him have Saw Judson, my other Burmese supply officer, and finally even took away my Lahu boy Aishuri to work with Brayton Case in supervising the truck gardens he was persuading the Chinese Army to develop—Brayton Case who practically single-handed had fed the Chinese Fifth Army during the first campaign.

When the last of the 38th and 22nd divisions' battle casualties had been discharged to duty, our hospital census dropped rapidly to about seven hundred. Then my real troubles with the nurses began. During our first busy months they hadn't had time to be more than normally homesick. Furthermore, everyone prophesied that General Stilwell's return would begin in November, 1942. But Stilwell hadn't been given the wherewithal in 1942 and the sudden disappointment, coming at the same time as the decrease in pressure of work, was more than the girls could bear. At first they found a great deal of pleasure in the recreation hall we opened, where they could gather together in the evenings with the enlisted men and play games. Then the Special Service officer brought over officers twice a week to teach the girls to dance. But the girls weren't accustomed to mixed dancing and didn't enjoy it. Paul Geren proposed that we learn Gilbert and Sullivan's *Mikado* and put on a G.I. show of our own, but just as things were becoming interesting, the male soloists in the Friends Ambulance Unit were transferred to China and with them went our pianist. So that plan also failed.

Then I made a bad mistake. I bought the girls two guitars, a mandolin, and a ukulele. Thereupon they gathered four or five to a room of an evening, strumming and humming the songs they used to sing in Burma. Someone would make a nostalgic remark; someone else would add another; a third would voice her sense of frustration at the postponement of the return to Burma, and the whole party would forthwith dissolve in tears.

One night after the 98th Station Hospital had been transferred to Assam and our group had been augmented by personnel on detached service from the 181st General Hospital, a sack of belated mail arrived for the new officers. Lieutenant Chesley soon came for me in distress. Hla Sein had been chatting with him on his veranda quite cheerfully until the new officers began shouting to each other excitedly about letters they had just received from mother or wife. Hla Sein, to the best of her knowledge and belief, had lost every member of her family except one brother who had run out into China and had never been heard of since. She stood it as long as she could and then burst into violent hysterics, screaming and crying as if her heart would break. Chesley had been unable to quiet her.

I walked over, picked up Hla Sein, carried her back to her room and tucked her into bed, sitting beside her till her wild sobbing ceased.

"I'm all right now, Daddy," she said. "I'm going to sleep."

"Good girl," I said. "Good night."

The nurses' psychology was much like that of other exiled persons. They had voluntarily left their country in order to share in the task of liberation. Now the return seemed indefinitely postponed. It was impossible to reach their people by mail; and though their families were probably unharmed they had heard so many true accounts of Japanese atrocities that they knew that some, at least, had suffered. Poverty was rife in Burma, foodstuffs being commandeered by the Japs and clothing material completely unavailable. The fact that the nurses were rapidly banking funds to help their families only made matters more difficult since they had no way of sending the money to them. Many of the families in Burma didn't know that their daughters were safe with me in India, and the girls were sick at the thought that their families might be despairing of ever seeing them again. As a climax to their other worries, they realized with dread that with our return, cities and towns would have to be razed to the ground and thousands of civilians unintentionally killed. What was to prevent their own people being of this number?

American troops found it hard to endure separation from their families while on garrison duty in a foreign country even though they knew their families were safe from enemy attack and could exchange frequent letters with them. My own position was halfway between the American soldiers and the girl refugees. I could hear weekly from Tiny, get frequent letters from the two older children and an occasional one from the two little boys. I knew they were out of harm's way. I was homesick but I had resources to combat my feelings which the nurses did not have. They had no Burmese books to read, no magazines, no newspapers. And the language in English books and periodicals was so difficult for all but a few that they could get no enjoyment from them.

Lacking my forms of self-anesthesia the girls tried to develop some of their own. A movie theater had been opened with three-fifths of the seats assigned to the Chinese and the rest to Americans. Both Chinese and American units rotated on assigned days. The nurses greatly delighted in these movies and to my utter astonishment began to imitate various actresses, as their tastes dictated. Big Bawk fell for an actress in one of the musicals who talked with a resonant, singing tone even when she wasn't supposed to be singing. For months Bawk concentrated on her own voice, developing its naturally lovely, sweet tones until every word she said rang like a chime through the entire area. By the time we reached Myitkyina she was more expert than the screen star. We were then operating on some of the ghastliest casualties I had ever seen and under tremendous strain. To have Bawk, at the instrument table, sing out in her wonderful, resonant voice, "Okay, retractors coming up! Abdominal gauze? Right away!" would jerk me out of my operating trance and irritate me more than the shells that whistled over us.

One of the girls, who was never well, capitalized on her infirmity by posing as one of the extremely bored, disillusioned, indifferent ladies of the screen. The girls, who were by nature clowns, became even more skilled in the art as a result of the movies. And they began to change their hair-dos, which would have delighted Tiny since the new styles were designed to remain neat for hours at a time instead of collapsing every few minutes in the way that used to irritate her.

But of most absorbing interest to them were the love scenes and especially American love words. They were learning English very rapidly of necessity and there is no better place for a foreigner to learn English than at the movies. Practicing love words on each other didn't have quite enough spice in it for them. Besides, the feminine nature is extraordinarily possessive. They had to "own" someone, and God help the person who said more than three words or looked more than twice at their "property." Each girl had at least one other girl who was her personal property already. Now she set about looking for some male to call her own. That was not so very difficult. There were plenty of volunteers among the Americans, both officers and enlisted men, and it was seldom that the girls made a mistake in the men selected.

One of the prettier nurses had a special problem. She already "owned" two of the other girls who were not nearly so attractive as herself. She dictated every act of their private lives. While the pretty girl had a trail of boy friends, the other two had none. That would never do. A Burmese girl would be conspicuous if she didn't do something about her less fortunate friends. So she "assigned" one man to each of the others and saw to it that all four "played the game."

In the contest of wits that continued throughout the campaign, the boys definitely came out second best. I knew this, for I censored the girls' letters. The boys never caught on to the fact that they were being used as foils to satisfy female possessiveness or as a help in the practice of English. The girls wrote incredible letters, full of an extraordinary variety of love words and phrases picked up hit or miss at the movies and thrown hit or miss into the "sugar reports." One phrase would be used over and over until the little Burmese girl felt she had mastered it—then she would start on another. Fortunately sugar reports didn't have to be grammatical. The boys used slightly better grammar, but as for spelling, the girls won hands down. Being Americans, the boys never thought to use a dictionary. Being Burmese, the girls always did—either the dictionary or the old man. One of the girls went so far as to make me write her sugar reports for her. She would bring paper and pencil, ask me how one said this or that endearing phrase in English, get the spelling right, and then copy it. I often wondered how much her various boy friends would have enjoyed those love letters if they had known that they had been written by the old man.

I was particularly amused by the three girls who had long waiting lists of boy friends and at the way they handled them. To the pretty one, it was an entirely callous affair. The men were graded in her estimation according to rank. When the lieutenant was around she gave the sergeant the cold shoulder. When the captain arrived she cut the lieutenant dead. Undoubtedly she picked up this trait, too, at the movies.

The other two girls, like expert bridge players, succeeded in finessing the old love out of the way before the arrival of the new. I have no doubt that each boy friend fondly imagined himself the only one upon whom his beloved ever permitted her thoughts to rest. These two girls differed in their line of attack. The first was quite careless in her dress when none of her pets was around, but as soon as one appeared she would apologize hastily for her dress, since she had "just come off duty" or had "just come back from a stroll." Then she would excuse herself for a few moments and come back positively ravishing in a symphony of color. The other took no chances on being caught off balance and managed to make herself perfectly stunning in a pair of oversize G.I. pants and shoes big enough for me. One day I discovered that she had acquired half a dozen boy friends that even I hadn't known about.

"Listen, girl," I remonstrated, appalled, "don't you have about fifteen sweethearts too many?"

"Why, Daddy! How can you say that? It was you yourself taught us in Namkham that there was safety in numbers!"

A great deal of publicity had come to us because we had been with Stilwell on his trip out of Burma. The largest group on the retreat had been our hospital unit. Correspondents, anxious to put the C.-B.-I. theater on the map, pounced upon the Burmese nurses as being unique in the United States armed forces. Most of these correspondents had never been to Burma but their job was to bring Burma to public interest. The nurses were all the Burma they could find to describe, so they described them— plenty and often. All this would have done little harm had it not been for the fact that American journalists liked to exploit individual names, nicknames, and personalities. The girls with cute names or nicknames and those who were brim-full of personality were featured in one article after another. Visiting photographers would call for them by name and photograph them, to the exclusion of nurses more important to the work of the unit. A hard job well done gained no publicity whatever. So the efforts of the correspondents, though perhaps good for the theater, almost broke up the unit. Girls who had worked themselves sick wondered why they had tried so hard. Girls who made headlines by their attractive individualism decided that that was all that mattered and became more and more temperamental. I came to fear the advent of photographers and correspondents more than I feared the outbreak of an epidemic of bubonic plague, but I had to be courteous and helpful to the press as one of my war duties. I smiled externally but internally I boiled.

Whether Sergeant Opas was trying to help me in maintaining nurses' morale or adopting a ruse to get work promptly and efficiently done, I still don't know. But he succeeded admirably in either case. He pretended that he couldn't tell the Burmese girls apart and that even when he could, he couldn't pronounce their strange Burmese names. So he nicknamed them all Susy. There was Susy No. 1, Susy No. 2, Susy No. 3, and so on. He himself became just plain Susy to all of them. The result was that when something had to be done in a hurry, Opas had only to shout "Susy" and everyone on the operating-room staff jumped to attention. There was so much laughter and delight over this in the operating room that the 98th Station Hospital surgeons couldn't think and we had to ask the girls to laugh in whispers.

From then on nicknames were given all around, some of them most appropriate. Ma Kai delighted in the name of Tugboat Annie, which, considering her shape and her winning ways, was most apt. Hla Sein became Chow-hound No. 1 and Lulu, Chow-hound No. 2. Captain Yen, a Chinese Special Service officer, became Father Monkey and Little Bawk became Baby Monkey. Nang Aung could speak Chinese so fluently and with such a perfect accent that even the Chinese were mistaken in her ancestry and called her Miss Wang.

But everyone didn't help us maintain morale. When a Chinese is really sick he is the best patient in the world. So is he a fine soldier when actually in combat. But when he is in garrison or only a little sick, he can be at least as troublesome as most other soldiers. The nurses, being Burmese "foreigners," were considered legitimate prey, especially by the goldbricks.

Before General Stilwell had given us his order to keep hands off the Chinese, a major in Chit Sein's ward had pulled a revolver on her, "Miss Burma, 1942." I promptly beat him up most thoroughly and General Sun put him in jail. Later, when our hands were thoroughly tied by the order, all I could do was call the Chinese guards and have them throw the offender out of the hospital. There came an epidemic of trouble which did not help morale a bit. One Chinese soldier struck a nurse so forcibly on her breast that she was incapacitated for days.

Burmese *longyis* are circular skirts folded neatly about the waist and tucked in. They have to be retucked every few minutes, since they loosen with movement. Soldiers often snatched at these *longyis* to make them drop off. The girls reacted by buying G.I. belts. Occasionally some hero would make a pass at a nurse and then brag to his mates about his "conquest." One of these braggarts was a major on my own ward. When I heard of his efforts I got his clothes, gave them to him and stood by while a Chinese M.P. dressed him and kicked him out of the hospital.

The following Saturday night, as we left the cinema and climbed into our truck, we noticed the major standing in a milling group of soldiers. Just as our truck pulled out, two stones, each as big as a fist, were thrown at us. One of the stones struck Little Bawk's forehead with a sharp crack, laying her out for the rest of the evening, and the other hit big, broad Captain Kochenderfer so violently on the chest that his breath left him in a loud grunt. The officers and men rushed to jump from the truck to repay the Chinese in kind, but I remembered General Stilwell's order in time and insisted on their remaining where they were. The next day I took the stones to General Boatner.

"Just how far do we have to obey General Stilwell's order to keep our hands off the Chinese, sir?" I asked.

"Right up to the hilt!"

"What about self-defense, sir?"

"What do you mean?"

I told him about two incidents of attempted rape and about the blows and about the *longyi* snatching and showed him the stones. Boatner reached for the telephone, called General McCabe and reported the incident. The generals agreed there had been enough abuse of cinema privileges and ordered the cinema closed to both Americans and Chinese. Then Boatner called his secretary and dictated a written order empowering me to use any immediate disciplinary measures that seemed necessary in such emergencies, reporting the incidents and my handling of them as soon as possible thereafter. I never had to use that order. Our worst troubles ceased immediately. Very rarely after that did a Chinese soldier attempt insult to these girls—except for an occasional bit of profanity, and the nurses had learned so much Chinese that they could cuss the soldier down in his own language every time, much to the delight of the other patients. But the damage had been done. The cinema was closed and with it went the best self-anesthetizing device the nurses had yet found.

At Ramgarh there were rumors that Stilwell's campaign, already postponed till February, would not begin even then. I began to wish I hadn't kept my promise to Tiny—to come out of Burma if it fell—but had done what I had longed to do: remain behind and organize guerrilla bands of my own. I rather fancied myself as a guerrilla. With my local reputation in the Shan States I might well have succeeded. I tried to wheedle General Boatner into setting the nurses and me down by plane on some meadow in the Shan States to let us see what damage we could do to the Japs. All I got for my pains was a big laugh.

As time dragged on I grew desperate. If I didn't soon get these girls at least part of the way home, they would go mad. Or if they didn't—I would. The outcome of my desperation was our expedition to Tagap. But the Naga Hills were no more Burma than they were the valleys of the moon, and the girls were so disappointed that they were soon pouting for the boy friends they had used so cleverly for distraction at Ramgarh. In trying to help the girls over their unbearable nostalgia, I had ended by hurting them in their sensitive—and possessive—hearts.

3

Garrisons in the Naga Hills

WHILE the 38th Chinese Division was moving to Hkalak to replace the colonials, a battalion was ordered to guard the flank of the West Axis at Hpachet Hi. Captain Webb's hospital group was ordered forward from Punyang with this battalion. There was a lateral road connecting the two axes running from Tagap to Pebu to Hpachet. Since it was necessary for Webb's group to pass through Pebu, I arranged to meet them there and see personally to the establishment of the new hospital. I had a secondary thought in this plan. Perhaps if I were away from Tagap for two weeks it would be good for the girls there and, again, I might be good medicine for Webb's nurses who had already driven that long-suffering hero almost out of his wits.

From Tagap one drops back to the Namyung River on the Refugee Trail and then goes up the river, crossing from one side to the other some fifteen times in the first twelve miles. There had been leeches on the wide Refugee Trail—lots, we had thought, compared to anything we had ever seen in Burma. But at that time I hadn't seen the Pebu Trail. This must have been the birthplace and ancestral home of the leech. There were three species, all of them of the "ground leech" type, an inch or so long when hungry, as opposed to the "water leech" or "buffalo leech," some three inches long before it gets to work. The brown ones were on the ground or in the damp grass waiting, so close together that your eyes had to be focused on the ground at your feet to find a place where you could step without landing on several of them. The red variety kept out of the mud on the stems of the elephant grass or small plants, and the green ones on branches about shoulder height from the ground. All three kinds fastened themselves on you as you went by. They seemed to direct themselves by a sense of smell. Poised on the small sucker at the base, the big sucker at the head end waved in the air leaning directly toward you. If you suddenly moved a yard to another position, the leech would immediately sway like a compass needle and still keep pointed right at you.

Every ten or twelve steps my Naga porters stopped and cut leeches off their feet with their long dahs. I had a pocket knife and tried cutting my leeches in two after I scraped them off. Then I was astonished to see both halves come for me. I tried flicking them off with thumb and middle finger. I soon found you couldn't budge them if you snapped at them while the head sucker was attached. But they would fly off into the bushes at once if you flicked just as the head sucker was about to take over from the tail sucker. This was a pretty lesson in timing. The flick had to be correct to the split second or you could flick in vain all day.

At our first and second ten-minute rest periods I took off my leggings, socks, and shoes and burned off about thirty leeches that had squirmed through my defenses. Remembering experiences in Namkham with patients who had leeches in the nose, throat, and urethra, I finally compromised with the leeches of the Pebu Trail, letting them get their fill elsewhere so long as they kept away from my face and the fly of my trousers. All in all I tried all the routines: brushing the pests off with sacks of wet salt and tobacco, burning them off with matches. I found that nothing compared with Skat. If you soak the fly of your trousers and your socks with Skat, tuck your trousers into your socks and smear Skat all over the exposed parts of your body, the leeches take one suck and quit. But on this trip I had no Skat. When I reached Pebu I made a fire and cremated some seventy beautifully gorged specimens and then bled so much all night that my sheets were covered with blood.

I also had nightmares all night long, for two miles short of Pebu I had suddenly ceased looking for leeches at my feet and glanced upward to see a long green snake hanging by his tail from a branch, his head on a level with mine and his beady eyes star-

ing inquiringly at me. People had been telling me that there were
no snakes in the Naga Hills. On their trip from Tagap to Hkalak
months later Grindlay and Chesley killed three: a cobra, a krait,
and a Russell's viper, the big three of poisonous snakedom.

The next day was Saturday. I didn't expect Webb's detachment until Sunday, so I loafed and enjoyed the yarns of the radio
boys who had been evacuated from Hkalak when the colonials
abdicated in favor of the Japs. General (then Colonel) Cannon
walked into camp the same afternoon, having taken the mountain trail from Tagap. Cannon was doing what I was: getting
familiar with the terrain and helping his Chinese battalions
choose garrison sites and get themselves dug in.

The air supply dropping ground at Pebu was on the top of the
mountain behind the camp. On Sunday afternoon I climbed up,
both to meet the colored Quartermaster boys and their lieutenant
and to meet Webb's detachment if it came in. Nobody turned
up. So I loafed in camp until Thursday, when I again walked to
the top of the mountain; just as I reached the brow, down tumbled the nurses of Webb's unit on top of me, clattering along in
the huge G.I. shoes Webb had secured for them.

Next morning we struck up the mountain to the west and the
nurses taught me how to climb at such a slow pace that I could
continue steadily for fifty minutes instead of stopping to gasp
for oxygen every few steps. We made faster time going slowly
than we did when we struggled forward too rapidly for our hearts
to stand. We had quite a happy day's trip. The girls chattered
continually about their journey from Ledo, laughing as they recalled the way roly-poly Roi Tsai had negotiated the long steep
path down the east side of the first range in the middle of a downpour. Webb had had to order one of the men on ahead to each
corner to grab Roi Tsai as she slid, scrambled, tumbled, and
dived down each slope, brake her and turn her head on for the
next slope, while he ran ahead to repeat the maneuver at the next
corner.

That night was the worst I ever spent anywhere for insects.

There is no place in the Naga Hills that is not infested with one or another insect plague. In Hkalak it was a small black fly, which cuts a clean hole in your skin and then injects a drop of a horrible itch-producing poison. They bite only in the daytime, but you don't know they're biting or even that they're on you until the poison has been injected, and then it's too late to do more than squeeze out the poisoned blood and hope for the best. At this camp, too, there were literally clouds of buffalo flies, insects so tiny that they can hardly be seen. They bite only at night and swarm through the meshes of the mosquito net. A single bite doesn't itch nearly so much as that of the black fly, but when myriads of them bite at once it is more than the nervous system can endure. I may have slept a total of two hours that night. Our huts were horrible old coolie shacks with roofs of dried withered leaves, and it poured rain all night. We fastened our ground sheets over our mosquito nets. I didn't seem to be very expert at that. During the first half of the night the head end of the ground sheet gave way repeatedly and then the foot end fell down and buckets of water poured in on me.

The next day's trip into Hpachet, a large village full of pigs, chickens, cattle, buffaloes, and dogs, was almost entirely uphill but the country was so pretty and the villages so interesting—Hpachet is on the edge of real Naga country—that we didn't mind too much the steepness of the road; and the natives hadn't run away from the West Axis.

The air-drop field was located at the top of the mountain above Hpachet, with the American barracks beside it. Beyond it the Americans and Chinese were encamped. Lieutenant Mitchell, liaison officer, and Quartermaster Lieutenant Robinson and his colored boys were not expecting us and must have thought they were seeing things when we arrived; but they were equal to the occasion and made us royally welcome. We were soon sitting down to a good hot meal.

Building materials were very scanty about Hpachet and it was several days before we could get our quarters and a small hospital built between the Americans and the Chinese. The camp was so high that there were few insects and the scenery was beautiful. But because of the height, there was almost no water—just a trickle from a spring. Bathing was next to impossible and I could feel the forthcoming gloom. You can deprive nurses of almost anything and they will smile, but not if you deprive them of their baths.

General Boatner was now in command at Ledo. While I was in Hpachet a radio came in from him: "Your mission is first to furnish hospitalization for all Chinese troops south of the line Tagap-Pebu-Hpachet; second, to give medical attention to all porters in the employ of the U.S. Army; third, to furnish medical attention to the natives as far as practicable in order to obtain their friendship for the U.S. Army."

It was the end of May. During the week at Hpachet the weather had been delightful, but it couldn't last. If I didn't hurry back to Tagap before the rains finally broke in earnest I wouldn't be able to use the "leech trail" but would have to strike for the mountains. I would rather have the leeches than the mountains any day. The rains actually broke before I reached Pebu but we made it anyway, cutting new trails here and there to avoid crossing the Namyung.

I arrived back at Tagap in time for another "battle." The shooting began at Nathkaw, several miles south, where a patrol of Japs had been reported trying to outflank our outpost. The outpost at Kumkidu heard the shooting and opened fire and then Tagap itself threw in everything it had. We kept ducking as all sorts of missiles whistled over us. Bill Cummings was a bit skeptical of there being any Japs near us so he set off with another officer to investigate while the nurses and I cut several American-made bullets out of Chinese bodies. On his return Bill told us that there hadn't been a single footprint in the valley through which "the Japs" passed. Bill had asked the Chinese captain which direction he had been firing.

Tagap Home Laundry

Medical Supplies and Food Were Dropped by Parachute at Tagap

Grenade
Fishing

Gurney,
Grindlay,
and
Seagrave

*Photos by
Bill Duncumb*

"Sir," the captain had replied with much dignity, "we fired in *every* direction!"

They had most certainly been firing in every direction. The first Chinese soldier to be killed was the sentry on the north edge of camp hit by a bullet fired across the camp by a sentry at the south edge. Machine-gun bullets had riddled the mosquito nets of the American radio boys, who luckily had dropped into their trenches at the first shot.

I couldn't understand how the troops under my friend Major Peng had gone so haywire at this late date, for on the occasion when they had opened fire on the herd of monkeys in April, Peng had almost immediately controlled the mass hysteria of his troops and they had subsequently been well disciplined. I soon found these were not Major Peng's troops. All but one company of his command had already left for a "rest" at Ledo—funny place for a rest, malarious Ledo—and the job had been taken over by another regiment. Peng was still at Tagap, however, and the moment Japs had been reported at Nathkaw he had radioed General Sun for permission to remain in Tagap with his one company so he could help give the Japanese another licking. That seemed quite typical of the man. He went off to Ledo in great disgust when he learned there had been no Japs at Nathkaw.

Grindlay's detachment was now due to arrive and we all decided to go meet them. Knowing that the rains would make the Namyung River unfordable, American engineers had had cables dropped by air, dragged them to the site by elephant, and built a suspension bridge across the Namyung gorge. There was a new road to this bridge and Bill Cummings claimed he knew where it was. Thinking we might have a long wait, we took our swimming suits and some hand grenades and a picnic lunch so we could enjoy ourselves while waiting. Our stomachs already rebelled at canned corned beef.

But Bill had been too enthusiastic about his knowledge of the right turnoff. He led us on the wrong path and we finally arrived at a river that was not the Namyung at all. We agreed we'd have plenty of time for a good swim, fishing, a picnic lunch and still be able to return to the Refugee Trail to meet Grindlay. So we cast all care aside, put on our swimming suits, and had a really good time. It was the first time the girls had worn occidental swimming suits instead of *longyis* and they were quite shy at first, though the suits were extremely becoming.

Bill went upstream to a deep hole under an overhanging cliff and threw in a grenade. Fish of all sizes up to eighteen inches floated down, and men and women went wild grabbing at them. Bill and my Chinese orderly Pang Tze (Fatty) got the biggest fish, but Chit Sein and Little Bawk won on total number, though Bawk was just learning to swim. Chit Sein, born on the banks of Inle Lake, the largest lake in Burma, could swim like a fish. Grabbing fish right and left and diving into the deep water for them, she thrust them into the bosom of her swimming suit and piled them into the tiny apron, came out of the water after each dive bulging in all the wrong places, rid herself of her fish on shore, and dived back in again.

I managed to catch one small fish.

When our three grenades were used up and we had caught enough fish to furnish the whole unit with a big meal, we started a fire, made coffee, ate our picnic lunch, then hurried back up the hill. As usual Grindlay was ahead of schedule and we found the crowd had just passed by. They were still getting out of wet clothes when we arrived back at the hospital.

It was a very happy meeting. Everyone jabbered about the experiences on the trail: how the leeches had been quite nasty to Grindlay's dog; how E Kyaing, in spite of her clubfoot, had refused the privilege of making the trip slowly with an escort, had thrown away her painful shoes at the first stop, and had kept up with the rest of the party barefooted; how Grindlay, who couldn't carry a tune, had taught them on the trail to sing "Alouette" and how the girls were singing in French as well as English and Burmese. Big Bill Duncumb had come back to us from the Friends

Ambulance China Convoy and he had taught the nurses to sing what they called the English pub song, "Green Grow the Rushes—O."

But shrieks of laughter burst forth as Koi described how she and Emily had bathed in the nude at Namlip Sakan. Arriving hot and tired, they were desperately in need of a bath but had no change of clothing along so couldn't let their clothes get wet. So they walked up around a bend in the stream out of sight of the camp and everyone else, and then, promising each other by the memory of their ancestors not to glance around, placed their backs firmly together—apparently they didn't trust each other's ancestors—and bathed, continually admonishing each other not to look.

For days, while we waited for permission to push on to Hkalak, everyone was busy and happy. Our bamboo walks between the wards had fallen apart, so the men dug up and crushed soft rock; nurses lugged it to the wards and we soon had paved paths everywhere. Squads of nurses hoed and planted a large garden with the types of vegetables that could be eaten as they grew. There is hardly a green thing Burmese girls don't love to eat; they eat pea vines, for instance, long before the peas flower and pod.

To prepare Hkalak for us, Dr. San Yee, two nurses, and a Chinese boy had gone on ahead. Now they radioed that quarters were built and medical work was increasing rapidly, so I set out with seven nurses and Pang Tze. Of the three Chinese garrisons, Tagap was the largest and Hpachet the smallest. Hkalak, of medium size, was farthest forward, and about twenty-five miles from Hkalak was Shingbwiyang, still in the hands of the Japs. Since Captain Webb and Captain Johnson were friends, I detailed Johnson to join Webb at Hpachet. Grindlay always got mad if he didn't have enough medicine and surgery, so I left him in charge at Tagap with Gurney, who now had his commission as captain, and Ba Saw. At Hkalak I would be farthest forward and in an intermediate position between our two other stations.

The road from Tagap was west along the Salt Springs Trail,
down, down, down, crossing two large streams like millraces to a
broken-down coolie camp at the Salt Springs. If we had only
known it, we could have gone four miles farther to a lovely little
camp that had just been built. Anyway, we spread our ground
sheets over the broken-down roof and slept on the broken bamboo floor. From there, the next morning, we walked many miles
continually uphill over an unconscionably miserable excuse for a
trail. In many places we had to guess where the trail was supposed
to be. There were innumerable fallen trees over which we had to
scramble, some of them four feet in diameter. We evolved a
special technique with these: one, look for leeches; two, turn
your back to the tree; three, push yourself up to a sitting position
on the top; four, swing your legs over in an arc; five, pray silently
that your knees can take it; six, drop down on the other side.

Halfway up the huge mountain, the strong wind had blown
down bamboos, forming arches about four feet high across the
trail. It began to rain and we had to stoop under the bamboo
arches and claw ourselves to a stop with our fingernails when we
started to slip back. About three in the afternoon we came to a
shoulder of the mountain that we thought must be the top and,
therefore, near our next proposed camp. The nurses were hungry
and cast eager eyes at bamboo shoots, the first we had seen in
two years, so we stopped every few rods and cut the shoots to
carry with us. The wind was very strong now and made us shiver
in our wet clothes as we climbed. The top was still a long way off.

When we finally reached the camp there was nothing left of
it but a few scattered bamboos. We were tired out but the girls
managed to put up a framework to support our ground sheets and
a lot of leafy branches. We stuffed ourselves on rice and fried
bamboo and got what sleep we could between the attacks of
buffalo flies.

By this time I discovered I had become the private property of
my Chinese soldier friend Pang Tze, who had been a sergeant
major in the Chinese Army before becoming an orderly in the

Ramgarh hospital. He had popeyes and a domineering manner, and I wouldn't have chosen him to come along with us. He chose me instead and insisted on staying with me. Now he was the real boss. He wouldn't allow me to carry even my musette bag or canteen. He strapped on my revolver and carried that as well. When I had trouble climbing over a tree trunk or huge boulder, his big paw would reach out, grab me by the seat of the pants, and heave me over. I used to have to argue with him to let me bathe myself. He brought me my food and almost insisted on feeding me; and if I tried to wash my own messkit he would become extremely hurt. The status of every man and woman in the unit could be judged by whether or not Pang Tze would take orders from them. Those who were at the moment out of favor with me had their orders ignored.

Our third day out of Tagap was much easier. The road was as much down as up. The only interesting feature was our crossing of a small lake on what appeared to be a floating island of sod. I hesitate to think what would have happened to us if we had stepped off the well-defined path. Then after one last horribly cold damp night beside a stream with still more buffalo flies, we were over the range and moving down into the camp we had left at Hkalak. Hla Sein and Lulu, Chow-hounds Nos. 1 and 2, came running out to meet us. Several little bamboo huts had been built for us, though mine was not yet completed. The site was wonderful, on a camel's back to the north of the Chinese camp. It faced directly east across the gorgeous mountain country we were later to cross on our way home to Burma. Two small rivers sprang full grown from the land—the one on the north to supply the hospital, and the other on the south to be entirely private for our personnel. There seemed to be only one fly in the ointment, a very real fly—our old friend the black or dumdum fly; but with Skat even this pest didn't bother us—much.

Instead of waiting for me to check in with him, the liaison officer, Lieutenant Stewart, came over to check in with me. Not far behind him was the Chinese battalion commander. I knew at once that there was to be one more fly in the Hkalak ointment. In my time I have come to know many officers, good and bad, in many different armies. I cannot permit myself to state my feelings with regard to Major X, except to say that he would disgrace an army in Hades, where he undoubtedly is now roaming restlessly around. The major's first act was to try to force me to "pull my rank" on Lieutenant Wallace, the Quartermaster, and compel him to issue American rations to his troops instead of the Chinese rations to which they were entitled by order of Chungking. When I refused, he tried to force me, "for safety's sake," to move the hospital into a hollow in the center of the Chinese camp. After my experience with trigger-happy troops at Tagap, I knew we would be safer outside the Chinese lines.

The night of our arrival, Wallace and his colored boys came over to give us a welcome concert. Wallace pretended he couldn't sing, but no sooner did his boys get off the first note when he jerked to his feet, put an arm around each of his sergeants' shoulders, and joined his tenor to theirs. They began with "Praise the Lord and Pass the Ammunition" and ended with "When I Take My Vacation in Heaven." Their voices were very good and their harmony superlative. Amo's eyes rolled, Grier's bass growled, Casey's tenor soared upward, and the Burmese girls sat by with throbbing hearts, completely fascinated. When Jimmy Ackerson opened up on "Shout, Brother, Shout," the girls' feet began to itch and they joined in the shouting in true revivalist fashion.

The boys always came to our Sunday-evening sings and gave us another concert after each service. When any new dignitary came to town they threw him a concert and party.

I was always greatly impressed by all the dealings between our enlisted men, both white and colored, and the natives throughout Burma. I wonder why psychological studies are not made on different races based on the dozen or so words each race will pick as the most essential to teach to foreigners or to learn from foreigners. With the English, the words of Hindustani deemed most essential are those for "Get out!" "Go!" "Stop!" "Left!"

"Right!" For the Indian the most essential words are "No papa, no mama, no brother, no sister—backsheesh!" In Chinese the words necessary for Americans are "Hao bu hao? Ding hao, bu hao!"—Good or bad? Very good, no good! The many Burmese languages are too much for the Americans, but what they teach the natives is "Okay. Come on, let's go!" whereat everyone digs in with a laugh and the job is promptly done.

It's the "Let's go" that spells the difference between the American and the colonial Englishman because it indicates the truth: that the American intends to work along with the natives and sweat the job out with them. It is therefore not surprising to hear natives everywhere say of the four races: "We fear and detest the Japs. We are afraid of the Chinese. We respect the British. But we love the Americans, especially when they leave our women alone."

General Boatner had given us the task of doing medical missionary work among the natives to win their friendship for the U.S. Army. But these American Quartermaster men were already doing a swell missionary job. It was high time I got busy. Ted Gurney and several nurses and Big Bill Duncumb had made one tour among the natives out of Tagap, circling first east, then north, and so back to the Refugee Trail. Gurney reported considerable success in treating natives in the villages, and many of the patients who needed hospitalization followed him back to the hospital or were carried to Tagap. Now Grindlay, too, was circling more directly east and south and, using the excuse that an American pilot had been forced down in a very wild section, he made a forced march alone except for a Naga companion to a high valley never before visited by a white man.

Grindlay is a funny cuss. To listen to his claims he is a growling, atheistic, profane hater of all mankind. In practice he is gentle, kind, inordinately interested in humanity, especially in its stranger forms. He sits for hours making the natives talk about themselves, their customs, their strange ideas. By the time he has done he has won them into feeling themselves his equals and they are eager to give him everything they have. Completely antagonistic to the very idea of missionaries, he is the best medical missionary I've ever seen.

I radioed Johnson at Hpachet to make a missionary trip south on the West Axis to the top of Mu Bum, halfway to Hkalak, where I would meet him with another party, exchange nurses, and let the two groups have a change from the monotony of Hpachet and Hkalak. I wanted to see the road that had killed so many men of the 22nd Chinese Division.

We dropped down rapidly to the foot of the Hkalak mountain, three nurses, my pal Pang Tze, and I, and found twenty miles of the smoothest trail we'd seen in all that country. The grades were easy, the weather clear, there were no leeches, the scenery was exquisite, and there were interesting native villages—a pleasant change, since the villagers around Hkalak were too sophisticated for us. They were well fed and well paid, since they worked for the Quartermaster. They had a market at ten times normal price for all the fresh foodstuffs the Chinese wanted, so they paid no attention to us and refused to sell us a thing. The only interest they showed in us was the height to which girls of their own race group had attained. The women of all the villages were completely fascinated by the nurses.

Our second camp was in a four-house village. Here we were lucky enough to find the headman's family all sick in bed— lucky in that we were able to be of so much assistance to him that he was later to prove a very great help to the garrison at Hkalak.

Early the next morning we began the difficult ascent of Mu Bum. The road was good again, the grade was entirely legitimate. But whereas we had previously passed not more than fifty or sixty Chinese skeletons, we were now passing groups of from ten to thirty skeletons every few hundred yards. Unlike the refugee

skeletons, however, these soldiers had not died completely un-
attended where they dropped, on the trail and at the water holes.
They were in small broken-down camps. Apparently their comrades had helped them into camp and tended them till they
died, and then pushed on themselves, too weak to give proper
burial to their dead comrades.

About five miles before we reached the top of Mu Bum, we
ran into Captain Johnson's party cooking dinner for us by the
side of the road. Their coolies had already started building two
thatch huts. Johnson and his nurses had made such good time
that they'd passed the top of Mu Bum before realizing it and
then had picked what Johnson felt was rather a good site for a
camp. We were so delighted to see one another that no one
realized till the next morning what a very extraordinary camp
site it was. What we had thought were a lot of thick bushes just
beyond the campfire and the huts were the tops of giant trees.
The camp was within a yard of an enormous precipice.

Wondering for what tasks the good Lord was saving us, we
exchanged nurses and started back. We had planned to go all the
way back to the village at the foot of Hkalak hill in one day and
sleep there, but we heard that there was a "safe hand" letter
from General Boatner for me at Hkalak and so we pushed on up
the hill that night.

During our first two months at Hkalak, Major X forced his
battalion to perform a prodigious amount of labor in building a
most elaborate system of defenses. He was obviously planning to
remain at Hkalak for the duration. Now his defenses were complete and he planned an inspection of three days to be performed
by me, of all people, and Lieutenant Wallace who was now
liaison officer as well as Quartermaster. Since I wasn't busy medically, and couldn't think of a valid excuse, I spent three of the
unhappiest days of my life inspecting every trench, every fox-
hole, every dugout and pillbox, not only in the main camp but

in the outposts as well. Wallace was a canny southerner and stood around looking at the scenery and, taking notes, pretending to be mapping the defenses, while I jumped in and out of trenches and foxholes, exclaiming about their individual "merits"—each was really worse than the last—gasping in astonishment at the marvelous intricacies of each dugout and pillbox. The climax came when Major X took me into the top story of his own pillbox. "This pillbox," he said proudly, "being my own command post for the day the Japs attack us, is, of course, the best of them all!" He leaned against the center post which promptly fell with a clatter to the floor.

Never have I seen anything so childish as those defenses. Though fortifying against an enemy that notoriously attacked from the rear, the major had outposts on all the roads into Hkalak except the one in the rear. The "outpost" on the road from the south was two hundred yards from the center of camp. Every pillbox or dugout had at least one line of fire directed exclusively against American barracks and installations. The line of fire of several machine guns was such that nothing could be hit but some enormous trees. The major was especially proud of the camouflage of his pillboxes, which could be seen from ten miles away in any direction. If I'd been a Jap platoon leader I'd have considered no assignment easier than to wipe out this battalion.

The third afternoon the major threw a huge dinner party for the entire camp. There were speeches. Then there were two volleyball games. At my request the Signal Corps team, in their contest with Major X's team, took a terrific beating, after which Wallace and his Quartermaster boys could safely and most thoroughly drub the Chinese. Then came dinner. It was really excellent, for it was composed of American rations, Chinese rations, and quantities of bamboos and mushrooms from the jungle. Major X had gotten gallons of what the Americans called bamboo juice, potent stuff, and everyone promptly toasted everyone else with the usual *kambei!*—bottoms up! After the banquet the Chinese platoons sang Chinese patriotic songs, and it was over.

Informers began to bring in reports that the Japanese were opening a series of supply bases on a line from Taro, outflanking us, and on to a point within twenty air miles of Ledo. General Boatner radioed that General Sun was ordering Major X to send a platoon to cut this supply line and ambush the Japanese. I was ordered to furnish two first-aid men to accompany the expedition. I had only two men, Sergeant Deaton and Chiou Seing, a former officer of the Chinese Army who was working with me. Neither of these men had seen action—and when anyone in my unit was to see action for the first time, I wanted to lead him into it—not drive him. I promptly radioed Boatner for permission to go. In the morning, back came Boatner's message addressed to all American liaison officers in the Naga Hills: "Any American who catches Seagrave more than five miles in any direction from Hkalak is hereby ordered to shoot him. Seagrave is not, repeat not, allowed to go on this expedition." Boatner told me later that General Stilwell came into his office just after the message had been sent and that he showed the general a copy.

"Change it," Stilwell growled, "change it to one hundred yards!" So I sat and cussed and cussed.

Then a message came from Boatner saying that the Chinese had been ordered to leave Wednesday morning and that all American officers were to get a hump on and arrange for porters and rations and help in every way to see that the platoon left on time. That meant me, for Lieutenant Wallace was off on a patrol to Shingbwiyang and I was the only officer around.

I walked over to see the major and to find out how many men there were in a platoon of Chinese so I could secure the correct rations and porters. He said a Chinese platoon consisted of forty-five officers and men. I therefore arranged for rations for forty-five men in a platoon. I promised that the rations would be forthcoming and that more would be dropped after a three days' march. That evening he returned and declared there were seventy-five men in a platoon. By Wednesday morning the number was eighty-five. He was clearly trying to use American "inability" to furnish rations for his "platoon" as an excuse for not sending the platoon on the mission. After three hours of argument I convinced him that General Sun would have his hide if he disobeyed his orders, and at noon he finally permitted his captain and lieutenant to start. Both the captain and the lieutenant were as fine men as the Chinese Army could produce and had been eager to be off. The captain was later killed at Taro and the lieutenant was brought to me with his femur shattered by a machine-gun bullet.

The major deployed the first two squads with fixed bayonets— the Japanese were only five days' journey away—and with them his Chinese "intelligence" section. These men, who between them were able to speak some fifteen or twenty Burmese words and in a frightful accent at that, he had dressed in what he thought were Burmese clothes, skirts of white parachute cloth— Burmese men never wear white *longyis*—and nondescript torn shirts. Since this was Naga and not Burmese country, he might better have disguised them as Nagas, in other words sent them off naked. As the rations were portered out the major himself counted the number of loads, and his only complaint was that I was sending Chinese rations instead of American.

The next morning, before I had had my second cup of coffee, he sent his personal interpreter, the worst scab in any army, barring the major himself, to tell me that he was furiously angry with me for having lied to him about the number of rations I'd sent. I coldly told the interpreter to go back and tell his chief that he had seen the ration loads go out himself and had counted them. Furthermore he might remind the major that in no man's army does a major call a lieutenant colonel a liar or get "furiously angry" with him. The major stormed for hours after my message reached him.

When Wallace returned the next day the major ran to him and asked if he did not wish to hear what a rascal I was. Wallace said he did not, probably because he already knew. That took the wind completely out of the major's sails. He sent me a message of apology and invited the whole American camp to a banquet of apology the following night to restore his "face."

A diversion occurred the following day when Lieutenant Topp walked in with a staff photographer and an order to do a story on the Seagrave Unit. I was glad to see Topp but not the camera. Since Ramgarh, cameras were a terror to me. The nurses had read some of the "stories" and had picked out places in them where correspondents had deliberately changed my answers to make the kind of story they thought the people back home would like. I never could persuade the girls that I hadn't told the falsehoods or selected the same photogenic group each time for the pictures. But Topp had been ordered to write the story, which later appeared in *Life*, so I explained to the girls the value the army placed upon keeping the theater in the eye of the public, and they cooperated very well. Topp not only got some wonderful pictures but gave us a very decent and subdued write-up.

The next evening at dusk Nang Aung, Emily, Tugboat Annie, and Pang Tze arrived, having made the thirty-mile trip from the top of Mu Bum to Hkalak in one day, a feat an infantryman would be proud of. Then the silly girls stayed up till after midnight, shouting, singing, and laughing as they recounted their adventures at Hpachet.

Letters reached me from Tagap saying that Pearl, E Kyaing, and Louise wanted to take a vacation at Calcutta, and I was in trouble again. These girls hadn't had a vacation for two years. Perhaps I was all wrong. Looking at the matter now I know I was wrong, for I had put the success of our job first in importance, the integrity of the unit second, and personalities third. When we first went to Ramgarh there hadn't been time for vacations, so only the sick were permitted them. About the time the work began to decrease we were unofficially alerted for a campaign to begin in November or December, 1942, so we only arranged for a rest camp in the mountains near Ramgarh. The girls had wanted to tour India. Then the campaign was postponed till mid-February and I sent off one party of nurses on a vacation to Agra and Delhi. If line officers would only give medical officers definite information, which they never do, I would have had no difficulty, for our work was easy and I could have sent off large groups of nurses at any time.

Now in the middle of the Naga Hills in the latter part of the rainy season, with our unit newly alerted for action supposed to begin the first week of October, three of the girls—one of whom had a clubfoot—wanted a vacation. I wrote back advising against it because, first, a total of twelve days' marching through deep mud would not make fourteen days in Calcutta a very successful vacation and because, second, we were alerted for a day earlier than they could possibly return; but I left the decision up to them. They decided to let the vacation go. But then girls who had not asked for leave began to gripe verbally and in letters, until I dreaded to see the mail runner arrive.

Then General Boatner ordered me to Ledo to discuss plans for the medical setup for the coming campaign. He had suggested by radio that he place three new portable surgical hospitals, fresh from the States, under my command and the 25th Field Hospital in close liaison so I could integrate the medical work of the entire front and, as he put it, get the new units away from the Park Avenue methods of running hospitals and get them used to the woods. Grindlay came to Hkalak to hold the fort during my absence.

During the whole rainy season Lieutenant Harris had been the unit's liaison officer between our different detachments. He had covered some twelve hundred miles over the ghastly trails, wearing out one pair of G.I. shoes every sixty miles. He was now in Hkalak and wanted to join us, so he, Pang Tze, and I set off together for Tagap. May the good Lord spare me from traveling the Naga Hills with Harris again. On the trail he would hold his arms away from his sides, like a cormorant drying its wings, and sail along. I would reach the top of each hill a half mile or so behind him and have to run down the other side hell bent for election to catch up with him. I wouldn't even have enough time to pull off leeches. By the time we reached Tagap our porters were completely disgusted and ran away.

From Tagap we followed the new trail across the suspension bridge over the Namyung. When American engineers built this bridge they shrugged off the approaches and let the Nagas build them unassisted. The Nagas cut steps from two to four feet high, right straight up the mountain. One step was so high that a half-inch rope had been fastened to a tree above, so the climber could pull himself up to the higher level.

The last day before we reached the roadhead at Nawngyang, Harris took sick and I actually beat him into camp. At Nawng-yang we hopped a jeep for the rest of the trip into Ledo.

At Ledo I discovered that Colonel Vernon W. Petersen, M.C., had arrived the day before, assigned to combat headquarters. Boatner's plans were therefore automatically canceled and I had made that horrible trip for nothing. Petersen not only outranked me but was a splendid officer of many years' experience in the army. They didn't need me any longer. The whole theater was lousy with medical units, and with many more on the way.

But my troubles weren't over. General Boatner ordered me off on a month's vacation.

"But, sir," I protested. "I've been doing nothing but sit on my fanny for months."

"I am the one who gives orders in this headquarters," he said.

So there I was, off for a month's vacation I didn't want, after having requested the Tagap nurses not to insist on theirs. On top of everything else, that was too much for them, and I wasn't surprised when I returned to Tagap to find that the girls had no further use for me.

PART TWO

THE LONG ROAD TO MYITKYINA

In 1943, forces of the United Nations climbed up the ladder of the Solomons. Early in 1944 they invaded the Gilberts and Marshalls and leapfrogged up the coast of New Guinea. Simultaneously a campaign for the control of the Hukawng and Mogaung valleys in Burma was fought by Chinese, British, and a small force of American troops. Fighting and cutting their way through the hills and jungles, the Chinese and Americans advanced toward the strategically important town of Myitkyina which the Japanese defended until August 3, 1944.

While the campaign for the Hukawng and Mogaung valleys was being fought, the Japanese launched two offensives on the Arakan and Manipur fronts in an effort to cut the Bengal-Assam railway to Ledo. Had they succeeded, the communication lines of the Chinese and American forces in northern Burma would have been severed. The repulse of the Japanese by the British Fourteenth Army at Kohima and Imphal—and the capture of Myitkyina—assured the eventual realization of General Stilwell's plan for the conquest and construction of a relief route to China.

4

The First Offensive

AFTER my unfortunate vacation I returned to Ledo four days late for the job at hand. The Chinese had been ordered forward in three columns. The first, from Hkalak, was to secure the right flank at Taro, then held by the Japanese. A detachment of our unit, minus nurses, was to proceed with them and serve that flank until replaced by a surgical team of the U.S. 151st Medical Battalion. The second column of Chinese would advance from Tagap to secure the left flank at Sharaw down the Tarung Valley. Another detachment of our unit, also minus nurses, was ordered to proceed with them. The third and main column would then advance directly south to Shingbwiyang and continue up the Hukawng Valley until stopped by the enemy. The main group of our unit, with our nurses, would follow this center thrust in three echelons. I assigned Captain Johnson and three Burmese technicians to the Sharaw flank—Major Grindlay, Major O'Hara, Lieutenant Chesley, and Dr. Ba Saw to the center. If I made a forced march of double stages, I could reach Hkalak in time to head that detachment with Dr. San Yee and three men. Captain Gurney and the nurses would remain at Hkalak until relieved there. Captain Webb's transfer from our unit to another assignment was a terrible blow, but he was being replaced by Lieutenant (now Captain) Antonellis already on his way to join Grindlay at Tagap.

Harris and Pang Tze were willing to undertake the double-stage forced march, so we set off with as small a kit as possible. When we reached Namlip Sakan we came upon Antonellis whose knees had soured on him. He had planned to rest there a day but decided to go on with us if we would let him take his time. I could well sympathize with him, for my own knees had squeaked

83

for three days after we first reached Tagap, for a week after I made the Hpachet trip, and for a month after we went to Hkalak.

At Tagap we left Antonellis for a few days of rest and started on for Hkalak. Reinforcements for Major X were on the road, sick and weary from their long march. One poor soldier with a high temperature was helping himself down from rock to rock in a part sitting, part crawling posture. We knew he could make that last mile to our hospital so hurried on by. It was wonderful to have the Hkalak girls come running to meet us with the old-style enthusiasms we had grown so to depend on. The Quartermaster boys came over immediately to give us a welcome concert.

One day late already, we hurried on the next morning and by nightfall caught up half a day on Major X's troops. Two of my men were with him so there was no further necessity for me to hurry. It was known that there were no Japanese north of Ngajatzup. If I arrived at the village two miles north of Ngajatzup the day the Chinese contacted the Japs, I would still be in plenty of time.

The second day out of Hkalak, Harris broke down. I didn't wish Harris any bad luck but I was quite proud of the fact that the old man had outlasted the young infantryman from the mountains of Tennessee. Stinky Davis was waiting at this camp with a fever casualty whom he turned over to Harris and then he went on with me.

After two more days we reached a little deserted village behind the lines and were eating our third meal of baked beans for the day when our first casualties arrived. One of them was a lieutenant who had a shattered thigh with a three-inch overriding of the bone ends. No forward unit had even an imitation fracture table, so it was up to me to arrange some sort of traction apparatus. It might be weeks before the lieutenant could be evacuated, so we had to give definitive treatment in the jungle. We set up on the dirt floor of the veranda of an abandoned Naga house in the midst of buffaloes and their dung. Naga houses have enormous posts and girders. Our parachute air-drop canvas bags were reinforced with two-inch-wide straps. We ripped off these straps and, fastening them to the girders above, suspended our lieutenant by the hips and shoulders a foot above the bamboo operating table. With cuffs of strapping around ankles and armpits and a lot of rope, we secured traction and countertraction on our patient by pulling against the posts of the house. The knee and thigh were held in the correct amount of flexion and abduction by additional straps fastened to the roof. It was then easy to put the patient in a plaster cast which incorporated the straps. The "fracture table" was such a success that I decided to patent it, though a Naga house might prove difficult to transport all over the jungle.

We didn't have a good night's sleep in that old house, for it was already far too well "occupied." In the morning we picked out two newer shacks, much smaller but cleaner, at the other end of the village. The village was built in a semicircle around the crown of a little hill, and the Air Corps transport planes were using this thirty-by-eighty-yard area as a dropping field. It was the first time our transports had dropped so close to the Japanese lines and the pilots were probably a bit nervous. They were also new to air-dropping so they were very erratic. Already we had lost one Chinese whose skull had been cracked like an eggshell when a sack of rice hit him. Now, all day long, we had to dodge as they threw rice, corned beef, baked beans, mortar shells, and small-arms ammunition at us. On the afternoon of our second day, there were only four houses left untouched by air-drop. A Kachin Ranger persisted in taking refuge under one of these while planes were dropping, refusing to learn the lesson of the ruined houses. As I stood watching, a case of ammunition burst loose from its parachute shrouds and struck him squarely on the head and shoulders. He was dead before I could reach him.

The third morning a plane came over whose pilot had gone completely haywire. Without the usual warning he buzzed down the length of the field and dropped about fifteen sacks of rice within a very few yards of where I was standing beside our hospital. Very well, I thought. If he's going to drop lengthwise I'll step over behind that house twenty-five yards to the side. Back circled the pilot. This time he shifted his axis thirty degrees and again the sacks came straight for me. I moved over another twenty-five yards but he came straight for me again. He was shooting pretty close. He must be trying to get me, I thought. Okay, I'll move once more. There was a tree behind which I had stood during previous droppings. It had a trunk nine inches thick. If the pilot threw them at me there, it would mean he was dropping on an axis exactly ninety degrees from his first throw. I stood a foot from the tree and peered out to watch. He was heading straight for me. Just as the sacks tumbled out I drew my body erect and turned sideways behind the tree. Sacks fanned my back and one struck squarely in the fork of the tree beside my head. The tree bent with the shock, hitting me on the point of my shoulder and fracturing the coracoid process of my scapula.

The pilot must have seen me tumbling down the hill, for he didn't change his axis again. Chinese soldiers grabbed me and put me in their trench while they stood guard over me. This would have been little protection if the transport had "bombed" us again, but the soldiers seemed to think it more important for their *Lao E Guan* (old doc) to be safe than for themselves to keep out of harm's way.

A half hour after the bombing the medical detachment of the 151st Medical Battalion arrived. I had been worried about how to keep people from finding out about my shoulder. If I had to operate in the next few days some American might see something peculiar about the movements of my left shoulder and report me. Then brass hats would order me back to Ledo just as the campaign was getting under way. The arrival of the 151st boys meant I could use the ten days of marching back to Hkalak and Shingbwiyang in teaching myself how to handle that shoulder. I took the captain into my confidence and he strapped it into position with adhesive tape so I wouldn't be tempted to swing my arm

as we marched. The next day went well. I had dreaded the climb
up the precipice to Lulum but even here I had no trouble, for
Pang Tze pushed me all the way to the top.

Traveling by double stages again, we reached Hkalak and
found that Gurney and the girls there thought I had been
wounded. They were more gently exuberant over my return than
ever before. If I'd thought it would have the same effect on the
nurses at Tagap, I'd have stayed out in the open and let the
"bomber" pilot have one more chance at me!

It was hard leaving Hkalak and the Quartermaster boys. We
had had happy times there. The boys came down to give us a
farewell concert and of course they ended with their "master-
piece."

> High above the Chindwin River,
> Near the Taga Hka,
> Stands our dear old Alma Mater,
> Hail to Hkalak Ga!
>
> Hail to the Seagrave Unit!
> Hail to the Burmese girls!
> There's not a sweeter bunch of ladies
> In the whole universe.
>
> Hail to the American Rangers!
> Hail to their Kachin scouts!
> They've frightened off old Tojo's army
> There ain't none hereabouts.
>
> Hail to the Q.M. boys!
> Here's to the ration can!
> It takes a special act of Congress
> To get anything but Spam!
>
> Faithful, loyal, brave, and true
> Through this luckless war;
> There's not a happier group in Burma
> Than ours at Hkalak Ga.

And now the refugees were leaving the Naga Hills and going down into the famous Hukawng Valley for the real test as to whether or not Stilwell had been able to teach the Chinese to fight an offensive war to win. We couldn't help wondering, as we left the Naga Hills, whether we would find a bit of real Burma in the Hukawng Valley or just some more no man's land. I was disturbed that the fight for the Hukawng was being entrusted to the 38th Chinese Division alone. If it was to be a hard fight for one division, then surely the 22nd Chinese Division would be the one to take on the job, since this was the territory out of which the Japanese had driven them, to the death of many of their comrades on the West Axis. But the colonials had reported few Japanese in the valley. It was thought a few battalions of the 38th would have no difficulty in pushing the Japs over the Tarung to the Tanai in a matter of three weeks. And certainly from what we heard at Shingbwiyang things seemed to be going according to plan, for the Chinese already had driven the Japs beyond Ningam to Yupbang. Grindlay had moved on to Ningam Sakan, and with my knees and shoulder it looked as if I would never catch up with him. Our morale was wonderful! Perhaps our return to Burma would take no longer and be no more difficult than our trek out with Stilwell!

But Grindlay was still at Ningam when we got there on November 11, 1943. Things had been moving so fast that we medics, at least, were certain we'd be marching on any day for Yupbang, Taihpa Ga, Maingkwan, and points southeast. Myitkyina by February, 1944, did not seem impossible at all. Since we were not going to be in Ningam long there was no use building new quarters. We used sheds with tarpaulin roofs and bamboo floors.

Grindlay had put up parachute tepees for an operating room and there were already three wards full of patients, for the unit had been quite busy during the first week in Ningam. The front line was in Yupbang about eight miles away. The road was not bad for foot travel. Evacuation of casualties from the front to

Ningam was by regimental litter bearers. At Ningam we were to act both as a surgical hospital and as a clearing station, evacuating the most serious cases to the 151st Medical Battalion at Shingbwiyang by litter bearers of the Chinese Transport Company under Major Thrailkill. The litter bearers from the front did their work most efficiently; our patients reached us from three to five hours after being wounded. In front of us were no American medical personnel. The Chinese battalion medical officers gave first aid and sent the patients back to us at once.

It became apparent immediately that these Chinese first-aid men had learned a great deal since the first Battle of Burma. In those days their first-aid work had been uniformly terrible. Now it was unbelievably good. I knew, back at Ramgarh, that Major Sigafoos, the first American liaison medical officer to the Chinese Army, had felt complete frustration when given his assignment to train Chinese regimental medical men. It had seemed to him what it really was: the toughest assignment in the theater. Liaison medical men had a thankless task. Their job demanded immense tact and self-immolation upon the altar of Chinese "face." Stories about them never reached the newspapers. No photographer wanted to take their pictures. They had no chance to practice medicine or surgery themselves. They were often shelled or machine gunned, but no one ever stopped to think about it. But Major Sigafoos, his associates, and his successors undoubtedly saved the lives of more Chinese soldiers than any single combat surgeon. Many of the soldiers whom the combat surgeon saved would never have reached him alive if regimental first-aid men, trained by Americans like Sigafoos, hadn't done a really good job. At Myitkyina there was actually little difference between the first-aid standards of the American and the Chinese units.

One of my first duties at Ningam was to build a fracture table and, since I had been unable to bring my Naga house along, to modify it so it could be made entirely out of bamboo. This proved quite successful, since it was possible to move the bamboos

around to suit the patient rather than move the patient around
to fit the posts and girders of the Naga house.

We had no electricity. Our Storm King gasoline lamps were
of India make and cracked on their first lighting. We had six
kerosene wick lanterns and some flashlights, but we could spare
no personnel to hold the flashlights. However, in actual combat
the U.S. Army was a huge family. Stationed in Ningam were a
company of antiaircraft men and a company of airborne engineers, as well as a few Quartermaster and Signal Corps men. We
didn't have to wait for a nurse to notify us that a casualty had
arrived. The American boys would spot a casualty a hundred
yards away and come thundering in to hold flashlights, act as
litter bearers, orderlies, or what not.

The smooth working of the unit at Ningam owed a good deal
to the assignment to us on detached service of two Chinese political officers of the 38th Division—Captains Yen Hsiao-Chang and
King Pe-Du. When Major Grindlay told me about the assignment of these political officers, who correspond to the Russian
political commissars, I feared the worst. I had heard too many
caustic comments on Chinese politicos. The entire unit, however, fell in love with both of them at once. Captain Yen spoke
good English and was soon adopted by the nurses and given the
honorary title "Monkey Father," which didn't seem to offend
him at all. Both Christians, they came regularly to our Sunday-
evening song services. Yen had a fine tenor voice and soon teamed
up with Paul Geren, Big Bill Duncumb, Little Bill Brough, and
Major Chao Kuo of the 38th Division in a glee club that performed in and out of season.

It now became known that the Japanese had many more troops
in the area than the Chinese. Both sides were sparring for time.
The fighting was not continuous and some days there were only
six or seven casualties. We had plenty of time for relaxation and
good fellowship. We swam in a little stream that ran by the hospital and sometimes grenaded for fish when it became impossible
to stomach corned beef and Spam. American rations lacked noth-

ing but flavor! Japanese corned beef tasted much better than American, simply because it was spiced a little more. I'd seen American soldiers vomit when given a package of K-ration. To avoid uncontrollable nausea I had to look far away and stop breathing when I saw Spam. But I am spoiled. All my life I've eaten the best of American, British, Indian, Burmese, and Chinese cooking, as taste demanded. In Ningam, with fish and many jungle vegetables available, even, occasionally, some venison, our food was good and a help to our morale. All this, together with the success of the campaign to date, made us feel so cheerful that our previous misunderstandings were being ironed out and in another month we would all have been ourselves again.

And then the blow fell.

In his firm determination to be nowhere near the Chinese camp, Grindlay had chosen a site for the hospital downstream and completely outside the Chinese perimeter of defense. While the hospital was in this defenseless position a small Japanese patrol broke through between Yupbang and Kantow. The Japanese patrol was less than a mile from the hospital when intercepted by a Chinese patrol. Major Boag, the American liaison officer, promptly radioed General Boatner begging him to order the Burmese women to the rear, which General Boatner immediately did. The nurses realized that without their help we wouldn't be able to carry out our assignment and ten of the Hkalak girls begged the general to permit them to remain. Their request was granted, but the remainder marched back to Shingbwiyang.

Thus within a month of the actual beginning of the second Battle of Burma the nurses were as much as told that they weren't needed, that they couldn't be counted on to work under danger, and that in all probability the second campaign would be full of retreats like the first. Again they were separated from me, so I couldn't take up their troubles one by one as they appeared. Instead, small gripes and misunderstandings piled up and were magnified into overwhelming proportions, added to which, at Shingbwiyang they had many "friends" who patted them on the back and assured them that all their complaints were justified. So I was not surprised when at the end of December fourteen of the girls resigned from the unit and went back to India as refugees. The only mitigating circumstance was that among the fourteen who left were five whose unsettled nervous systems had caused trouble many times since leaving Burma. Even for them, however, I could feel only the deepest sympathy, for all the thirty-three nurses who had retreated with us to India in 1942 had gone through hell.

After the resignations, Ruby and five other nurses came back to Ningam with official permission. Ruby came to talk to me the first evening.

"Ruby," I said, "why do you Tagap girls all seem to dislike me so much?"

"Well, for myself, Daddy, all I know is that you hate me."

"Hate you?" I exclaimed. "What gives you that silly idea?"

"So-and-so told me you hated me," she replied. "That's how I know. She said she heard you say so."

"Yes, and she has lied about me before. Just the other day she lied about me to one of the girls with whom she happened to be angry. You know very well, Ruby, that when you girls get upset with each other you misquote people just so you can hurt each other the more. People of all races do that. You yourself have been misquoted, haven't you?"

"Yes, indeed."

"Do you still believe I hate you?"

"No, I know you don't; I knew it all the time but never had a chance to talk to you by yourself. If you had talked to the other girls by themselves, Daddy, they would never have wanted to leave."

But that was the one thing I hadn't had a chance to do ever since Ramgarh. First there was the separation at Tagap, Hkalak, and Hpachet, and then the enforced evacuation to Shingbwiyang just when things were beginning to smooth out.

Losses never come singly. O'Hara had been refused a deserved promotion to a lieutenant colonelcy simply because our unit wasn't big enough to merit two lieutenant colonels. I had protested the fact that a superior officer like O'Hara should be penalized for being a member of a small unit. The army was O'Hara's career and he ought to have gotten his promotion even if it meant our losing him. Now his promotion came through. At the same time Major Grindlay and Lieutenant Chesley were transferred to Ledo, and later, because of long service in the theater, sent back to the States. To replace them we were given Major Milton A. Dushkin and Captain Bachmann; but the unit wasn't the same any more.

Officers of all sorts of units were continually trying to persuade me to treat our unit personnel in the "orthodox" G.I. manner. If our civilians got upset about something or other, their advice was simply to bat them down, lock them up, bust them, dishonorably discharge them, do anything but reason with them or let your heart bleed for them. But to me this treatment was not only foreign to the things we were fighting for but too often demonstrated lack of personality and leadership on the part of the commanding officer. Mediocre officers could use the power entrusted to them to bluster their way out of personal failures and shout down those whose only fault was being human. Stilwell didn't do things that way. Major Grindlay was so unlike other officers that he complained about my being military at all. Somewhere there was a middle road and it was up to me to find it.

The possibility of danger threatening the unit was forestalled within twenty-four hours of the evacuation of the nurses by the antiaircraft unit and the airborne engineers who voluntarily threw a system of foxholes and trenches in two perimeters around us.

A peculiar thing was now holding up the Chinese attack: lack of cough medicine. The floor of the Hukawng Valley is less than a thousand feet above sea level, but it is a hundred air miles or more north of the Tropic of Cancer and there is a heavy damp fog blanket over the valley until late in the morning. The Chinese, never heavily clothed, in muddy cold trenches all night and day, suffered from bronchitis almost to the last man. By their incessant coughing they gave themselves and the Chinese positions away to the Japanese. Gallons and gallons of cough mixture—goodness only knows what the mixture contained—were finally issued and the situation improved rapidly.

And then General Stilwell himself came to town, and wherever Stilwell went something happened. In a very few days the Chinese began again to attack.

With Stilwell's arrival the triangle between Sharaw, Yupbang, and Ningam was cleared permanently of the enemy. Almost simultaneously the 22nd Division pulled a surprise encirclement on the Japs at Taro and wiped out the garrison. Annoyed that the 22nd had beat him to it, General Sun threw his men of the 38th Division into a final assault at Yupbang and captured that town. Many Americans wondered why the Battle of Yupbang was considered so important. It was not that the Chinese had demonstrated their ability to fight a prolonged offensive campaign at Yupbang. They had not. It took Taihpa Ga, Maingkwan, Mogaung, and Kamaing to do that. But to us Yupbang was important because here the Chinese passed their final examinations and graduated from the course of instruction Stilwell had begun for them at Ramgarh.

From Taihpa to Shaduzup, the Chinese would be having their postgraduate "internship," with the assistance of General Merrill and his famous Marauders. Then at Mogaung and with other engagements north of Mogaung, Colonel Lee and several other distinguished Chinese regimental commanders demonstrated conclusively that they had become expert tacticians. They proved, as Stilwell always claimed, that with proper food, training, and sufficient weapons the Chinese could really lick their weight in Japs.

I don't pose as a military genius. Whenever I'd say a word

about military matters in General Boatner's hearing he'd burst
into loud laughter and proclaim Doc Seagrave the world's worst
strategist. Wherever in this book I make references to maneuvers
of any sort, they must be understood for what they are: a doctor's
ideas about a campaign he happened to take part in. And more,
they are the ideas of a doctor to whom, aside from General Ted
Wessels at Myitkyina, not one line officer ever told a single fact
about what the blazes was going on.

On Thanksgiving Day, 1943, the promise of Congress that
every United States soldier in the world would have turkey for
dinner was not fulfilled at Ningam. American personnel at Ningam felt badly about this oversight and, fearing that our Christmas turkey might also fail to appear, I radioed General Boatner
that if he would furnish ten pigs and the trimmings, our unit
would put on a barbecue and entertainment for all American
personnel and Chinese officers.

The pigs arrived on the dot by parachute. We recovered nine.
The tenth pig started squealing as his parachute opened and
some hungry soldiers had the poor brute killed, cooked, and eaten
almost before he hit the ground. Everyone took an extraordinary
interest in that barbecue. The butchers were sufficiently repre-
sentative and impressive: Colonel Laughlin, the liaison officer,
Sergeant Jacobs of the Signal Corps, and our own Englishman,
Little Bill Brough. The Veterinary Corps was represented in the
person of Major Haley. Not realizing what a good pastry cook
we had in the person of Sergeant Brown, I started to bake the pies
myself and then quit when I saw that Brown was almost as good
as my wife. All our new enlisted men sweated at the barbecue pits.
Paul Geren, the nurses, and, most especially, our three Englishmen—Captain Gurney, Big Bill Duncumb, and Little Bill
Brough—worked up a half-hour program that was a hit.

And General Stilwell and General Sun were there.

The festivities began, very properly, with the Chinese and
American national anthems. I started to make a welcoming

speech, as the only American who had ever before spent a Christmas in Burma, when the Chinese Army carried off the honors by presenting General Stilwell with the first prisoner of the campaign. As I left to take a look at the wounded Jap, General Stilwell called out, a twinkle in his eyes: "Don't give him any ether!"

I know where I would have landed if I'd obeyed that order!

After the barbecue almost the whole army repaired to our operating room to watch the operation, and each man wrote on the Jap's cast his personal remarks—most of them unprintable.

In the fall of 1943 a swarm of unattached medical officers appeared in the theater unannounced, assigned by combat headquarters. Not knowing what to do with some of them at that time, General Boatner asked me how many I could use.

"Sir," I explained, "our nursing personnel is only sufficient to handle the work for the medical officers we now have. We can use as many more officers as you care to assign—providing you can give us ten enlisted men for each new officer."

General Boatner and Colonel Petersen undertook to find out whether we might be given the Table of Organization of a clearing company. In the meantime he sent us some fifteen men, many of whom had been with us in Ramgarh.

As these men came in, hitchhiking over the Refugee Trail, their barracks bags were free-dropped by airplane at Ningam. Air-dropping could be very funny. The parachutes on cases of corned beef and Spam never failed to open. But those on cases of peaches or coffee or milk frequently remained closed or their shroud lines ripped off and the supplies would come hurtling and crashing down. This had already happened to much of our own stuff. Parachutes didn't open when they dropped the nurses' suitcases at Tagap. The shroud lines gave way on my own suitcase at Tagap, so on my vacation I invested in a new high-priced one and filled it with my most valuable stuff. When it was dropped at Hkalak the unopened parachute came down with it as a little packet, and the Quartermaster boys picked up my stuff from all

Burmese Nurses on the Irrawaddi Ferry

Princess Louise

*Photos by
Bill Duncumb*

Grandma Naomi

Photos by Bill Duncumb

Nurses Resting

over the field. A pressure sterilizer dropped at Tagap came down the same way, and it took Colonel O'Hara a month to fix it so it would hold steam. To see three shipments of canned beer free-dropped to the enlisted men at Tagap and Hkalak had been an experience, for the cans exploded and foamy beer fountained into the air and flowed off in tiny streams. Now our men's barracks bags were being dropped quite expertly—into the river.

Almost at the moment of losing the fourteen nurses, we discovered two of our other old girls, one in India and one in China. Naomi had come for training to Namkham in 1932. She was a Taungthu girl with a fine sense of humor, a born mimic; she was also the best educated girl I had trained. She remained in Namkham as head nurse for two years after graduation. But she had several younger brothers and sisters, one of whom was Nang Aung (Miss Wang), who needed education, and she left our Namkham hospital to work in the civil hospital at Taunggyi where the government paid her more than twice what I could afford.

When the British evacuated Taunggyi they gave Naomi twenty-four hours to bid her folks goodbye. She hurried to her home village only to find that her father and mother were away on a visit so, without seeing them, she was flown from Shwebo to Calcutta, and later was evacuated to the Punjab where she lived a completely humdrum existence on a small pittance from the Burmese Government. One day, languidly turning the pages of a London illustrated weekly, she was startled to see pictures of myself and the nurses at work "somewhere in India." For months she searched for an American officer who could tell her where we were. Finally, long after we had left Ramgarh she was given the Ramgarh address.

And now in January, 1944, we had her back as chief nurse. Like a good chief nurse, Naomi watched quietly for several weeks, relearning our American ways and studying the psychology of the younger nurses. She was intensely annoyed at the trifling complaints of the nurses who had left, because she knew what real trouble was. She was some six or eight years older than the other nurses, and when she had them diagnosed she began to win their friendship by displaying her old sense of humor, mimicking everyone in sight. The girls began to call her Grandma.

One day when a younger girl was nearing the ragged edge of control and in a few more minutes would have had a tempest well organized in her teapot, Grandma Naomi suddenly exploded with a gruff "S'*taing ga!*"

"What do you mean?" the girl asked, startled.

"S'*taing ga!* You're posing!"

The girl thought it over, recognized the correctness of the diagnosis, laughed, and it was all over.

S'*taing* is the Burmese transliteration of our word "style." To the occidental, style is important. It changes every year or every month and one must change with it. In other words, one must pose as everyone else is posing at the moment. To the oriental mind, style, which is a temporary custom, is perfectly ridiculous and something to be embarrassed about. Custom, the custom of your ancestors for generations, which the Burmese and every other race in Burma call *htonzan*, is everything. To give up the *htonzans* of centuries for the s'*taing* of the moment is disgusting or at the very least laughable. S'*taing ga!* from now on became a byword of the unit. The enlisted men used it as well as the nurses and officers. Everyone's delinquency, from that of the old man down, was recognized as a pose and laughed off. Many of the personnel would catch themselves posing and admit it with a shouted S'*taing ga!* before anyone else could catch them at it. Insincerity can be pretty well overcome when brought out into the open and laughed off.

The other girl to come back was Wasay, who entered training four years later than Grandma Naomi. A Karen girl of strong physique, almost never ill, priding herself on being able to stand as much as a man any day, Wasay had been in charge of my Kokang hospital on the east of the Salween River, the largest of my branch hospitals. When the Japanese attacked Rangoon in 1942 and Mr. H. N. C. Stevenson, political officer in Kutkai, began to organize Kachin guerrilla bands, Wasay volunteered to go with one company if these original guerrillas ever went into action. They did not. She stayed with her job till she heard that the Japs had broken through the Chinese Sixth Army and were on their way to Lashio. Then she set off on foot hoping to join me at Namkham ahead of the Japs.

When she reached the Salween crossing at Kunlong she found, to her dismay, that the Japanese were already on the other side of the river—so she hurried back to Kokang, hastily collected the most important drugs still in her possession, and, with her assistant nurse and the Karen pastor and his family, hurried out to the Lisu Mountains just as the enemy pulled in. She said two women were left behind by the townspeople to watch their property, women whom they assumed the Japanese would leave alone: a crazy woman and one who was six months' pregnant. The Japanese raped them both and the pregnant woman aborted.

From then, May, 1942, till December 23, 1943, the two nurses and the pastor's family lived between the Japanese armies and the Chinese armies on the Salween front. They settled in a friendly Lisu village about fifty miles over jungle paths from Namkham. The people gave them a small plot of ground on which to grow potatoes and corn. With their few medicines, they cared for sick villagers and even for some Chinese casualties from the Salween front, receiving an occasional peck of rice as a fee. When their medicines gave out they filled the bottles with water and kept on caring for the sick.

Finally in December, 1943, an American liaison officer discovered Wasay and, through Colonel Condon and General Dorn, radioed me asking if I wanted her. I replied that I certainly did. Wasay found a horse, rode many days until she reached the Burma Road east of Paoshan and was given a jeep ride to Kunming to catch a plane for Shingbwiyang. She was rather ragged when she arrived and it took about three months to get her over her experiences, but as assistant chief nurse she became most useful.

Up to this time in the campaign there had been no liaison between front-line units and the big base hospitals. Surgeons at the front didn't know the outcome of casualties they'd operated on, and base institutions had no conception of the circumstances under which front-line surgery was performed. To remedy this the 20th General Hospital sent us first their Major Norman A. Freeman for a month's detached service with our group and later Major Henry P. Royster for six weeks. Both were marvelous surgeons and helped immensely to improve our technique. I believe they enjoyed their stay with us also. In any event, during the months that followed they wrote us frequently, telling us about the outcome of some of our most interesting cases and also quite frankly pointing out our grosser errors of therapy, knowing we would appreciate rather than resent their so doing.

During January the U.S. 13th Mountain Medical Battalion arrived in the theater minus equipment. The campaign had not yet developed sufficiently to warrant giving them an assignment, and their commanding officer, Lieutenant Colonel Faller, came to Ningam to find out if I would accept a company or two from their battalion on detached service and let them learn some jungle medicine while waiting for their first assignment. Realizing that this would help us over the period of reorganization of our unit's teamwork following the resignation of the fourteen nurses, I gladly accepted the offer. Captains Whedbee, Bomse, and Andrews, and Lieutenants Gladstone and Beebe soon appeared with a hundred men.

During the cold season the Hukawng Valley is very cold and very wet at night. A fairly large number of casualties occurred during the battle that resulted in the final capture of Yupbang. Shock had reached alarming proportions by the time casualties reached us. We now had a new operating shed, covered by a forty-foot-square tarpaulin, in which were six operating tables. We built four more shock tables with very low head ends in front of the operating room. On these tables the casualties were given plasma and other treatments for shock before being taken to the operating tables. One of our boys put up a smaller tarpaulin in the form of an almost airtight tent heated by a gasoline stove, where our blankets were hung and brought out warm to cover the chilled bodies of the casualties. A small-power light unit reached us, and the boys made blackout shades out of empty No. 10 cans. My third "Hukawng Model" fracture table was more of a success than the earlier models, but the American boys immediately introduced some improvements of their own. Tired of continually running after the *hkai shwei* (hot water) which the Chinese demanded all day and all night, the nurses filled empty plasma bottles or enema cans with water and hung them to the roof beside each patient, with the rubber tube within easy reach of his mouth so that he could suck to his heart's content.

Since Stilwell had proved to everyone that the Chinese could fight, Ningam became a Cook's Tour for officers in the rear. Many a curious medical officer arrived, and Major Dushkin, who acted as our triage or disposition officer, collared them and made them perform a minimum of one surgical operation each, whether they were surgeons or not. It was amusing to see pediatricians, obstetricians, and psychiatrists learning to operate in the jungle.

Motion-picture cameras also began to arrive and the army honored us by having a newsreel made of our hospital and surgical work which was used for educational purposes in the training of medical officers in the States. Newspapermen, too, began to pour in. One correspondent called on me the day I was finishing our report for the entire Battle of Yupbang. He asked me a lot of questions, one of them regarding our mortality figures. I pulled out the report and showed him that whereas on January 7 we had been running 4.8 per cent, we were now running slightly over 2.6 per cent. Six weeks later, as I was driving a jeep south of Taihpa Ga, an officer waved to me to stop and came over to talk. He was censorship officer for war correspondents at Delhi and a correspondent had sent in an article about our unit that contained statements he didn't believe could be true. Of course he realized, he said, that the correspondents had stretched things a bit to make good reading for the folks back home but he couldn't pass things that weren't facts. Would I read the article?

"That contains practically nothing of the usual exaggerated nonsense," I said, as I folded up the article and handed it back.

"Do you know what the mortality rates were in the last war?" he asked.

"I can't quote them exactly but I believe they were well over 10 per cent," I replied.

"That's right. Yet you claim you are getting only 2.6 per cent."

"That report is on file at headquarters. You can look it up any time," I said, getting a bit irritated. "If the report has any errors it will be in understating the total number of patients treated, because our registration clerk failed to register some of the minor cases. Deaths have to be reported too many times to too many people to permit of errors." I didn't go on to point out that his rates for World War I were final figures. Ours were those of a front-line surgical unit and a clearing company. Probably he hadn't heard of plasma or the sulfa drugs or the closed plaster treatment of large wounds.

"The article quotes you," he continued, "as saying that Chinese by custom do not readily give blood for transfusions, yet the 20th General Hospital says they obtain lots of Chinese blood."

"The 20th General," I replied, "has been working with the Chinese for less than a year and under military circumstances, when Chinese will give blood on command. I have been working with Chinese for twenty-one years. Take your choice."

I was always apprehensive when correspondents came around. You could never tell what would come of it. Even if the correspondent didn't misquote or misrepresent you, someone would resent the disparity in publicity given you over other equally deserving units. Because we were an unorthodox unit, with some very photogenic Burmese nurses, we were given a hundred times more publicity than we cared for or merited.

5

The Hukawng Valley

WITH the Japanese wiped out at Sharaw, Yupbang, and Taro, the next objective was the triangular area of ground between the Tarung and the Tanai, which form the Chindwin River, and the village of Taihpa Ga, which guards the motor-road crossing of the Tanai. So far the Japanese hadn't worried much about Stilwell's Chinese accomplishing more than a pinprick. Now they threw in a good part of the Japanese 18th Division, which had helped capture Singapore, and pulled up some 150-mm. guns. This gave the Chinese something to think about, for the 150's could stay in safety far beyond the reach of the Chinese 75's and raise havoc. Most soldiers, I have heard, prefer being bombed to being shelled by big guns: the guns are far too persistently regular and, if properly used, seem to be able to hit a tenpenny nail on the head. They are extremely hard on the nervous system. There has been much loose talk about the Chinese as soldiers, but when it came to nonchalance in the face of shelling, I believe the Chinese could win hands down. On many occasions I saw our own Chinese, as well as Chinese on detached service with us, get up on high ground just to watch the shells hit. You could swear at them in five different languages for doing it but their heads would pop up again the minute you looked away. The Chinese way of fighting may be exasperating but the rank and file of Chinese troops did not lack courage.

The entire Chinese 38th Division was now in the main Hu-kawng thrust and officers were busy training new replacements from China. One regiment was in garrison at Ningam, one began the sweep down the triangle from the Sharaw-Yupbang line toward Taihpa Ga, and the third was ordered to cross the Chind-win at Kantow to outflank the Japanese in the Taihpa area. A detachment of our unit was ordered to accompany these troops in the Kantow flank. Captain Gurney and Captain Antonellis, Dr. Ba Saw and Dr. Taubenfliegl went on this mission with our enlisted men. On the arrival of Major Royster from the 20th General Hospital, the command of the group was turned over to him. Not only was Royster a great surgeon; he was a born teacher as well. In their six weeks of surgery with Royster, Antonellis and Ba Saw learned more surgery than they'd thought it possible to know. Royster made himself the "assistant" and the young men the "great surgeons" and their self-confidence increased immeasurably.

Dr. Taubenfliegl was a Polish contract surgeon. At the beginning of the war in Spain he joined a medical unit with the Republican Army and served till the end of the war, after which, with other foreign doctors, German, Czechoslovakian, and Polish, he was evacuated to China. There the group spent troublous years serving the Chinese armies, with little or nothing in the way of equipment and medical supplies. All spoke Chinese well and had learned how to live with the Chinese and like it. Under Stilwell they had been transferred to Ramgarh to work with Major Sigafoos as liaison officers with the Chinese regiments. Taubenfliegl was a grand person to have around. Although he had taken punishment the like of which few American officers have ever experienced, he was never known to complain and had a sense of humor that was leaven to the whole group. At Myitkyina when Colonel Petersen offered me my choice of any liaison medical officer as a permanent addition to our unit, I chose Taubenfliegl.

The remainder of our unit continued to run the clearing station at Ningam until the first echelon of the 25th Field Hospital could set up a semipermanent hospital there. A surgical unit of the 25th was hurried forward to newly captured Yupbang. Major Thrailkill, post commandant at Ningam, thought that this team, setting up for the first time in the jungle, might be saved a great deal of trouble if one of my officers were to go along with them in an advisory capacity. I selected my executive officer, Major Dushkin, a fire-eater who seemed determined to take vengeance on the Japanese for all the sins of the Axis against the Hebrew race.

Dushkin and Bill Brough reported to Thrailkill the next morning and started off with the detachment. It became immediately apparent to Dushkin that the captain in charge was determined to have nothing to do with him. But you couldn't do such things to Dushkin. You couldn't keep him quiet if you put him in a padded cell. At Ningam, in order to keep everyone from going mad, we had to issue an order forbidding him to pull any wisecracks before 3 P.M. Dushkin blithely changed P.M. to A.M. and kept on going. Now he chatted and joked and finally asked the captain what the grouse was about.

"Everyone knows that as long as Seagrave is around no one else will have a chance to do any combat surgery," the captain said.

Dushkin lost his breath for nearly five minutes. This statement, plus the rigors of marching, almost got him down. Then he began a half-hour's dissertation on how we had made the visiting medics operate, even against their will; how he had had difficulty, as triage officer at Ningam, making me operate whenever there was a chance to teach a younger man to do the operation. Finally the captain yelled for quarter and asked Dushkin to apologize to me for his unwillingness to look over our hospital at Ningam or even to shake hands.

Soon after our surgical detachment had set up beyond Kantow, General Stilwell sent me orders at eight one morning to have the group move forward several miles to the regimental headquarters so that the evacuation of casualties would be more rapid. I sent Gurney and four nurses to handle the evacuations and the new operations and to transmit Stilwell's orders to Royster. They reached Royster at noon and by eight in the evening he and his group were set up and operating at the new site.

As the battle increased in intensity, I had Royster reinforced with nurses and more enlisted men and later with still another detachment of the 13th Medical Battalion. A week later I walked over to see how everyone was getting along. The installation was crowded into the smallest area of any ever occupied by a surgical hospital anywhere. It was completely hemmed in by Chinese troops. One hardly dared take a deep breath for fear someone else would be forced out of the enclosure. There was only one cook, Wong Jack, one of my Chinese sailors, who was cooking two diets simultaneously, Burmese and American, and making both delicious. Our personnel would grin even at a flank assignment if they knew Wong Jack was to go with them.

The girls were excited over the battery of Chinese 75's that was firing only a hundred yards away, so we walked over after supper. We had heard many a shot fired in anger but this was the first time we had actually seen artillery in action. The Chinese put on a good show for the ladies; too good, for it provoked the Japanese and they threw a lot of 150's back at us.

A few days later Royster wrote that the Japanese shells had come so close while they were operating on casualties that he had ordered the nurses into the dugout, to their great disgust. One officer, thinking the girls must be frightened, went down to comfort them and found them nonchalantly playing contract bridge. After that the girls were not ordered underground while surgery was going on.

The 22nd Division had now mopped up the entire Taro valley and a regiment suddenly appeared at Kantow with orders to march around the 38th Division's right flank to get in the rear of the Japs who were holding them up. General Liao of the 22nd didn't believe in using existing trails because the Japs were too well acquainted with them and could shell the trail or ambush troops on it, so he ordered his troops to cut a new trail over the foothills. He had his trail cut and his troops in action in the Japanese rear before anyone discovered that he had no medical unit with him. When Stilwell heard of it he sent a small detachment of our unit under Captain Antonellis to support Liao with a surgical team, until the surgical team of the 25th Field Hospital could be transferred there from Yupbang. Antonellis and his men made a forced march, dug in, and were operating on casualties by nightfall.

In the meanwhile the 38th Division had pushed the Japs across the Tanai at Taihpa Ga, and our unit was ordered to leapfrog Yupbang and set up on the Brambrang River three miles north of Taihpa. Since there were still many snipers wandering around in the jungle the nurses were forbidden forward until Dushkin and his men had dugouts ready for them. It is interesting to note that in spite of all that Stilwell and his Chinese had thus far done (it was still only late February, 1944), his American officers had so little faith in his getting much beyond Taihpa that they ordered us to start our hospital as the first section of a permanent installation where the 25th Field Hospital would spend the monsoon from May to October. Dushkin had a large group of men with him but the Japanese seemed determined to keep him from building anything permanent. Howitzer shells came over at regular intervals. Dushkin and his men got underground in short order and had enough dugouts to accommodate us all by the time we arrived. For the first and only time in the war we lived underground with sand in our hair for days, while we built wards and bamboo shacks. Since it was most painful and most un-American to the entire army for me to have no fancy domicile in which to live, Pang Tze and the Burmese boys built me another charming twelve-foot-square bungalow. The Japs, of course, now began to run, and not till the Battle of Myitkyina did any semipermanent medical installation catch up with Stilwell's front line. So much for the lack of faith which, added to his lack of supplies and troops, made Stilwell's burden in Burma complete!

Even Dushkin wasn't convinced that the 150's were gone for good. He found a stray bulldozer wandering down the road one day and borrowed it to scoop out a huge underground ward. The bulldozer did its work in a day and Dushkin threw his hundred Chinese labor corpsmen into the job of roofing it. They had it half finished when we were ordered on. The men couldn't decide what the major had built, a garage, a ward, a swimming pool, or a garbage pit. Whatever it was, it was gorgeous. We named it Dushkin's Folly.

The name Brambrang stands out in my memory as the place where our unit's basic equipment finally caught up with us. Colonel Williams, the theater surgeon, had ordered a clearing company minus personnel in August, 1942. We were told the equipment had left the States in October. In February, 1943, we learned the ship had been sunk and that Williams had ordered us another complete outfit. In September, General Boatner, sending me off on the unwanted vacation, ordered me to locate the equipment no matter where it was in India. I traced it across the breadth of India and found it stored and forgotten in the dark corner of a warehouse in Karachi. It had been there since May. All but one of the trucks had been commandeered by other units. Delhi approved the immediate transportation of this basic equipment by air to Ledo. Planes were actually assigned when again something went wrong, and the equipment left Karachi by coastwise vessel for Calcutta. There the fates were still against us, for instead of coming on to Ledo by rail, it was put on barges and towed slowly up the Bramapootra River. At long last, our lost vehicles having been replaced by ordnance at Ledo, our equipment rolled into Brambrang, but almost immediately the men of the unit were ordered on flank moves and had no chance to use the equipment or ride in the vehicles—and the main unit went into an eclipse that lasted for two months.

For the Battle of Taihpa Ga was over. The Japanese had been thrown back on Maingkwan, capital of the Hukawng. From now on the 22nd Division would be responsible for the main drive down the valley, reinforced by Colonel Rothwell Brown's tanks, while the 38th Division, spearheaded by General Merrill's Marauders, took responsibility for the wide left flank and its encircling moves. Ever since the first days in Ramgarh I had done my medical best to please General Sun of the 38th, a much easier man to know, since he spoke English, than General Liao, the French-speaking commander of the 22nd. And now I was apparently being punished for succeeding too well. Although our motorized equipment had arrived, General Sun insisted on our unit moving through the jungles with his division. But American officers refused to let the nurses move through the jungles and ordered the real Seagrave Unit to bivouac along the motor road and wait and wait and wait—while our enlisted men and officers performed one difficult flank move after another.

One regiment of the 38th was to start south from Makaw and another on an inner flank from Ritu to the south and east. They were to back up the Marauders when they set up their roadblock at Walawbum. I sent Major Dushkin and Captains Johnson and Bomse on the outside flank and Captains Gurney, Bachmann, and Gladstone on the inner flank. With the battalion that was ordered to guard Pabum, where the Tanai breaks out of the mountains, I sent Dr. Ba Saw with Captain Andrews and a few men. Then we turned over our hospital to the 25th Field Hospital and moved to the south bank of the Tanai to vegetate.

All through the months since the 13th Medical Battalion had joined us at Ningam, Captain Whedbee, the senior officer, had stuck to me like a brother, sharing the awful boredom of inaction, hoping, as he put it, that when he started learning front-line surgery it would be with me. But always the group with me was a clearing station and not an active surgical unit. Now without a single chance at surgical training, Whedbee and Beebe were rushed off to Taro to join a battalion of the 22nd Division on a flank move of four months' duration through the jade-mine area.

So our unit sat on the Tanai with the war going by all around us and with not a thing to do. I sent off six girls at a time for a two weeks' rest in Calcutta. With San Yee, Antonellis, and Dr. Kish, another contract surgeon, to help me, I would still have a powerhouse to go into action if and when I could persuade someone somewhere to want us.

It must take a special type of psychology to enjoy army life in peacetime. When you're actually fighting and helping wipe something nasty out of the world, the army is the only place to be. The excitement of danger and the feeling of usefulness make up for the loss of democratic privileges. But when there's no danger and nothing to be useful about, the army is horrible. All my adult life I've been my own boss, often to the consternation of the American Baptist Burma Mission. I've planned my own grand strategy and determined the tactics by which I would accomplish each phase of my campaign to develop medicine in the Northern Shan States. I've moved my pawns if and when it suited me. As I saw one "battle" about to be won, I would complete preparations for another and swing into it before boredom overwhelmed me. Life was always interesting and worth living. I've had to use my brains at least ten hours a day and have been able to sleep at night with a more or less clear conscience.

In the army, of necessity, you have none of these privileges. Grand strategy is determined with no help from you. Medical tactics are sometimes left to you, but not if anyone can help it. You can't move until every other unit involved in the particular phase of the conflict is ready to move also. Supply is so complicated that experts have to do everything. As a result, most of the time you may not use your own brains more than two or three times a day. In fact, you're better off without brains for then you don't have to think.

At the Tanai we had chosen to bivouac in what seemed at first a rather nice old Japanese camp. There were foxholes under huge banian trees. The jungle had been cleared away. But when we began to brush away the leaves the site turned out to have been used by the Japanese cavalry. Manure and dirt were everywhere, and untold millions of flies. At least we had found some work to do even if it wasn't medical. The few men we had with us didn't like the thought of the work because back in the States, policing up camp had been a form of punishment. But the nurses got at the job and between us we managed to get tired enough to get some sleep at night and forget our troubles for awhile. The boys worked at repacking supplies and repairing vehicles.

While we were working the first morning, Grandma Naomi asked me what Colonel Williams and I had been talking about on his visit.

"I asked him what his plans were for our unit after Stilwell conquered northern Burma," I said.

"What did he say?"

"He said he might have us open up some station hospitals on the Burma Road such as we had before the war."

"Aren't you going with the army until they capture Tokyo?" she asked.

"That's what I intended to do."

"Then why the station hospitals?"

"Colonel Williams said he was sure you girls wouldn't be willing to go on with the army after we leave Burma."

"Why not?" Grandma asked. "Now that we're in the war we'll stay with it till it's over."

"That's what I told Colonel Williams most of you would say. The trouble with you girls these past two years is that you've not been in contact with your families. You haven't been able to send money to them or know that they're safe and well. When we get beyond Burma there'll be a mail service back and you can keep in touch, and your army salaries will be a wonderful help to your families in rebuilding their lives and their ruined homes. But," I added, "some of you girls will be getting married. You're already much beyond the age most girls in Burma start housekeeping."

"Maybe some of the girls are foolish enough to want to get married," Naomi replied, "but they will get married one at a time, not all at once!"

"And whom are we going to marry?" asked one of the younger girls.

"One of the handsome men of your own race, of course," I replied.

"All our handsome men are married or gone to war," she said. "Besides, I'm never going to marry a man of my own race. If I marry I'm going to marry a Chinese officer!"

"What on earth for?" I exclaimed.

"Our men always beat their wives with sticks. Do you suppose I'm going to let any man think he can beat me?"

"No, I certainly don't," I said, thinking of the numerous times I would rather have taken a beating from this five-foot nurse than have her lash out at me with her tongue, as she could when things got her down.

"And that's not all," the young lady continued. "There isn't a school in Burma that teaches boys all the practical things you've taught us. And now for two years we've been associating with hundreds of really big people who have been treating us as their equals. We've lived in foreign countries, traveled in airplanes. We've helped save thousands of lives. We've been through hell just because we thought that was what we'd come into this world for. Now do you think I'm going back and marry a man who never in his life was more than a few days' journey from home— and let him beat me?"

"All right, all right," I capitulated. "You're not. But why the Chinese officer? Have you got a new sweetheart I don't know anything about? I thought you already had that American boy in Ramgarh and the colored sergeant in Hkalak. Have you already forgotten about them?"

"Oh, I have more boy friends than that!" the little vixen replied. "But I never keep more than one on the books at the same time. When I *admit* a new boy friend I *discharge* the old ones. Sometimes I *readmit* them, too. Right now I have one white boy friend, one black, one yellow, and one brown. I enjoy variety!"

The conversation was definitely getting beyond me. Yet I could sympathize. Years ago my mother had grieved because the Karen boys and girls she had put through high school and college never married each other but went back to their villages to marry someone with no education at all. For a college girl to marry a man who could barely write his name seemed a pitiful waste, but only by so doing could she hope to become boss in her own home and avoid a life of semiserfdom. I could understand the frustration these nurses of ours must be feeling.

I turned again to Naomi. "Wouldn't you girls like the Burma Road station hospital assignment?"

"Sure we would," she replied. "We'd be in our own country and perhaps they'd let us help our own people, too. But it wouldn't be nearly so exciting."

"Perhaps," I said, "they won't need us after Burma is conquered. There are lots of new American medical units coming in all the time, you know."

"Well, if there's nothing special they need us for we wouldn't enjoy just going along."

Already we seemed to be at that stage. There were three portable surgical hospitals leapfrogging each other down the road, busily active while we stagnated on the south bank of the Tanai.

Our supreme commander, Admiral Lord Louis Mountbatten, put on a little show for us, personally coming to inspect what Stilwell was doing. All American units were ordered to be present in columns of sevens for Lord Louis' speech. Our unit appeared with the men in full regalia, tin hats and all, and the nurses in their best silks and satins. After all that had been said about our unit's not seeming to be a real part of the army, it was very heartening to have Colonel Willey tell three different officers that we had the most military behavior of any unit present. In his speech, Lord Louis hinted that before long the British would be giving Stilwell the support he deserved.

Next morning I was standing bored and despondent at the entrance to our area when Stilwell's aide, Captain Young, drove a jeep in; and there was a patient for me, Lord Louis himself! He had been driving when a bamboo had sprung loose and struck him across the left eye. Examination showed a hemorrhage in the anterior chamber of the eye. Here was real trouble. Stilwell had long waited for the admiral to come and watch the Chinese in action, travel over the Ledo Road, and see how well the Americans had accomplished the "impossible." And now, before the admiral could see either the Chinese or the road, it was my certain duty either to send him back to Ledo by air to Captain Scheie, the ophthalmologist at the 20th General Hospital, or else be responsible for the loss of the eye. There was no question at all that Lord Louis was as unhappy to be sent back as I was to send him. But the nurses were thrilled at having a chance, however slight, to serve a cousin of their king.

Major Dushkin was a wonderful letter writer—to his wife. He used to write her such wonderful letters that he lost his censorship privileges for three months! He wrote to no one else, not even reports to his C.O. I soon learned that once Dushkin got away from me on a flank move, he and his detachment would be completely lost, then suddenly appear again half a hundred miles away. It was no use worrying about him. He would undoubtedly take good care of himself, or his boys would see to it that he didn't get hurt.

Gurney, however, was something else again. No sooner would a courier leave his regiment when Gurney would send a note by him reporting on his men and his work. He had plenty to report this time, as it happened, for before they reached Ritu, their jumping-off point, the Japanese began to shell their path. A Chinese soldier was blown apart next to some of our boys and a small shell fragment struck one of our 13th Medical Battalion sergeants, piercing the right frontal lobe of the brain. Gurney performed the minimum operation and sent the boy back to the experts at Ledo. He was back on duty in six weeks.

One noon a radio message arrived: Merrill's Marauders had captured Walawbum on the motor road fifteen miles beyond Maingkwan, only thirty minutes behind schedule. About a mile east of Walawbum the Americans had come to the edge of a rice field across which the Japanese were entrenched. The Marauders were not green troops. They set up machine guns, screamed tauntingly, "Tojo eat ——! Tojo eat ——!" and mowed down the Japs as they sprang to the defense of Tojo's lost reputation.

With the establishment of Merrill's roadblock, the Chinese 22nd Division rushed into action spearheaded by Rothwell Brown's tanks, and for the first time in Burma the Japanese were massacred. Headquarters moved immediately to Maingkwan and I obtained permission to move forward to a new bivouac on the Nambyu River near Walawbum. My first act was to put up a sign, "SEAGRAVE UNIT," hoping that the powers that be might see it and give us a job.

Passing through Maingkwan we saw the first P-40 plane shot down by the Japanese. The pilot, they said, had been rescued, while his pals, circling the field, had kept the Japs at bay. The plane was a complete loss. So was Maingkwan town. But already American engineers were putting in a transport landing field. Beyond Maingkwan the fields were ripe with harvested Japs.

Our new bivouac area was as nice as a bivouac area *can* be. The Nambyu is a medium-sized stream, clear, fresh, and deep enough to provide good swimming. We were on an old village site. No houses remained but there was a parade ground, almost like a lawn, where we played baseball. Orchids were in bloom and the girls brought in lovely clusters of gold and purple ones that would have been worth a fortune in the United States. The country was beginning to look a bit like Burma at last. There were actually a few fruit trees, mangoes, lemons, and pomelos, even raspberries and a few poor-quality plantains. These, together with fresh fish, when we could beg a grenade from someone, gave us a welcome change from corned beef and Spam.

Just beyond our bivouac area we discovered the deserted camp of a Japanese regiment. It was half a mile from the main road and was built in dense forest with no destruction of the local trees and bamboos. All building material had been brought from a distance. Even the road to the camp had been cut through underbrush, its entry a mile farther south than convenient. No wonder the air force hadn't been able to find the Japs. Camouflage was perfection itself. Beside the bamboo houses were underground shelters, many of them yards deep under the trunks of huge banian trees. A direct hit by a five-hundred-pound bomb would have hurt nothing but the trees. Everywhere was evidence that the Japs had lived very well indeed. Anticlimax was evident only at the exit onto the highway of one of the many small roads. There thirty Japanese had gone to see what was causing the great clatter on the highway and had met point-blank fire from Brown's tanks. They had met such sudden death that they hadn't had sufficient time to plant the mines we found beside them. Until then I had never been close enough to see men lie as they fell, hit by bombs, shells, machine-gun or rifle fire. The sprawling, awkward postures of the dead are amazing. But nothing so amazing as the countless millions of maggots that flowed in a stream from the bloated, purple corpses, while myriads of bluebottle flies hovered about, buzzing and laying eggs themselves, to hatch and swell the ranks of the all-conquering maggot.

Even at our new site we were away from the sound of firing, for the Chinese were pushing forward so rapidly that the front was already at Tingkawk Sakan, the last village in the Hukawng Valley. The only shots we heard were those of the 38th Division soldiers who, having finished their share of the Walawbum battle, were resting across the river and practicing with tommy guns and bazookas. Many tommy-gun bullets whizzed over us, but the bazookas were providentially pointed in another direction. As the Marauders pushed on across the mountains to establish their second roadblock in the Mogaung Valley, only one regiment of the 38th supported them. Dushkin, Johnson, and Bomse accompanied them, but Gurney's detachment returned to us and helped us keep sane.

Whenever half the 38th Division went into bivouac, it put on Chinese operas to which General Sun gave us a standing invitation. The master of ceremonies held up the performance for half an hour on the first day to give us time to jack up and out of the mudholes on the route; and then he made us a flowery speech of welcome.

An American should, of course, show a bit of tolerance for his first Chinese opera. There is no scenery. Props are of the simplest. But the Chinese have a right to be proud of their opera. There really is a plot and, usually, a fairly good one. The costumes are gorgeous and the acting in most cases superb. The music, which most Americans would not call music, *is* music. For three hours they sing and play without a note in front of them yet every note is correct and, with no maestro to direct or baton in evidence, each attack is perfect.

All the Chinese actors were men, but the make-up of those taking female parts was so superb and the acting so very good that in the love scenes, even my sclerotic arteries skipped a few beats. One soldier was incredibly perfect in his imitation of a shy, coy, coquettish Chinese girl with her first lover. And these were soldiers, not a professional troupe imported for the occasion. I argued with two Chinese colonels for an hour about the amateur status of the players but they assured me it was all 38th Division local talent.

There was always plenty for me to think about in the Nambyu bivouac, even though a feeling of helpless uselessness is not conducive to constructive thinking. Pamphlets kept coming to me continually from the government of Burma at Simla containing charming pictures of prewar Burma and the government's idea of the kind of propaganda against the Japs worthy of being distributed to the Burmese refugees. The pictures, presenting as they did scenes that will never be the same again, brought an unbearable nostalgia. The publishers undoubtedly realized the scenes would never be the same, for the theme of the pictures was,

"Look what the Japs are desecrating!" And how did they happen to be desecrating Burma? It takes two parties for an invasion to be successful: a strong invader and a weak, unprepared defender. The invader is wicked in sins of commission but the weak defender is wicked in sins of omission.

My unhappy thoughts at the Nambyu bivouac were not entirely caused by the apparent determination of the Burmese Government to learn nothing from the "hell of a licking" given them by the Japs. The American Baptist Mission seemed determined to learn nothing also. They, too, sent pamphlets.

The Burma missionaries were refugees like ourselves, eager to go back to the country and people they loved, to help them throw off the disastrous effects of Japanese conquest and rule. But the government wouldn't permit the missionaries to return for a period of years unless they donned uniform and went in as part of a military unit. The missionaries divided into two groups: those who were willing to put on any kind of uniform or join any sort of unit just to get back to Burma, and those who, just as eager to return, still lived strictly by their principles. They felt it was sinful to wear a uniform or to be identified in any way with war. If the people of Burma saw them return with a military unit, what would they think? Would not the natives be disgusted with missionaries who took any part in war, even patching up its wounds, and lose faith in their quondam preceptors?

Always the same old stupid story! It was common in Christian circles, in the last two decades, to be pacifist in word and deed, but especially in word. Pacifist phrases were the style everywhere. It was stylish to condemn such grand old hymns as "Onward, Christian Soldiers" and "Stand Up, Ye Soldiers of the Cross." I remember well a heart-rending diatribe published in *Missions* by a Burma missionary in which he bewailed the presence of these two hymns in the Burmese hymnbook. He described how he had had either to tear them out or to order them left unsung in order not to compromise Christianity with the peaceful Burmese. Of all the crass hypocrisy I ever met, that's the worst. Neither of those hymns extols fighting that is destructive of people's bodies or souls, but rather exhorts "soldiers" to fight against invisible forces of evil. The Burmese, every race of them, dearly love those songs and never misunderstand them.

A much better example of a pacifist was our Bill Brough, the Friends Ambulance Unit leader who served with us in the first campaign. Conscientious objector that he was, Bill put on the uniform of the Friends Ambulance, rather than be drafted into a fighting unit, and served in London during the great blitz. Later he was assigned to the unit's China convoy and reached Burma just in time for the Burma War. Learning that things were going a bit quietly in China, he requested transfer to the Burma front under Stilwell and so joined us. After evacuation in India he was again ordered to China and worked feverishly through all sorts of dangers and difficulties south and east of Kweilin. During 1943, he was actually within sight of Hong Kong. But still he wasn't satisfied with his contribution to the war. Learning that Stilwell was about to begin his return trip to Burma, Brough, who had been a detachment commander, came to Ledo and enlisted as a buck private in the U.S. Army, asking to be assigned to me. With me, during the Hukawng and Myitkyina battles, he was under fire, ambushed and shelled more than anyone else in our unit except Captain Johnson. He complained if he wasn't first on the list for every difficult assignment.

While serving on Dushkin's flank move, the Marauders were ambushed and shelled one evening and there were several American casualties. Japs were still shelling and no one had time to get wounded men under cover. Everyone was scooping out earth and getting himself into safety. Surgical operations were impossible because of the proximity of the enemy which even prevented the use of flashlights. So old pacifist Brough with Mitchell Opas, my chief technician, heedless of their own safety, took out their entrenching tools and, still under fire, dug each American casualty a shallow trench to protect him from additional wounds.

But Bill still had a deep unrest in his soul. What Japan did to

Burma and China was beyond the endurance even of a sincere pacifist. Giving anesthetics, helping at operations, and even performing minor operations himself—all this was splendid training for a man who expected to enter medical school on V-J Day. Perhaps that was where the discontent lay. He was too safe with us. He was learning things that would help him after the war. He might be saving lives, as he did when he won the Bronze Star and the Oakleaf Cluster with the Marauders—but that was only an attempt to alleviate the evils of war. He was doing nothing to destroy the cause of all these things. The battle for Myitkyina was only half over when Bill came to me with regret in his voice.

"Sir," he said, too good a soldier to continue calling me "doc" after he enlisted, "I've got to get into a fighting unit. I'm sorry. I'm not doing my share here."

So I lost Bill to a fighting unit. That is real pacifism. I, too, am a conscientious objector. I detest war. My idea of my mission on this earth is to stop misery and pain, prolong life and happiness. Yet I couldn't get released from medical work in World War I, and by World War II, I knew how little I would be worth in any but a medical unit. So I can't preach about one's real duty being in a fighting unit rather than a rehabilitation unit. But surely in the face of what Germany and Japan have done to the world, the pacifism that will choke over the idea of wearing a uniform in a reconstruction group is something the world can do without.

Letters began to come from good Baptists back home in America who were very shocked that a few cusswords had been reported in my book, *Burma Surgeon*.

It seems to me that swearing is sometimes a very excellent safety valve and keeps one sane and on the job. At other times it amounts to a prayer and I am convinced God recognizes many oaths as such. If one couldn't see God in that story of mine he wouldn't believe me if I'd protested on every page. Somehow it never seemed to me that a man proved his real Christianity just by proclaiming it to the world in a loud voice. Even the Pharisees did that about their religion.

Old "Dad" Harris of the Karen Mission, the last of the great missionaries in Burma, stood up for me, backing me up with the Bible. "If anyone gets after Gordon for those swear words in the book," he said, "he should refer him to Galatians. Saint Paul did plenty of swearing in Galations!"

My family are practically charter members of the American Baptist Mission. It was about one hundred and fifteen years ago that my two great-grandfathers came out to Burma as missionaries, and some twenty-eight members of our family have since been missionaries in Burma. Each generation found the work of a missionary so satisfying that they urged the profession on their descendants. We love the country and its people. It is a great thing to help a people grow. There is no more satisfying job in the world. But never have I urged my children to return to Burma as missionaries, for unless missionary work is broadened to include more practical help to the people of the east, I believe it has little future in the postwar period.

In Namkham we had Bible study out of school hours and many Buddhist children came early just to be present. If no one wanted to be converted I didn't care, for we were thinking in terms of generations. I don't love people who become "Christian" too easily. We are, or we should be, out to change a race; help the race to grow hundreds of years in a generation. I never required any of my Buddhist nurses to go to our religious services. As a result they went to all of them.

In Myitkyina our Princess Louise came to me with a solid gold crucifix on a chain.

"Daddy, I want to buy this."

"How much do they want for it?"

"Two hundred and fifty rupees."

"It isn't worth half that and you know it."

"I know they want too much for it but I must have it. I have got to have it."

I didn't object to the girls buying jewelry for what it was worth. That's the way the people of Burma bank their money. But ordinarily I urged the nurses to save their money to rehabilitate their relatives when they returned to them rather than buy trash. But when this mature Buddhist girl asked me for permission to buy a crucifix at double cost, I didn't feel like demanding her motives.

"Okay, Louise. It will take me a couple of weeks to get the money from Ledo. You will have time to think it over."

Two weeks later Louise came to me again. "Daddy, they say the money is here. I want that crucifix!"

She wore it everywhere.

While all these things were going through my mind, the Chinese Army gave Stilwell a birthday present of the Jambu Bum Pass into the Mogaung Valley, and headquarters moved to Ting-kawk Sakan. The battle of the Hukawng was over; the armies were at last in real Burma, but we, the refugees, were left stranded in the horrible, dark, foul, stinking no man's land they call the Hukawng.

"Girls," I said, "we are nothing but a bastard unit now: no papa, no mama, no brother, no sister, no friends—backsheesh!"

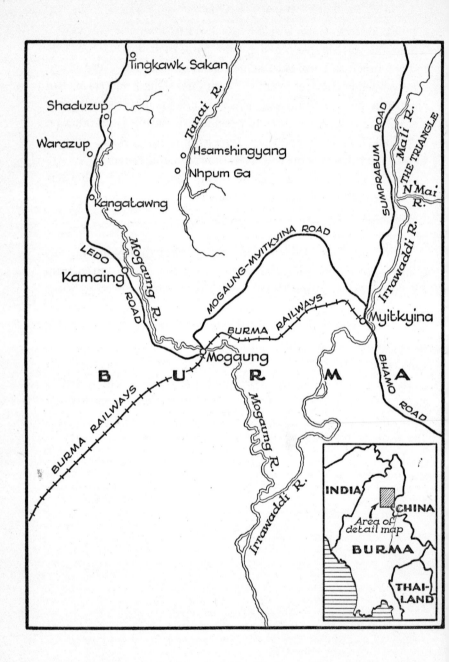

6

Myitkyina! Myitkyina!

I HAD another birthday at the Nambyu River. Our Special Service
radio was working for once and gave me a most wonderful birthday present: news of the airborne landings of General Wingate's
Chindits behind the Japanese lines in Burma. Lord Louis had
kept his promise. The radio gave some conflicting reports about
where the airborne commandos had landed, but to an old-timer
it was easy to locate at least one of the landings as having been
near Katha. Stilwell was receiving a bit of support at last. At
Katha it would be possible for the British to cut both the river
and the railway. The Japanese were crossing the Chindwin west-
ward, reported the radio, but nobody seemed to realize what a
blow the Japanese were attempting against India and Stilwell's
lines of communication. The Japanese must certainly be afraid
of Stilwell and his two Chinese divisions. Rather than try to wipe
him out by frontal assault, they threw several divisions against
the British at Imphal and Kohima in an effort to get behind Stilwell. The British held on with their teeth and fingernails and
saved India and, incidentally, Stilwell's forces. But that's not a
part of my story.

I made one last try for a place in Stilwell's campaign by driving
south to Tingkawk to see Colonel Petersen. There Petersen informed me that Major Dushkin's detachment had finished its
flank assignment and would be on the road in twenty-four hours.
I was worried about rumors that Stilwell was flying in some new
Chinese divisions. It would have been entirely in keeping with
army thought at that time to push me back to process those divisions rather than give the Burmese girls a combat assignment.
So I pretended that our unit would remain assigned to the 38th

Division and went forward to contact Dushkin and select a site.

It was delightful driving down into the Mogaung plain. As soon as you pass Jambu Bum you smell real Burma. Even rainstorms stop at Jambu Bum. On the Hukawng side it may be pouring. On the Mogaung side it's typical Burma weather—in April bright and clear. None of that Naga Hills stuff. I inspected some of the Japanese defenses in the pass. How the Chinese ever drove the enemy out of them is beyond the powers of a simple imagination to comprehend. Walking up a tributary of the Mogaung River I bumped into Dushkin.

"I thought you'd be coming after us!" he said. Never have I been paid a better compliment.

I took Dushkin back with me, arranging to send back transportation for our men the following day. At Tingkawk I reported to Colonel Petersen, realizing that I was in for it.

"The 50th Chinese Division is being flown into Maingkwan this week," he said. "The Seagrave Unit will proceed to Maingkwan at once and open up a hospital for them."

That meant we were to retreat twenty miles. How I wished I had never joined the confounded American Army! If I'd stayed on in Burma and organized guerrilla bands I would have been my own boss. We were Stilwell's first surgical unit. We had joined him when he hadn't a single medic but us. Now, instead of letting us help at the front, we were being sent back again. Had we really become a nuisance instead of a help in Stilwell's war? But where had we failed? What had we done wrong? The last time some of us had been ordered to retreat we had lost fourteen girls. How many would we lose this time? My objection to the assignment was, of course, due to being afraid of women. What man isn't? But in the U.S. Army you obey orders.

So we went back.

"It's your own fault," Dushkin said. "You said in your book that you asked Stilwell to give you the nastiest jobs he had."

"Okay," I said. "I'll shut up."

God bless those girls! They could see that the old man was

heartbroken about it and this time not one of them griped. Their co-operation at Maingkwan was immense. From that point on our unit perhaps proved itself worthy of General Stilwell's tolerance of us. We had lost fourteen of our girls, but from Maingkwan on we turned out a bigger job than we ever did with the original unit except during the first two months at Ramgarh.

The 50th Chinese Division was to camp five miles north of Maingkwan along a fair-sized stream. We were given a tiny stream two miles closer to Maingkwan. There was an open field available but one could never tell when the Japanese would start bombing again so we had to camouflage and disperse our wards. If the colored engineers hadn't lent us a bulldozer we could never have put up our wards and quarters in time to be of help to the 50th Division, for the jungle was the thickest, most matted, thorny, and impenetrable it was ever my ill luck to see. The engineers pushed the jungle away, our men put up the ward tents and built bamboo beds with the help of a few Chinese, and the nurses and Pang Tze and I built a hut for me and erected a ward tent for nurses' quarters. Then the nurses took over the ward work and sick call as the Chinese streamed in.

It was plain that Stilwell wanted us to do as we had at Ramgarh: get the sick into wards as rapidly as possible, cure them, and rush them out again for combat. We couldn't do this effectively unless we held sick call ourselves. American liaison officers, working through Chinese dispensaries, could never do it rapidly enough. Holding sick call would be a horrible job for our few officers and nurses in addition to ward work, but if we had been chosen because the job was important to Uncle Joe, extra work was nothing to complain about. Only one officer did complain. I added insult to injury by sending our trucks to the Chinese camp to pick up outpatients. That was a bit of shrewd psychology because these were Chinese who had seldom seen or ridden in a truck and lots of patients came with minor complaints just for the ride. The doctors sorted them out rapidly until we had three hundred beds filled, the number I had calculated a new Chinese division would need. There were an additional three hundred in sick call every day.

More than a hundred of our worst cases had very severe relapsing fever. Since the Chinese had been deloused in Chabua as they changed planes, we had the perfect chance to wipe out relapsing fever immediately, before the Chinese again acquired lice and spread the disease among Stilwell's fighting troops. The relapsing fever was the worst I'd seen, and there was a small epidemic of pneumonia also acquired by troops in a weakened condition flying over the Hump. We cured the two diseases when they occurred separately but lost a dozen cases that had both diseases simultaneously. Malaria wasn't too bad. There were some venereal cases and many chronic ulcers and, of course, the inevitable Chinese fistulas-in-ano. Beriberi was present even in April, two months before the beriberi season, for these troops were half starved. Many of the beriberi cases were partly paralyzed. Luckily for them we had secured a large shipment of thiamine which resulted in visible improvement daily, while thousands of multiple vitamin tablets soon wiped out the rest of the beriberi. During the real season for the disease at Myitkyina we had only a few of the minor cases and no severe beriberi.

The new Chinese needed Indian-type typhoid and cholera vaccines as well as smallpox. Liaison officers lined the men up by the regiment and we went to town in the old Namkham way. As we gave the shots we found no plump Chinese but many emaciated ones. After one week of good and oversufficient food the Chinese came back for their second injections without that starved look. In the wards it was the same as at Ramgarh. Patients fattened so rapidly that their intestines didn't have sufficient room to circulate freely in their abdomens and they were continually whining about abdominal pain. Apparently none of Stilwell's new Chinese had had full bellies on consecutive days since birth. Now their abdominal weight increased more rapidly than that of a woman during pregnancy.

Just after we passed our peak Colonel Petersen came to visit

Little Bawk Prepares a Meal While Naga Boy Looks On

Open-air Mess Hall

us. Merrill's Marauders were crossing the range to attack Myitkyina from the north. They were to be supported by a regiment
of the 30th Division of Ramgarh-trained Chinese, with whom he
was sending the U.S. 42 Portable Surgical Hospital, as well as by
a regiment of the 50th Division, with whom I was ordered to
send a medical detachment from our unit, composed of men only.
As we polished off the 50th Division, I was to evacuate the
chronics and bivouac until Colonel Petersen found something
for us to do. Dreading another bivouac I begged for permission to
hold onto our chronics so we might have something to do. Petersen agreed, but warned me that he might have to order us to
move suddenly. Sudden moves didn't frighten me; what did were
sudden and prolonged sits.

Lieutenant Colonel Combes was liaison officer to the regiment
that Dushkin, Gurney, and Antonellis and their men were to
support. In co-ordinating our moves with his, I discovered that
the Chinese were to march twenty miles the first day down the
blistering motor road to Wesu Ga in the jungle beyond Walawbum. Then there would be three days of forced marching until
they caught up with Merrill, though at that point there would
be considerable shade through the jungle. With most of the
soldiers just getting on their feet physically and many just discharged from our wards, I was convinced that the men would
collapse in the heat of the sunny motor road and the value of our
work at Maingkwan destroyed. Combes permitted us to con-
tribute our sixteen motor vehicles to see if they would be of material help. Early in the morning our men started off with our
own equipment and with as many of the weaker soldiers as they
could crowd into the trucks, drove them to Walawbum, then
came back to the rear of the column to pick up stragglers and
carry them through to Wesu Ga. Shuttling thus all day long gave
every Chinese soldier a ride of from three to twenty miles, longer
in proportion to his weakness. The only group that received no
help was the group with the heaviest loads: trench mortars and

kitchen equipment. Always the toughest men in the Chinese Army, these men staggered along with impossibly heavy loads and invariably got there. In my strongest days I couldn't have carried a load like that for a single mile even in winter. Yet these men carried them over twenty miles on a blistering hot highway.

It had been punishing work for our enlisted men, driving all day in the heat and then having only a few hours of rest before beginning a very difficult trip over the mountains, but there were no complaints. We didn't have many enlisted men in our unit but those we had were superb and deserved the bronze stars they earned on this trip. They stood up to punishment magnificently.

It was lonesome in Maingkwan after the boys left, but one day Brigadier General Sliney, who had trained the Chinese artillery in Ramgarh—the artillery was the best part of Stilwell's Chinese Army—came in to chat and we had a long bull session. And one day I looked up and there was General Boatner. It was the first chance I'd had to talk to him since the first of January.

"Doc," he said, "Delhi has decided that your unit is to have no Table of Organization. You are to remain a nameless, unorthodox, bastard unit."

"Okay," I said. "I've been calling our unit that anyway. No papa, no mama . . . backsheesh!"

"I hope you don't object," the general said.

"Sir," I replied, "if I interpret the reasons for that decision correctly I consider it a compliment."

"That's exactly what it is."

"As I see it, Stilwell wants us to remain plastic so that if he's short a station hospital or a field hospital or a clearing company or a portable surgical hospital, he can throw us into the vacancy without a by your leave. This thing we're running now is a field hospital."

I then took the opportunity to beg the brass hats to abandon the idea that Burmese nurses must not be allowed into danger zones and to give us a combat assignment.

"Sir," I said, "I wouldn't want one of these girls hurt for anything in the world. I've known some of them since they were babies. But they entered this war with their eyes open. They've been in plenty of danger and proved they can take it. Their morale has never been hurt by danger or hardship. Nothing hurts their morale but retreats."

"What do you think you want? Kamaing and Mogaung? You can't have them."

"No, sir. Let the portable surgicals and the 13th Medical Battalion have them. But I want first priority on Myitkyina, Bhamo, and Namkham."

"You don't want much, do you? I promise you that you'll go into Bhamo with the first troops. I can't promise that with regard to Myitkyina. How big a field hospital can you run in Myitkyina during the monsoons, if we take it?"

"With our present staff, five hundred beds, sir."

"How would you like Sumprabum if we don't capture Myit-kyina?"

"A poor second best, sir, but one of our girls lives there."

The day after Boatner was with us Harris returned from a trip to Ledo much worried. So was everyone else in Ledo, he reported. Tokyo Radio had just reported that Colonel Seagrave and thirty Burmese nurses had been captured in the Hukawng. I laughed. Tokyo was paying us a real compliment by thinking it worthwhile to "capture" us. I could wish all other Japanese prisoners of war were as happy as we were, as well fed, and as free to move around.

A report came in that an English-speaking Kachin refugee had been seen marching up toward Yupbang answering to the description of Lebang Lu's father. Lebang Lu was one of the girls who had left us, but for all that, several of us climbed into a jeep and drove back to Yupbang to verify the report and to help the gentleman financially if he were in need. We drove by our old bivouac on the south bank of the Tanai, by the Taihpa Ga airfield and the site of the hospital at Brambrang where the 25th Field Hospital had planned to spend the rainy season. Everything was abandoned. Not a sign of war anywhere. Natives were returning to their areas and making first preparations for a new rice crop. I hoped the American officers who thought Stilwell couldn't accomplish what he said he could were properly ashamed.

There were hundreds of Kachins in the refugee camp at Yupbang, and though Lebang Lu's father wasn't among them, Kyang Tswi bumped into an old friend and learned that her own family as well as that of Kaw Naw were well, that they knew their daughters were with me and safe. The trip was well worthwhile. As we stood waiting for the tea the English Civil Affairs officer was preparing for us, an American soldier—I was not wearing my insignia—approached me.

"Do you suppose those girls are some of 'Seagrave's Burma Nurses'?" he asked.

"Yes, they are."

"Gee, they look good! Do they speak English?"

"Not quite as well as you do," I replied.

"This is Colonel Seagrave," introduced Brayton Case, who was standing beside me.

Thereupon the soldier bolted and ran.

Back at Maingkwan we found Ba Saw, just flown back from his flank assignment in Pabum, and Captain Johnson, back from a much-deserved vacation.

Early on the morning of May 17, 1944, as I was tossing sleeplessly on my bed wishing it were time to get up and that there were something special to do when I did get up, one of those incredible hunches hit me. Something was cooking. I hustled the boys out of bed and ordered them to evacuate all our remaining patients to the Chinese regimental hospital. While they emptied the wards, the nurses, our few Chinese, our Burmese boys, and I pulled the tents down and rolled them up. When the trucks returned we loaded them with equipment for a surgical hospital. Everyone thought the old man had gone mad.

After breakfast the following morning I sat waiting for the

telephone to ring. It rang at eight-fifteen. On the other end of the wire was Colonel Petersen.

"How long will it take you to evacuate your patients?"

"I evacuated them all yesterday, sir."

"How soon can you start for the airfield at Maingkwan?"

"In an hour!"

"Hurry down there. Three C-47's have been assigned to pick you up."

"Yes, sir. Goodbye!"

The men and women of our unit needed no detailed orders. They had worked too long as a team for that.

"One suitcase and one bedroll each," I shouted. "We leave at once."

I was the last to be ready and even then a couple of the girls had to help me. Fifty-five minutes after the telephone rang we were at the field. Hour after hour passed. Planes were darkening the sky and a few landed on our field but they were on other missions. They had never heard of Seagrave. At noon the boys we were leaving behind with our equipment and vehicles brought us down a hot meal.

A liaison plane flew in and circled to land. "That's Colonel Petersen," I said to one of the boys. "Meet him and show him where we are." Those were my psychic days.

"What made you think it was I?" the colonel asked.

"I know you fairly well, sir. I knew you would come if you could steal a plane."

"That's just what I had to do. Yesterday Merrill's men took the Myitkyina airfield. You will report to Colonel Hunter."

"Yes, sir. Will I have to radio you for instructions as to evacuations and so forth?"

"Whatever medical measures need to be taken in the Myitkyina area will be determined by you," the colonel replied. "You are to arrange the entire medical setup with Colonel Hunter."

"Yes, sir."

"The planes seem to be held up. Medical needs are third priority today. I will have to return this stolen plane at once."

"Lieutenant Harris will telephone you when we leave, sir."

The boys played horseshoes. The girls fluttered around here and there looking for fruit. I sat. I had sat so many months I felt I could tolerate a bit more without going mad, for Myitkyina— Myitkyina!—was at the end of this wait.

Out of a jeep climbed a Chinese in an American uniform, covered with dust that had caked with his sweat.

"Are you Colonel Seagrave, sir?" he asked.

"Yes."

"I'm Corporal Wing, sir. Medical Department. Colonel Breidster assigned me to your unit and I have just come in from Ledo."

"Are you an American-Chinese?"

"Yes, sir."

"You're Cantonese, aren't you?"

"Yes, sir."

"Then you don't speak Mandarin?"

"Yes, I do, sir."

"You don't write Chinese, do you?"

"Yes, I do, sir."

"Somebody catch me while I faint! Where's your barracks bag?"

"Here, sir."

"Stick around. We're leaving for Myitkyina any moment. What do you know about medicine?"

"I'm a dental technician, sir."

"You aren't any longer. You're registration clerk to the Seagrave Unit. God help you. I'm going to work you to death. A Chinese-American who speaks Mandarin and Cantonese and writes Chinese as well! God is good! God is good!"

Little Bawk had too much thyroid secretion for her own good. About four o'clock she came to me for the umpteenth time.

"Darn it, Daddy, why don't the planes come?"

"I don't know, I tell you. Listen, woman. Everything that's

happened during the last two days shows that the good Lord is at last taking an interest in us again. I don't like to wait any more than you do, but I'm willing to bet you real money that when we get to Myitkyina we'll find that it was a good thing we didn't get there any sooner."

A C-47 circled in to land. After it had taken off again one of the Signal Corps boys from Hkalak sauntered over.

"Sir," he said, "the radio reporter on that plane says the Japanese bombed and strafed the Myitkyina field a little while ago. An American casualty that was being put on the hospital plane was killed and an American nurse shot in the leg."

"Bawk," I yelled, "just listen to this!"

We didn't have much longer to wait. A plane landed and the pilot admitted that he had heard of Seagrave. A third of the nurses, a third of the Burmese boys, a third of the supplies, and I got on board. Johnson, Ba Saw, and San Yee would come in the other two planes.

I looked down on those awful hills as we crossed the Chindwin-Irrawaddi divide: the hills that our men had negotiated on foot. Then I felt my still-creaking knee joints. And I thought the Lord didn't care about me any more, I thought, shamefacedly.

A railroad. The Burma Railways. The Irrawaddi again. Myitkyina. Myitkyina airfield from which half the unit had taken off for India two years before. May le bon Dieu forgive all my sins. The refugees are back again in real Burma. God is good!

We circled the field. What if a Jap sniper did hit us now? We were in Burma. I had always wanted to die in Burma.

A smashed C-47: was anyone hurt? Several crushed gliders: I hoped the passengers weren't killed. A dead Jap, sprawling, grotesque in the fading light. A Zero half buried in the ground: our boys got to work in a hurry.

We landed. Burma at last. Burma. Burma!

"Where will I find Colonel Hunter?" I asked a nonchalant American soldier.

"Across the field, sir," he said, pointing.

Hunter was minus a front tooth and wasn't ashamed of it. He was a real American officer who cared about nothing but the job in hand.

"Lieutenant Colonel Seagrave reporting, sir. Seagrave Hospital Unit. Four medical officers and eighteen Burmese nurses. Where do you want us to set up, sir?"

"My God! Women!"

How often I had heard that phrase shouted in joy! But Colonel Hunter's tone was one of complete disgust: hadn't he had enough trouble?

"We ask for no special security, sir," I said.

"Go over to the revetment next to the first-aid station across the field. I suppose you want rations. I haven't had enough food for seven days."

"We have three days' rations with us, sir," I said. "We shall be glad to share them with you."

"No, thanks. We'll get along."

"Yes, sir," I saluted and took my leave.

It was about four hundred yards from our plane to the revetment that Colonel Hunter had assigned us. Major Shudmack, at the first-aid station, regretted that his men were too tired to help us properly; they would do what they could to move our baggage into the revetment.

"Please, Major," I said, "our unit is here to help, not to cause trouble. For months I've begged the brass hats to give us a real assignment. Let us do this alone."

The major insisted on helping me with a couple of loads and then his tired feet gave out. Ba Saw's and Johnson's planes parked near our revetment. The airstrip was lit up by flares, for planes were coming in all night. Snipers' bullets whizzed over us as we carried our equipment down the field piece by piece but the refugees didn't care. They were back in real Burma at last. We laid a tarpaulin over some upright litters and crawled in. Only two casualties came in during the night and they were dead on arrival.

Our first task was to boil our instruments and set up operating tables for casualties. Anything approximating an operating room was out of the question. There wasn't a bamboo or a stick anywhere to support a tarpaulin. We set packing cases up with litters across them for operating tables and were soon ready to go. Before long the Chinese found us, and Ba Saw, San Yee, Johnson, and I were busy. At noon Dushkin and Gurney arrived with their detachment, the thinnest, dirtiest, weariest bunch of men I'd seen for a long time. The sun was blistering hot and our skins began to burn, for we were naked to the waist. Then a squall of rain blew up and a nurse held an umbrella over the operative field while I removed a man's shattered spleen. Apparently there were photos being taken and weeks later I heard that Howard Baer had done a sketch of us; but we were completely unconscious of it all. Correspondents never interfered with medical units when they were really busy with surgery.

Dushkin immediately began acting as triage officer, and Gurney and Antonellis, tired as they were, set up two more litters and joined in. Our men stretched electric wire over upright litters, cut holes in empty No. 10 cans to act as black-out shades and as night fell we had electricity. The men put up several parachute tepees for patients, while they covered others with ground sheets. We operated on one hundred and twenty patients that day and crawled under our tarps with patients all around us.

It's hard to praise adequately the job that was done by the C-47 pilots during the battle for Myitkyina. For many days the big transports flew around the clock. They came in on mornings when ceiling was zero and seemed to smell their way to the field. The hospital planes didn't fly in very bad weather but nothing held back the transports. For some time we were forbidden to put up more than three ward tents because of the danger of Japanese planes. But when we had patients to evacuate, the transports took them. It was for patients and patients only that the transport pilots would consent to delay their take-off. For them they would wait an extra half hour.

On our second full day the men put up three operating rooms of triple-layer parachutes and several more tepees for patients. Then Bill Brough located a lot of bullet-riddled gasoline barrels and some moth-eaten bamboos and three by six timbers. Using the wall of the revetment to hold one end of the bamboos and gas barrels piled three high to rest the other, the men stretched out tarps and we had a place to keep dry at night. On Sunday evening the Japs began throwing 70-mm. howitzer shells at us. Colonel Hunter thought us too close to the field so on the fifth day we moved two hundred yards nearer town. Here there was a much larger and higher revetment, the best near the field.

We were lucky to have three light days in succession—only twenty or thirty patients per day—to make the move. We had acquired a few local coolies to help, plus the detachment of litter bearers that had accompanied Major Dushkin. By the end of three more days we had put up a ward tent for the nurses against the east wall of the revetment toward the town, and our colonial-style, gasoline drum-pillared tarpaulins against the south and west walls for officers, enlisted men, and operating room. Later the men erected several pyramidal tents for themselves in the center of the revetment and at its mouth. The litter bearers built shacks for themselves west of the revetment. As the rules were relaxed we put up three ward tents for Chinese casualties and one forty by forty tarpaulin for Americans and British. A month later we were allowed a total of seven ward tents. In the operating room I had thirteen litters set up as operating tables, two for each surgeon, and one "Myitkyina Model" fracture table. This decreased the time lag between operations and offered opportunities to guest surgeons who dropped in from time to time.

The only fault with the revetment lay in the fact that it was on lower ground than the rest of the area. The only drainage was into the huge pits outside, from which earth had been taken to form the revetments. The drainage ditch by the operating tables was continuously running red with blood, and the pits soon became unspeakably foul—so also was the mud we churned up as we operated. On wet days the mud was ankle deep but didn't stink quite so much, while on hot days the mud dried and stank. One night during a heavy downpour a huge ditch in front of us collapsed and all the water from the airfield, instead of being carried away, flowed into our area, filling the pits and our revetment a foot deep. By morning our suitcases and shoes had floated some distance away. But the accident flushed out our stench very properly.

Our large number of casualties was increased through the hysteria of poorly trained troops in their first battle. As at Yupbang, the Japanese would fire a few rounds of rifle, machine-gun, and mortar fire and then climb down into their dugouts and laugh as both Chinese and Americans let loose with all they had for an hour at a time. For there were green Americans in the fight now, combat engineers and infantry fresh from the States who were replacing the worn-out sick Marauders, few of whom were still able to fight. We soon learned to distinguish the sound of hysteria in the rattle of machine-gun and rifle fire and to gird our loins for the inevitable casualties caused by American-made weapons. During the first three weeks they were more numerous than those that were caused by Jap fire.

About a week after we reached Myitkyina, Sein Myaing, one of our nurses who lived in that town, heard from her uncle that our unit was back in Burma again. One dawn she made him lead her out from Myitkyina through the Japanese and Chinese lines. I could understand the Japanese letting them through, for at that time they were anxious to get civilians out of the way. But I couldn't understand why the Chinese didn't shoot them down. Sein Myaing's nonchalance was amazing.

When we came out of Burma, Sein Myaing had been a bit fed up with me because I had chosen her as one of those to stay behind and help run the Namkham hospital for a few months rather than go to the front, little realizing that the battle would be over almost as soon as it started. There were other things, too. So when, on my instructions, Bill Cummings told the nurses at Namkham to decide whether they wanted to fly to India or stay in Burma, Sein Myaing decided to stay, and set off for her home in Myitkyina. The first Japanese commander there was a Christian and had enforced order among his troops, treated the people with kindness, and even organized Christian services on Sunday. Sein Myaing had been ordered to serve in a hospital for civilians in town and had been well treated.

After the refugee nurses had almost hugged her to death, Sein Myaing gave us the surprising news that Sein Hla Tha, headmaster of my Anglo-Vernacular Middle School at Namkham, had been in Myitkyina the night before the airfield was taken. Impressed by the Japs to act as interpreter he had come straight up there from Namkham, starting for the south just as the Americans came in. So Sein Myaing was crammed with news of Namkham, and very fresh news, too.

"Your own bungalow is untouched and the Japanese general lives there," she said to me. "One wing of the nurses' home has been hit by a bomb but no bomb has yet touched the hospital. On the other hand, the Japs have torn up floors and wooden walls and doors and windows and have used them for firewood and to build sheds." This after we had obligingly left the Japs more than a hundred cords of firewood conveniently cut and stacked!

"E Hla [*head nurse at Namkham*] and her husband Ai Lun are running a hospital for civilians at Muse. Dr. San Yee's wife and baby are well. [*Cheers and tears from San Yee.*] Sein Hla Tha and Rosie have a fat baby boy. [*Cheers from me. I had operated on that woman three times to cure her sterility and then had had her abort her first pregnancy during an attack of malaria.*] Than Shwe's father Po Nee and the Karen headmaster at Kutkai are pro-Jap and are lording it over Lashio and Kutkai. [*Groans.*] Dr. Ba Saw's father and mother and doctor-sister are safe in Shwebo, working in a civilian hospital there.

"Hkawn Tawng and her little sister are in Myitkyina now,"

she continued. "Do you remember she got angry with you for not taking her to the front and ran off with a Shan-Chinese trader? Well, he took a commission as a captain in the Japanese Army and is somewhere south near Katha. Hkawn Tawng has one baby girl and is six months' pregnant now."

"Where is Nang Seng?" I asked.

"She's here in town."

"Has she any children?"

"No."

"Where is Toi Roi?"

"She ran off to the mountains and is safe. Her mother divorced her father and married again and is living on the big island in the river just below town. Her father was killed by an American bomb."

"How have the people fared under Japanese rule?"

"The Japanese continually went off with everyone's rice which now costs eighty rupees a basket. [*About thirty dollars a bushel.*] We haven't been able to buy any cloth and not even cotton to weave our own clothes. That's why I'm so ragged. The Japanese would have been better liked if they hadn't constantly slapped and kicked everyone with or without provocation."

Not long after that episode, a Kachin scout serving the Americans across the river was flown to us in a liaison plane with a minor injury. As I was treating him I discovered to my astonishment that he was Toi Roi's older brother.

"Doesn't Toi Roi want to come back and work with us?" I asked.

"She will when she learns you're here," he replied.

"Can you get her down to your American officers? If you can they will fly her to us."

"I'll try."

Three days later, in walked Toi Roi. She was pale and thin and told a long story of semistarvation and malaria, with no drugs available for treatment. It was good to see her again. Then one day Nang Seng No. 2 and Nang Seng No. 3 herself appeared together. No. 3, whose husband was in Rangoon studying medicine, was nursing in the government's new hospital for civilians. No. 2 had several children, acquired since she had been forced some years before to stop training and marry a man who didn't want her.

Something should be done to change the marriage customs of the people of Burma, especially pernicious among the Kachins and most pernicious of all among so-called Christian Kachins. All marriages are marriages of convenience—convenience of the parents. The likes and dislikes of the children, especially the daughters, are never taken into consideration. For a financial inducement, for a bit of imitation rank, or simply to marry someone in the right clan, a priceless daughter will be given to a determined rake whom she utterly despises, or a son will be forced to marry a girl for whom he feels not the slightest respect or affection. The lives of each son and daughter of the two most famous Kachin "Christians" of Bhamo District were ruined by the headstrong cupidity and stupidity of their parents and grandparents. It is no wonder the girls and boys will take their happiness when and where they can find it.

I was especially glad to see Nang Seng No. 2. I had a problem to talk over with her.

"The nurses are wasting too much time on jobs that require no skill," I said. "Don't you think you can find some boys and girls who would like to work for us? I'll pay them five rupees more per month than the army pays coolies. They will have good food and a civilized place to sleep and Christian people to work with. If they prove to have the knack of nursing they may go on with us when we leave Myitkyina or stay behind if they choose. Even if they stay with us only while we're in Myitkyina, they'll pick up enough nursing to be a help with their families all their lives."

Not many days later Nang Seng appeared trailing three Karen girls, three Kachin girls, and a couple of Karen boys after her. One of the girls was her own sister, Nang Pri. Soon girls began to trickle in by ones and twos and a few more boys appeared. One day Ohn Hkin's entire family walked in from a village north of town and left Ohn Hkin's younger sister Ohn Yin to work with us. Even Hkawn Tawng turned up, with a sheepish grin on her face for having married the wrong man, and left her twelve-year-old-sister Roi Ji with us. I hardly recognized Roi Ji with her short hair and boy's clothes. Like Hkawn Tawng she had a fascinating smile and a mincing way of walking as if she were wearing high heels. This, in a twelve-year-old, presaged years of heartbreak for the males of her world.

And then a Karen doctor, Mildred Pan Hla, walked in and asked for a job. Working in the government civil hospital at Lashio she had started on the run a few jumps ahead of the Japanese, who caught up with her at Myitkyina. The Japanese refused to recognize her medical degree and ordered her to work as a nurse.

I've never regarded graduates of the Rangoon medical schools as knowing much about medicine. What Dr. Ba Saw and Dr. San Yee knew—and they were skillful surgeons—they learned after coming to us. But I was curious to see what it would be like to have a woman doctor in a combat surgical team, so we took her on. Mildred was hurt when I insisted she learn her first lessons from nurses, but before long she came to realize that she was learning things about medicine of which she had never dreamed. She worked placidly under fire, marched over difficult trails with the best, and when the unit moved to a new location she did coolie work with the rest and with indefatigable good humor.

All of our new additions were useful. Having lived through American bombings and shellings they paid no attention whatever to Japanese 70's. But unlike her sister, Nang Pri seemed to have been born at an operating table. She was a "natural," just like Little Bawk. In a week she had learned the names of surgical instruments and supplies and in two was assistant to the graduate nurse at the instrument table. Naomi took a fancy to her and at the end of three weeks gave her a chance, after midnight when most of the other girls were in bed, to act as second assistant to

me at an abdominal operation, acquitting herself with great credit
—much to the disgust of the girls who had gone to bed early.

On the day the airfield was captured it seemed that Myitkyina
would be ours within a week. We were told on good authority
that the Japanese had actually evacuated Myitkyina except for
snipers, not knowing just how big a force Stilwell had thrown
against them. But Colonel Hunter had only his depleted, weakened Marauders and two regiments of Chinese, who also were
not only tired out from their forced march over the mountains
but were fighting their first battle. There had not been nearly
enough troops to guarantee both airfield and town against unknown odds. Of the two, the airstrip was by far the more important. So while we hurriedly flew in reinforcements, the Japs
moved back into Myitkyina and dug in. We had to fight for it,
blast and burn the enemy out of their dugouts under road and
river embankments and deep under huge banian trees and bamboos.

7

Surgery at the Airstrip

WITH a long battle ahead of us we organized our work to the peak of efficiency possible in the jungle. Two operating tables for each officer cut down the time lag for surgeons, until they had time for only half a cigarette between operations, during which they had to write up the previous case on the inevitable toilet paper to send back to base with the patient the next day. To make our surgical instruments go further and save time of nursing personnel, we set up one large instrument table at the angle of the V-shaped operating room, like the serving counter of a huge restaurant, from which "short orders" were served out at a moment's notice to the first assistants of the surgeons at all tables. Two nurses were on full-time duty with plasma and glucose, getting shocked patients into condition for operation and keeping them alive as we operated on them. One Chinese sailor ran the autoclave all day, sterilizing linen washed free of blood by two of our soldier-orderlies. Two other Chinese orderlies were continually hauling water to keep our G.I. cans filled. Two nurses injected each new arrival with morphine, atropine, and tetanus antitoxin, reporting the nature of wounds and the patient's general condition to Major Dushkin, who acted as triage officer and assigned cases to the individual surgeon's tables. Nurses who were not assigned elsewhere cut and folded gauze into sponges. At least we didn't have to wash out and use again the blood-soaked gauze, as we did in the first campaign. Sergeants Probst and Stolec organized the men into the "Myitkyina Plasterers' Union," and soon they were putting on plaster casts most efficiently, with only an occasional glance from the surgeon. This proved its value one day when there were fifteen hip spicas to be put on men with badly shattered thighs. Two men with hand brushes and basins of

soap and water rushed from table to table as patients were anes-
thetized, scrubbing out the wounds and cleaning skins of the
mud and grime of war. Then nurses applied alcohol and iodine,
draped towels, and the surgeons began to cut.

And up and down the operating room were cries for "Grandma.
Grandma!" "Pang Tze. Pang Tze. Pang Tze!" "Wing. Wing.
Corporal Wing. G.I. Wing!" as the three most essential people
in the unit were called to straighten out difficulties everywhere
at once. Grandma Naomi, unruffled, calm, efficient, pulling wisecracks in two or three languages, stood in the angle of the V,
supervising the cleaning and resterilization of instruments, assign-
ing nurses and American, English, Burmese, and Chinese technicians to scrub up as operative assistants or to anesthetize patients, smoothing ruffled feelings, and always casting a critical
eye around to spot some gross break in technique on the part of
the younger personnel.

"Pang Tze, get this patient off the table for me and bring me
another, will you?" "Pang Tze, scrub!" "Pang Tze, hold this leg
for me!" "Pang Tze, *tang cha ping* [*litter bearers*], *tang cha ping!*"
"Pang Tze, I want a box to sit on. My back is breaking!" And
again and again, "Pang Tze, what the Sam Hill was the number
of that last patient I operated on?" And Pang Tze, running for
a look at the strip of adhesive glued to the patient's forehead,
would shout back, "*Sickasa fifa tree!*" or, "*Nina sickasati pour!*"
Poor Pang Tze's hard-earned fat began to melt out of his pores
and he hitched his belt a quarter of an inch tighter every day.

Once, during a short lull, Pang Tze lay down on the revetment
beside me with a sheepish grin on his round face. "*Wo kun jao
bu kou!*" he said. "I haven't had enough sleep!" One of my sergeants caught him at it and tickled his nose with a straw. Like a
chow dog, Pang Tze turned with a snarl and snapped at him
with his teeth. Yet I could rouse him from a deep sleep at any
time and he would jump to his job with an apologetic laugh.

Wing was the only person we'd ever had in the unit who could
write Chinese. Until he came we'd never tried to get the patient's

name for our records. We'd tried it at Ramgarh, spelling out the name as best we could in English, but no two people spelled the names the same way, and no matter who had written the name, the patient wouldn't recognize it when read back to him. But Wing took over our admission clerk's work and wrote the names in Chinese, and his records were a pleasure to work with. If he'd been a lesser man he'd have gone insane those weeks at the field. While admitting one patient or preparing him for evacuation, other casualties would come in behind his back. Because the surgeons could allow no time lag before beginning the operation, Wing was in continual demand. At first the Americans were very polite to this "foreigner" in the U.S. Army and called him Corporal Wing. He wasn't ruffled. When they dropped the title and called him just Wing, one felt that the enlisted men were beginning to like him. Finally they began calling him G.I. Wing or just G.I. To them Wing was now not just another American soldier but the best kind of American soldier.

In the supply hut we had a new American boy named Gilbertson who had never been on a combat mission with us before. Though he had no teacher he somehow learned in no time at all just how much of each article we would need during each phase of the battle. With Stinky Davis collaborating—chumming with C-47 pilots and hospital-plane surgeons, grinning his twisted smile at the right moment in his censorable yarns—the supplies would flow in from base. One morning, when we were almost out of ether and plasma, Stinky and Gilbertson so worked on the tender feelings of the pilot of the hospital plane that quantitites of both necessities were delivered to us only six hours later.

Two nights after we moved to the larger revetment, we had just crawled into bed when an incredible storm of wind and rain hit us and nearly blew away our tents. Every bit of starlight was blotted out of the sky. Suddenly, as the storm swept past, there was a tremendous burst of machine-gun fire all around us, the lighter, snappier noise of the Japanese small-calibered weapons. Then the clatter of the heavier American-made weapons replied, as the Americans and Chinese opened fire. Even the machine guns of the English antiaircraft battery just across the way from the open, unprotected side of our revetment began to blaze away, and we knew it was the real thing and not hysteria. These English were old-timers who had seen action all over the world. Tracers streaked over us from all directions. One Japanese machine-gun squad had sneaked up under cover of the storm and was located between us and the landing strip.

But there was no panic. Dushkin quickly assigned men to sentry positions and to barricades of packing cases at the entrance to the revetment, while the nurses crowded around me for whispered instructions. "Get down flat on your beds at this end of your tent," I ordered. "No lights, no talking. Two girls on each cot."

Hours later, when the shooting had died away, I told the girls to climb back into their own beds. As Ruby and Louise brushed past me I noticed they were sopping wet and muddy and shaking with cold.

"What on earth happened to you?" I asked.

"You told us to get down flat, so we did—under the other girls' cots!"

At the open end of the nurses' tent I found our Burmese boys and a couple of enlisted men on guard with carbines, tommy guns, and rifles. As I added my automatic to the arsenal, I warned, "Don't shoot on any provocation until you've proved conclusively that what you're shooting at is a Jap, and even if it is a Jap, don't shoot on a line between us and the British antiaircraft!"

It was well we were warned, for soon a body crowded under the northeast corner of the tent wall and I could hear weapons being thrust to shoulders.

"Who's there?" I stage-whispered, dramatically.

"Don't shoot! It's me, Wentz. Sergeant Brown and I were sleeping out in the kitchen with the Chinese cooks when the shooting started."

"Where's Brown?"

"Right behind me. The Chinese dropped into the revetment pit."

Soon there was another shuffling and a muttered curse that sounded like Chinese, then a fierce challenge in Chinese from Bill Brough. If Brough was taking care of them it was all right, for he was a crack shot. We breathed easily again. Minutes later Bill crawled under the tent wall. "Chinese litter bearers with a casualty," he said. "I thought they might be masquerading Japanese so I asked them where their home towns in China were. They knew their geography and their Chinese accent was all right so I let them in. The casualty has only a flesh wound and will keep till morning. I gave him plasma. We can't have lights anyway."

Those Chinese litter bearers deserve a lot of credit. They worked under fire just like American medical corpsmen. With our four thousand Chinese casualties at Myitkyina we averaged only 3.8 per cent mortality in the cases that reached us alive, though some were gasping their last breath. Very few died in the plane on their way to base and two large base hospitals assured me, months later, that only ½ per cent died after reaching them. This was a record to be proud of in view of the ghastly wounds the casualties at Myitkyina had sustained. The wounds were no more horrible than those of other battles, but in other battles they didn't reach us alive. That they did so in Myitkyina was due not only to the fact that we were never more than two miles from the fighting but also to the efficient service of the Chinese litter bearers.

A great deal has been said—and I have said a great deal myself —about the callousness of one Chinese to the sufferings of another, a callousness epitomized in the story of the American pilot who saw a group of Chinese soldiers push one of their number out of the open door of a C-47 as they were flying over the Hump and then stand back and laugh immoderately at the joke. But at

Myitkyina we saw hundreds of casualties carried in and laid tenderly on the ground by their regimental litter bearers—who then burst into profanity as our own litter bearers less tenderly jerked the patients over to the American litters. Every American casualty knows that it was more comforting to be carried on Chinese litters by Chinese than on American litters by Americans.

If our own *tang cha pings* were perhaps a bit more rough, they also astonished us daily. They were from the 50th Chinese Division, yet, contrary to Chinese custom, they served us equally well, whether casualties were from the 50th, 14th, or 30th Chinese divisions, from the Marauders or from British units. For some reason most of our patients persisted in arriving in the evening and we were frequently operating until two and three in the morning. No matter how late we were, there were always *tang cha pings* on duty, and no matter how early we started in the morning, we found them standing by.

Inevitably I wondered how our unit would act if bullets and shells came near. I was and still am curious to know how I myself would react if we were really in danger. People talk about our medical unit's having been under shellfire more than any other, yet we knew nothing of danger as the men in the lines knew it. I never actually saw a man struck by a bullet or a shell. No one was killed within a hundred yards of me. Still the shells came rather close at Myitkyina. Several of the men and three of the officers dug themselves trenches beside their cots, into which they flopped when the shells began to scream over. The rest of us dug nothing. If the Japs shelled when we were not operating we all crouched by the east wall of our revetment. If they shelled while we were operating, we went on operating.

I recall one evening when they brought in an American boy with a bullet wound from temple to temple which had left only a few shattered remnants of his eyes. Paul Geren was giving him pentothal and Chit Sein was assisting me. I had only a few more stitches to take when the 70's began shelling. "Go over to the revetment wall," I said. "I don't need either of you any more. If he begins to wake up I can shoot in a bit more pentothal myself."

Both of them ducked under the table as they heard another shell scream and then came back to duty positions as it exploded beyond us, only to duck again at the next scream of a shell. I should have rebuked them for disobeying orders, but I was fascinated by my last few stitches into the American boy's torn face, and in any case their demonstration of courage helped my own nervous system along and, I hoped, made the involuntary ducking of my own head less apparent.

One evening Japanese reinforcements pulled a 150-mm. gun to the north of us and started shelling. A few shorts exploded just to the north, while most of the shellbursts were just south of our installation, shrapnel flying back over us into the revetment. Then the Japs in town opened up with 70's which fell to the west of us and with large mortars which hit to the east. There was a ring of exploding metal all around us and we didn't know which way to duck.

I still don't know the answers, but to me fear is the result of a too vivid imagination. If you spent your time thinking that the next whine of a shell would see your body bursting apart, like the bodies of the Chinese and Americans on whom we operated every day, you could soon work yourself up into a frenzy of fear and imagine shells bursting all night long, much to the impairment of your usefulness to the army. Some of the self-styled fire-eaters got it the worst. There was that enlisted man at Ningam who breathed fire at the thought of all the unlucky Japs he was going to send to their eternal punishment. One week of shelling at Brambrang and he wouldn't come out of his dugout unless ordered, and only then with three grenades, a dagger, a bayonet, and an automatic strapped to his belt and a carbine over his shoulder. Rigged up with this terrific assortment of American firepower, he would scrub up to assist at surgical operations.

There was also a medical officer who wasn't satisfied until he made a tour of the Chinese front-line trenches just as the Japanese opened up with machine guns. Then he was altogether too well satisfied. After that the sound of a Japanese gun would start an uncontrollable attack of dysentery, miraculously cured by putting a few miles of space between him and the Japs.

So far my only "wound" from Japanese shellfire was received one evening as I stood watching Ted Gurney operating on an abdominal casualty. There were two Air Corps men right behind me. At the whistle of the first shell they plunged for cover, thrusting me aside so forcibly that I fell over an operating table and was completely winded.

Most incomprehensible was the man who, to escape a theoretical wound, would inflict one on himself, in the hope that a certain wound would let him escape from a possible one. There were epidemics of this practice when new troops went into action. We had it in the Fifth Army troops during the first Burma campaign in 1942 and again in the new Chinese and American troops in the battle for Myitkyina. The Americans did it a bit better than the Chinese, putting a bullet through the base of the smaller toes of the left foot—we had half a dozen of these at Myitkyina when the new troops went into action. A platoon slept in our revetment one night. In the morning a soldier "accidentally" shot himself in the left foot just twenty yards from me while I was looking at him.

An American can get along in life with a limp or an artificial leg. A Chinese can get along without an arm or hand but he must have two good legs to make a living. So the Chinese self-inflicted wounds were always in the left hand or forearm. The best Chinese anatomists shot themselves very cleverly between the two bones of the left forearm, missing both bones, both large arteries, and the important nerves. Personally I would rather be hit suddenly and unexpectedly. It hurts less.

But no medic has a right to preach at hysteria in combat troops even if he serves in a combat medical unit. Someone was always fussing over the medics, urging them to take care of themselves and throwing out defense systems around the medical installations, whereas it was just the opposite with fighting troops.

The U.S. 42nd Portable Surgical Hospital under Major Harris had come over the mountains with the 30th Division and was set up in regimental headquarters north of town, so close to the enemy that they couldn't use lights to operate at night; already one of their technicians had a fractured spine from shellfire. At the time I was still medical boss in Myitkyina, so I invited Harris to come over and work beside us. It would be easier for us to keep them supplied with sterile goods and make all our work more efficient. Harris agreed and we had ten delightful days working together. Their Captain Bone performed a magnificent nerve-block anesthesia. He blocked the shell-torn faces I was trying to put together so well that the operations were easy and our enlisted men began to call me a plastic surgeon! By taking turns at the surgery, officers and men of both units were able to get some much needed rest.

Then one morning one of our fighter pilots zoomed over us and, testing his controls, accidentally released two bombs that missed us by what seemed like inches. We were operating at the time and wondered what made those guns sound so loud. Had the Japs brought up another 150-mm. gun? General Boatner and Colonel Willey rushed to the door of their command post. The general was convinced that that was the end of both medical units and sent Colonel Willey over on the double-quick to see.

Next morning the 42nd Portable Surgical Hospital was ordered to move to a new site on the other side of the field, thereby ending a most delightful companionship. The 58th Portable Surgical Hospital had just arrived from the States and was ordered to serve the American lines north of town on the Myitkyina-Mogaung Road, while we served the Chinese who were attacking the town from the west and south. The officers and men of the 42nd, almost overcome by fatigue and illness, were to begin taking furloughs, helping in the care of American patients until the 44th Field Hospital took over.

During the first two months of the Battle of Myitkyina we had confined our air support to the use of fighter bombers to pinpoint targets, then strafe, hoping we might save part of the town for our own use later. Soon fighters were based on our field. On days when work was light the nurses would climb to the top of the east revetment wall and watch them take off to bomb, screaming with delight as one plane after another peeled off into a power dive, dropped its load, and shot up into the sky again, then circled and strafed with his machine guns blazing. Any decent missionary would have reprimanded the girls for their actions or reminded them that perhaps the bombs and bullets were hitting their own relatives and friends in the city. But all I could remember was the unspeakable misery these girls had suffered as refugees in India waiting for the chance to help drive the hated invaders from their country. And as to the bombs and the bullets hurting their relatives and friends—I wanted them to forget it.

But still the Japanese defense didn't collapse—so B-25's were sent for. They came in squadrons, dropping so many sticks of bombs that their explosions sounded like the rattle of a super machine gun.

One day a prematurely aged man and an eight-year-old boy walked in. It was Esther's Uncle Boganaw and his youngest son. Boganaw had been headmaster of the mission school in Myitkyina and had elected to live out the Japanese occupation. At the time of Sein Myaing's and Dr. Mildred's escape from town he also might easily have escaped to the safety of the American and Chinese lines. Why he didn't do so I still don't know. Possibly he was skeptical of our ability to tear the Japs—and the town—apart. Perhaps it was only the apathy and fatalism of the Orient. Perhaps it was the oriental's determination to stick by his home. And, of course, it is very possible that, being the senior mission official of the district, he felt it his duty to stick it out and prevent as much as one man could the looting of mission property by the Japanese or the Allies. One day, when he and his youngest son were away from home, our B-25's came over and one bomb dropped squarely in the trench occupied by his wife and five other children. When Boganaw returned home there was no sign of his children or wife except a small piece of flesh hanging on a nearby telephone wire. That was the end. He slipped out of town—a much more difficult feat as the battle drew to a close than at the beginning. The Civil Affairs officer set him to work recruiting Kachins. He finished this assignment in October, sick with malaria and half crazed by the loss of his family, and begged to join us as coolie, orderly, or errand boy, just to get away from the hateful memories of the last days of Myitkyina.

Many other civilians had experiences like Boganaw's. Ma Yi, one of our new girls, was the wife of a Burmese actor touring somewhere in the south. She and her oldest sister hid from our bombers in foxholes some distance apart on the Irrawaddi bank. A bomb missed Ma Yi and blew her sister apart, right in front of her eyes.

I've talked to a great many people who suffered the loss of family, friends, home, and property at the hands of our air force or big guns. As far as I know there was only one instance where any blame was laid on us. A Burmese woman, crazed by the loss of everything she had in the world, ran to the first American sergeant she saw after her escape, pounded his chest with her little fists, screaming, "You killed all my family. I hate you!"

The contrary, however, was the rule. Everyone, as did Boganaw and Ma Yi, admitted the right of the British and Americans to drive the Japs out of Burma and the necessity of using bombs, shells, and machine guns to do so. They blamed themselves for not having the common sense to clear out of the battle area when the war drew close. Long experience had convinced them that the allied planes and guns were aimed at legitimate Japanese targets, even if they didn't always hit the target on the nose. Civilians were hurt only when they helped the Japanese or when they remained too close to them.

There was one heartbreaking experience toward the end of the battle. Some gaunt, haggard, and starved prisoners of war had effected an escape from the Myitkyina concentration camp. They were Anglo-Indians and Anglo-Burmese whom Chinese and Americans had picked up as they reached the allied lines and hauled to the areaway in front of our operating rooms. One was an old man of seventy with tuberculous lungs and an enormous inguinal hernia that reached to his knees. I came out at the completion of my operation. On a litter on the ground was the most beautiful woman I'd seen in many months, an eighteen-year-old Anglo-Burmese girl whose figure would have taken Hollywood by storm.

"Great Scott," I said. "I know you. I've met you somewhere. Where was it?"

"At Bhamo, three years ago, Dr. Seagrave," said a gaunt woman by her side. "I am her mother. My husband was in the service there and on one of your trips to Bhamo, when you were building the great stone church there, we asked you to come and prescribe for several of us who were ill."

"How did the Japanese happen to catch you?"

"We tried to get out of Myitkyina by plane during the evacuation but there was never room for us."

"How have the Japanese treated their prisoners of war?"

"Most of the time they didn't treat us badly," broke in the old man with the hernia. "I hate the Japs but you must give the bastards their due. Our food was never good but we were given enough until the Americans captured the field. After that we received practically nothing and they were very harsh to us."

"My husband was taken somewhere by the Japs a few weeks ago and I haven't seen him since nor have I any idea where he is," the mother continued. "My younger daughter is rather scatterbrained and cares nothing about us. She always manages for herself well enough with the Japanese and Burmese and English. She is off somewhere now with the Americans."

"What happened to this girl?" I asked.

"She was wounded by your bombs seven days ago. The Japanese refused to do anything for our wounded so we decided to escape. We were almost safely away when they machine-gunned us. That was three days ago."

"How did you manage to get out today?"

"They seem to want to get rid of us now," she replied.

"Didn't the Chinese fire at you?"

"No, they stopped firing the minute they saw us and let us into their lines, then sent us back by jeep."

I turned back the ragged blanket. The lovely body was clothed in very scanty and foul Burmese rags. There were three huge bomb-fragment wounds which had fractured the left arm and both thighs. There were several less significant machine-gun-bullet wounds of soft parts. Wounds were covered with clean fresh Chinese first-aid dressings but under them the shrapnel wounds were so foul that I could hardly breathe. The girl herself didn't resent the ghastly bomb wounds but, all through my examination, her weak plaintive voice cursed the unnecessary machine-gun wounds.

There were some serious Chinese casualties to whom I gave priority at the operating table. Finally they brought the girl to me. It was too late to operate radically. To do too much would be more dangerous than to do nothing at all. With a nurse holding an ammonia sponge to my nose to keep me from fainting from the incredible stench of the wounds, I gently cut away the rotten flesh, removed rotten fragments of bone, arranged for drainage, and put the three limbs in plaster. After our surgery was over for the day I went back for a last look and found the girl out of the anesthetic and sleeping peacefully. I was climbing into bed when I heard her stir and call. I sat on the edge of my cot for a second to make sure the enlisted man on night duty was on his toes. He answered the call immediately so I rolled over into bed, thanking the good Lord for giving me fine men and women to work with.

The next morning one of the nurses brought me my breakfast.

"Get up," she said. "Your Anglo-Burmese girl is dead."

"She can't be." I struggled to my feet. "She was perfectly all right when I went to bed."

"She's dead, all right!"

I couldn't eat. "Send for the night man."

"She called me just as you went to bed, sir," he said, "and asked for some water. I got the water and she died suddenly just as she started to drink."

Pulmonary embolism! How often I had seen those large clots filling the veins of shattered Chinese limbs as we amputated, sighing with relief that I had not caused embolism. Perhaps the girl would have lived if I'd amputated both legs at the hips and the left arm at the shoulder. Perhaps I might have done so, as the easy way out, if it had been a man or an old woman. But perhaps this young and beautiful woman would have heaped me with gratitude for not condemning her to live so mutilated.

Since there were no Chinese casualties at the moment, I tried to erase the matter from my mind by looking after the needs of the other escapees. The old man with the hernia was only suffering from starvation and the Civil Affairs officer agreed to fly him out to his people in India. One whole family of Anglo-Indians was very weak with amoebic dysentery and the mother had advanced beriberi. We could save everyone but the mother. The right thigh of an Indian had been almost torn off by shrapnel. I sent him in to Gurney for an amputation. American Kachin Rangers brought in a Kachin scout with a shrapnel wound of the right face of ten days' duration. The various parts of his face that had not sloughed off were growing back to the wrong parts of his skull. I sent him to my own table. Someone ran after me to say a Karen nurse—not one of our graduates—who had escaped with her husband after the bombing of the day before had entered the second stage of labor and that the baby's head was in sight. I detailed Wasay to supervise the delivery by one of the pupil nurses who had not delivered her quota—and started pushing around the pieces of the Kachin's face. Soon there was a squawk from the delivery table and the nurses had a new mascot to cuddle.

General Merrill was in the hospital. General Boatner flew in to take command with Colonel (now Brigadier General) Willey as chief of staff. Lieutenant Colonel Hiehle of the Medical Corps was flown in to act as task force surgeon with a Medical Administrative Corps officer to open up a task force medical supply depot and take supply worries out of our hands. Since I detested administrative work and loved surgery and since my executive officer, Major Dushkin, disliked surgery and loved administrative work, all routine matters were handled by Dushkin with Hiehle direct. Now Dushkin and Hiehle got along well enough face to face but not at all well over the phone. Every time one called the other up there was a dogfight; the wires would burn for fifteen minutes, and then I would have to spend a lot of time calming down the two warriors.

"He may outrank me," fumed Dushkin, "but he doesn't outrank you. When I'm talking for you I have your rank."

Hiehle, I thought, probably figures he draws his rank from General Boatner whose surgeon he is.

I had to see either General Boatner or Colonel Willey one afternoon so I walked over to the command post, cataloguing in my mind what I would say and what I would leave unsaid. I found them both together in front of the command post and was about ready to take my leave when Colonel Hiehle stormed up, his face a purplish red.

"What the unprintable is the matter with that unprintable executive officer of yours?" he thundered. "I call him up about some simple matter and he starts shouting at me over the phone as if I were a buck private. I don't have to take that kind of stuff from a major!" And Hiehle gave me a five-minute dissertation on Dushkin's errors.

Colonel Willey and General Boatner, I could see from the

corner of my eye, were watching me quizzically with grins of anticipation at what reply a missionary, well-versed in Biblical and bazaar profanity, would produce to this tirade from a junior officer in front of the top brass of the task force; so I smiled until Hiehle's less complete stock of forceful words was exhausted.

"There's nothing wrong with Dushkin," I said slowly, "except that his nerves are a bit ragged after that awful march over the mountains." Hiehle had flown in, as I had.

"Doc," said Boatner, disappointed, "why the four blanks don't you ever lose your temper?"

"I do, sir," I replied. "I lose it for half an hour before I ever dare come over here!"

About a month before the town fell, Boatner got malaria and Brigadier General Wessels took his place. Wessels was rare in that he was one general officer who kept his medical units informed of the tactical plans. It was a relief to know what was actually going on and not have to lay one's medical plans on underground rumors. Either Wessels or Willey dropped in once a day to make sure everything was going well. It was during the beginning of the end that our unit reached its all-time high on total number of operations in one day—one hundred and ninety—and still we had six hours of sleep. Forty of the cases were skin-deep minor wounds. Our high-ranking technicians had had so much experience helping with major operations that removing the tiny shell fragments from these numerous "nuisance" cases was a treat for them. Bill Brough had a man whose flank had been struck by a .45-caliber bullet which, proceeding just under the skin, had come out near the navel. Under my direction Bill connected the two wounds with a long incision so as to be able to debride the muscles underneath and sew them together cleanly to prevent hernia. When he was done he called all his pals to show them the "abdominal" operation he had performed. "I took out his liver and both kidneys," he declared.

It was during this greatest inflow of casualties that a plane came in bringing with it the largest collection of American brass

Bill Duncumb

Dushkin, Johns, and Antonellis

Supply Department at Myitkyina Airstrip

Max Gerber

Intravenous Department

Photos by Bill Duncumb

Operating at Myitkyina Airstrip

Burma ever saw. I was just finishing an operation when two major generals appeared so I went out to chat for awhile just as I was, in nothing but a pair of G.I. slacks and shoes and my rubber gloves. The generals refused to let me find a shirt.

They were astonished at the pigsty character of our operating room and the informality of our operating without gowns except for abdominal cases. I explained that in jungle fighting, medical officers have to sort out rapidly those things in surgery that are a sine qua non of success and those that are nonessential refinements. Many a capable American surgeon knows that 80 per cent of modern techniques are refinements not absolutely essential to success. The first thing American medical units had to do in the jungle was to shelve these nonessential "Park Avenue" methods, as the army calls them, and learn to do good surgery without them. Our unit could make this change more easily than those fresh from the States, for Gurney and I had been learning through years of poverty in mission hospitals that many things are nonessential. We never masked the nose, for instance, even for abdominal operations—only the mouth. In surgery on casualties other than abdominals we didn't bother to mask the mouth. Sterile gowns are hard to get in the jungle so we used them only for abdominal cases. For others the body naked above the waist, or with only an undershirt, was sufficient. In the effort to keep his own body clean the surgeon keeps the patient's clean as well. A litter makes a good operating table. One fly hovering over a surgeon even when he's operating in a pigsty will cause a burst of horrible profanity, while nurses, technicians, and orderlies run for the Flit can or pyrethrum bomb. But the myriads of insects at night arouse the surgeon's ire only when they bite him in a place he can't accurately locate for the back-scratching nurse who's always on duty. If these night insects become so fascinated watching the operation that they drop onto the intestine during an anastomosis, the surgeon wipes them away with gauze and doesn't turn a hair; for the patient will get well—also without turning a hair. Even the maggot, which should justly become the golden symbol of war, rarely causes irreparable damage and sometimes helps the patient get well.

A combat surgeon had to learn to shrug off maggots if he wanted to keep from going mad. From May to August the real owners of Myitkyina were not Japanese, Chinese, British, or Americans—but the maggots. Chinese and American G.I.'s were in the lines for days at a time, their clothes constantly wet with sweat from the awful heat of the sun and from the frequent rains. Omnipresent flies laid myriads of eggs, and the uniforms of the casualties that came in, American boys as well as Chinese, were such a mass of maggots, tiny, medium, and full grown, that if you took the shirt off it would crawl away under its own power. Very definitely, if he wanted to remain sane, the surgeon in the jungle had to learn what are the essentials and what the nonessentials of surgery.

The generals saw another load of casualties arriving by litter and took their leave while I went back to work. Not much later, while I was painfully sweating out a most difficult case, our dentist, Lieutenant Breger, came up and in an awed undertone informed me that a lieutenant general, three or four major generals, and five or six brigadier generals were visiting us—a veritable galaxy.

"Darn it," I said, not realizing that General Sultan was within earshot, "I haven't time for any more generals. I'm busy." I went on operating, not caring at that moment whether they court-martialed me or not. The generals looked us over from a respectful distance and then walked away. There were times when I'd have almost given my soul for a few words from Stilwell, but that man could tell at a glance how difficult an operation you were engaged in. If it were a minor operation he'd stand by and chat and ask you tricky questions that would force your whole attention lest you tell him a lie. If the operation were moderately severe but not critical, he'd stand a few moments and chat and you'd feel strength flowing back into you. But if it were a major operation, he wouldn't even reveal that he was around.

General Wessels was like that, too. If we were just clearing the
slate of a few leftovers, he would sit and chat for fifteen minutes
at a time and let you in on the secrets of what the war was all
about. But your life in the army wouldn't have been safe if you'd
tried to talk to him while involved in a major operation. It was
young medical officers making Cook's Tours of the front who'd
tear you apart while you were working on something big.

A few days later an important major on the general's staff came
to "shoot the bull" one afternoon. He was a devoted friend of
the unit, though he had definitely not started out that way. It
had taken months at Ramgarh and a severe bout of illness to
make him like us at all.

"Colonel, why don't you recommend two or three of your outstanding Burmese personnel for civilian decorations?" the major
said. "Your recommendations would most certainly be approved.
You're not being fair to them."

"They told me that at the end of the first campaign—both the
Burmese Government and the U.S. Army," I replied. "I took my
life in my hands and classified the group according to special
effort in the face of danger or unusual technical skill. Not a word
was heard from the Americans on the subject and the British gave
each civilian a pat on the back in the form of a certificate saying
they'd done something or other constructive. To the best of my
knowledge the girls threw the things away. The fact is that except
for Naomi, who makes a superb chief nurse—and that isn't a
purely military trait—our work hasn't succeeded because of the
work of any single Burmese girl or boy who stands out above the
others. It has succeeded because we're a group of teams that form
a larger team that's a powerhouse. It's not the Burmese girls or
the Burmese boys or the American enlisted men or Gurney, Antonellis, Johnson, Dushkin, Ba Saw, or Hsang Yee, and it certainly isn't me that gets us by. It's the teamwork of them all.
What they and I would appreciate most of all would be to have
Stilwell line them up and give them each a handshake and a

couple of words. But Uncle Joe is so shy around these girls that I know he'll never do it."

"There are such things as presidential unit citations and unit citations from the theater commander," the major said.

"Those would be too good to be true," I replied. "There are many medical units that deserve such citations more than we, for to them the jungle is a real hardship, whereas to us it's home. If Stilwell is too shy to give us a formal nod and a couple of kind words, maybe General Wessels would do it."

Shortly thereafter a letter came in from rear-echelon head-quarters saying that bronze stars were to be given to Dushkin, Gurney, and Antonellis, the officers who had led the detachment over the hills in the attack on Myitkyina airfield; that I was to make out a story at once of their labors on that trip. I complied. Then I wrote the following letter:

1. It has come to the attention of the undersigned that decorations are to be awarded to three officers of this unit for their meritorious services on the move which resulted in the capture of Myitkyina airfield.

2. The undersigned wishes to call attention to the fact that the following enlisted men accompanied these officers, sharing their dangers and difficulties.

3. On the occasion when the regiment served by this detachment resumed the march without notification and the detachment was abandoned in enemy-infested territory, these men, although not trained for that type of work, made litters and carried American and Chinese patients, who had also been abandoned, over mountain trails many miles to the nearest liaison strip whence they could be safely evacuated to base.

4. This action on the part of the enlisted men reflects great credit on the Army of the United States.

Months later Lieutenant General Sultan paid a visit to our hospital on the Irrawaddi bank.

"It seems almost every member of your unit is about to receive a decoration. I can't understand it," the general said with a twinkle in his eye.

"I can't understand it either," I said soberly.

That week orders came out awarding the Bronze Star Medal to all the officers and men of that detachment and the Oak Leaf Cluster, in lieu of second bronze stars, to Sergeants "Susie" Opas and "Bill" Brough. And on top of that came the notification that by presidential order, bronze stars were being granted to all our nurses who served in the first battle of Burma.

General Wessels' first two attempts to take Myitkyina were foiled by the general of the 30th Chinese Division refusing to obey orders. He either attacked a day early or a day late, refusing to support other divisions and consequently not being supported on his own un-co-ordinated moves. His men were accordingly massacred, though by this time the Japs were out of 70-mm. shells.

Stilwell ordered the recuperating Boatner to fly back, get the general and ship him to Chungking for investigation. The day after the Chinese general left, Myitkyina was ours. Mogaung had fallen to the 38th Division and Kamaing to the 22nd. Stilwell had proved not only that the Chinese, when well trained and equipped, can fight, but that a war can be fought in Burma during the rainy season. The English, not to be outdone, had sent in their 36th Division, experienced English and West African troops who had fought in Ethiopia and elsewhere, and were carrying the fight down the railway south of Mogaung, while Chinese and Americans took a much needed rest.

PART THREE

RETURN TO NAMKHAM

AFTER the loss of Myitkyina, Japanese resistance in northern Burma crumbled. New Chinese, British, and American units were coming into the battle. Changes were made in the over-all command, but the original Stilwell plan remained unaltered. On October 28, 1944, Lieutenant General Daniel I. Sultan assumed command of the American forces in the Burma-India theater. China became a separate American command under Lieutenant General Albert C. Wedemeyer.

From Myitkyina on, the allied advance was rapid. Bhamo fell to Chinese troops on December 14, 1944. The Ledo Road was now pushed forward to a point where it joined the old Burma Road. Chinese forces entered Namkham on January 15, 1945, and a few days later cleared the last Japanese roadblocks on the Burma Road at Wanting and Mongyu. On February 4, 1945, a convoy of American trucks, led by Brigadier General Lewis A. Pick who built the Ledo Road, rolled into Kunming, China.

8

The Taste of Peace

It took us two days to finish off the last of Myitkyina's casualties. General Wessels offered me a trip over town in a liaison plane and first priority in choice of a site for the field hospital we were to run for the rest of the rains.

We flew back and forth over where Myitkyina had been. Nowhere was a house intact. The shelling and bombing had been extraordinarily well done. Everywhere were pockmarks, especially around the railway station and other military targets. Near the riverbank on the northeast corner of town were two buildings that looked as though they could be repaired. The Baptist Mission area appeared hopeless. I flew back and pointed out my choice on the map. Two days later General Willey and I rode around there in a jeep. One of the buildings had an almost intact shingle roof, but the plastered mat walls had been blown out and the floors were ordinary wood. The tile roof of the other was completely off, but the upstairs floors were teak and downstairs teak tile over cement.

S.O.S. and combat commands all needed sites, and General Stilwell had ordered a house on the bank of the Irrawaddi saved for himself, so Willey could give us only the tile house, the floors of which would be better for an operating room. For the hospital we were given a hundred yards of the riverbank south to a tall steel tower whence the telegraph wires to Tengchung, China, jumped across the river. During the fight for the city one of our fighter pilots in his dive had struck the top of this steel tower. The engine of his P-40 lay in front of our house on the edge of the riverbank. The propeller and one wing were at the base of a huge mango tree near the crater of a thousand-pound bomb that had just missed the house. Bits of the engine, fuselage, and

169

the other wing were scattered over the hospital area. We hoped the Japs had given the pilot a decent burial.

The task ahead of us was formidable, for we had to move the hospital as a going concern. We had stopped air evacuation with the close of the battle and had some two hundred patients in the wards at the airfield. For making the move we had only one broken-down jeep and trailer that we could call our own. Our enlisted men, having worked continuously all those months at the field, had not yet recovered from their forced march over the mountains. We had ten Burmese and ten Kachin coolies working for us under an Indo-Burmese boss and four Indian sweepers. With these men, our Burmese and Chinese boys and Dr. Hsang Yee to help me, we drove over to our new location to start cleaning up, while Captains Gurney and Antonellis and Dr. Ba Saw finished up the medical and surgical work and saw that our jeep was loaded with priority goods for each shuttle trip.

Upstairs in one bathroom I had noticed a flushing toilet completely modern and in perfect condition. The amoebae I had been incubating since the first days at the strip began to die at the sight of it! The other bathroom was a wreck except for one porcelain bathtub that had survived a 75-mm. shell as it passed through the bathroom wall. While the rest of us worked on the largest downstairs room, which I had set aside for surgery, the Burmese boys climbed to the roof to throw down the broken tile and gather the intact pieces together. I assigned one of our new men to tour the town and look for loot.

The future operating room was a horror. The Japanese had used it for food storage. Near the brick fireplace—the first one I'd seen in three years—were huge heaps of potatoes, rice, dried peas, and dal. After our shellfire had blown the roof off, rain water had seeped through the upstairs floor and soaked and rotted the foodstuffs, and then flies had come. Now maggots in incredible millions were streaming out of the food all over the floor and up the chimney. As a matter of fact there was a distinct Japanese odor about the room and we fully expected to find one sleeping his last sleep under the potatoes and rice as we carted them out. I say "we." Personally, in such matters I'm a confirmed gold-brick. I searched hastily around for some job requiring "brains" that I could perform just out of range of my olfactory nerves.

The proper men to get the stink out of the room were the Indian sweepers. The lowest caste of "untouchables," they had been the scavengers of India and Burma for untold generations, so theoretically their olfactory nerves were atrophied. The sweepers went to work with a will. But so did our Americans and Chinese. I still claim I had some of the best Americans and Chinese in the American and Chinese armies.

Out in the yard were two Japanese dugouts, fifteen or twenty feet deep. The one near the operating room had the mysterious scent of a ten-day-old hara-kiri arising from it. We didn't go down to explore lest we trip on the cunningly concealed wire of a booby trap but dumped in bushels of similarly scented rice and potatoes on top of the Jap so he would have plenty of rations for his journey to Shinto heaven. Then we gave all a proper burial. The Chinese had "buried" two more Japs near the water's edge by throwing clods of earth over them as they lay on the ground. Here also the scent was somewhat strong so our coolies erected mounds in their memory.

Leaving a few boys to scrub out the operating room with soap and disinfectant, the Americans climbed up on the roof to re-lay the good tile. I had seen marvels before but nothing like the speed with which that roof began to look like a roof. I set the Chinese to hauling water from the well and took the sweepers upstairs to sweep and scrub the teak floor. Then I took a peek into the good bathroom, just to gain strength from another look at that beautiful flushing toilet, and such a wave of anger swept over me that I couldn't even swear. What I did was go to the veranda and gaze at the beauty of the Irrawaddi, with the majestic mountains of the Triangle, and of China rising beyond it—until the trembling passed off. My Burmese boys had carelessly filled the toilet bowl full of broken clay tile and smashed it to a pulp.

There was no help for it: I would have to take those emetine injections after all!

It took three days to make a start at cleaning out a house that a Japanese general had used as his quarters. But on the second day a quarter of the roof had been retiled and one could see in spots the lovely teakwood of the upstairs floor, so I sent for a dozen nurses to come over and help. The men were by now hauling in tile from other houses that had been irreparably ruined. To bring over our hospital equipment, G-4 lent us a captured and very decrepit Japanese truck, while in their spare time the 1,888th colored engineers drove over their six by six truck, which had been flown in from Ledo after having been sawed discreetly apart and later welded together. By the third morning so much of the roof had been covered with tile that one forty by forty tarpaulin could cover over the untiled area, and all but four of the nurses came over.

By this time some twelve scrubbings with disinfectant had removed all but a faint, mysterious aroma from the surgery and downstairs rooms. While the girls with dahs and sickles mowed down the yard-high grass from what had been beautiful lawns in the days of the English, our men and coolies filled in the numerous shellholes on our land, began erecting pyramidal tents for our male personnel, and put up the first ward tent.

The enlisted men whom I had detailed to bring in loot had located many broken and bullet-pierced tables, sets of shelves, almirahs and bureaus, four operating tables, and the framework of a settee just like those we had furnished the nurses in Namkham. Regretting the absence of the woven rattan seat and back, I made new ones out of some thin teak boards, only to find later that the Chinese orderlies had the seat and the Burmese boys had beaten me to the back. I settled for a nice big downstairs room with a bathless bathroom on the end opposite the operating room. Gurney and Antonellis shared a smaller room in the middle. Gilbertson and Bullock appropriated the former dining room and pantry for supply and office. We fitted up the central entryway as a recreation room and library, and the girls took over the entire upstairs floor. In order to give them enough room we disconnected the porcelain bathtub and put it on the back veranda of the operating room to store water.

One of our sweepers was a tall, white-bearded Punjabi Sikh. He took one look at my cubbyhole of a "bathroom" and disappeared. Hours later he reappeared covered with smiles. In one hand was a framework of a commode and in the other a gorgeous chamber pot which he had looted from somewhere in town. After that I didn't dare use the officers' latrine for fear of breaking his heart.

All my life long I have utterly despised and detested the type of sweeper-served toilets that seem so fully to satisfy the inner desires of the colonial English. They always stink. Furthermore the sweepers are inevitably dirty and lazy goldbricks. They're always underfoot when you don't want them and never to be found when you do. But these sweepers were different. Only once before had I seen a sweeper I had any respect for—the Christian sweeper who worked for my mother in Rangoon for years. These men were incredible. Anything they knew, from years of experience, that white men wanted sweepers to do—they did very efficiently without being told. We had to teach them to do only those things Americans insist on in addition. The bearded Sikh swept and mopped my floor at least three times a day and cleaned the bathroom oftener than that. Not realizing the difference between Americans and colonial English his servile respect was a constant embarrassment to me. He would no more think of passing between me and another person than he would of desecrating me by touching my messkit or canteen cup. Even when he passed behind me he doubled himself over almost to the floor.

For days our sweepers could hardly eat, amazed at being served in the chow line by American enlisted men, who made their dark skins blush still more hotly by calling them sahib. Then they caught onto the legpulling and made up for lost time. After everyone else was served they came along, each with a plate and cup. Into the cup went coffee and amazing quantities of milk and sugar. Onto the plates went enough rice for four ordinary people; then quantities of Spam, tinned vegetables, nurses' curries, soup, bread, butter, and jam, everything finally drenched with canned fruit. How they could stomach the mixture I don't know, but they never left a morsel.

Our fourth day was bedlam. Patients came over by the truckload and occupied the one ward tent, while the one they'd just vacated at the field was hurriedly put up in readiness for the next truckload. New nurses and coolies alternated mowing down grass for new ward sites. Older nurses received patients, sorted them and their charts, and gave the day's treatments. In the center of the area between our driveway and the river was a broken, crumbly cement floor, an ordinary type of construction in Burma where cement and sand have been padded with a lot of river mud to line the contractors' pockets with more money. Apparently no house had ever been built over it—certainly not more than a bamboo house. We put a ward tent over it and had a very effective receiving office and sick-call room. We were clearing the tall grass away for our tenth and last ward tent when one of the coolies touched something and yelled for me. It was an unexploded five-hundred-pound bomb. Unfamiliar with the mechanics of those things, I ordered the crowd out until the engineers could come and cart it away.

When the natives began to stream out of the Myitkyina area to seek haven with the Allies, the British Civil Affairs officer had to put them where they'd be out of the way and yet near enough to help the allied war effort and so pay for the free rice and salt they demanded. All were herded into a tiny village called Pamati, a couple of miles from the airstrip, where they lived in most unsanitary fashion, on the ground under parachutes or poorly thatched roofs. Medical care was administered in the civilian hospital at Pamati.

My interest in civilian medical care in Burma is a matter of long standing. When I express an opinion on the way certain medical matters were handled there, I stand on my record in Burma.

I doubt if any other foreign family has given Burma as many centuries of service as mine has. That service can in no sense be connected with exploitation—unless you can call education, medical and surgical care, and a bit of Christian preaching "exploitation." My family has not taken a cent of money out of Burma. On the contrary we brought into Burma many hundreds of thousands (lacs) of rupees of American money in the form of our salaries and appropriations for mission work, money that has improved the financial condition of a good many thousands of the people of Burma.

In Burma it was the practice to rotate doctors from one area to another every three years. But in any country a doctor has to root himself into the soil and struggle until the people nearby know him, especially if he is a surgeon. People the world over will go to quacks for medicine but not for surgery—not if they can help it. They want someone whose skill is known to themselves and their friends. And if that is true of the Occident how much truer it is of the Orient where the people still have to have the excellence of western medicine and surgery shown to them.

True government of a less fortunate people consists not in giving them what they demand but in teaching them to want better things and preparing those things for them in advance. This is what the missions, at their best, did for Burma as a policy. Was it or will it be the government's policy as well?

When an outstanding surgeon makes a name for himself in a district he should be left there or promoted in the same division. This will decrease rather than increase graft. His fame will bring in so many honest shekels that he won't need to resort to extortion. To avoid the smearing of his own reputation he will be much more rigid in supervising the professional work and morals of his subordinates.

You can't help loving the people of Burma if you honestly

work for their good. The real surgeon would love his district and use his utmost ingenuity in laying out programs for its medical welfare. He wouldn't be satisfied to keep up the placebo (make-believe) hospitals he might have inherited. For the sake of his own reputation he would make his district shine in medical matters instead of using the sins of his predecessors as an excuse for inefficiency. And surgeons who fail at their initial assignment should be given one in an entirely different area; for one part of Burma can psychologically and medically be so different from another as to seem part of another country.

While we were at the strip and the battle was still going on an Indian lad with a shell fragment in his chest wall was sent to me. He had been operated on a number of days earlier at the civilian hospital but he had continued to drain blood and had a very high temperature. That was all we could find out about him. When I examined him he had a small incision where the fragment had struck in the anterior axillary line level with the nipple. The entire right breast area was enormously puffed out and fluctuating all the way up to the clavicle. With the temperature and history this should have been an abscess—always assuming, of course, that the surgeon knew what he was doing when he performed the first operation. When everything was ready I pulled at the "drain" when, to my horrified amazement, it turned out to be a gauze cork plugged tight into the skin wound. A pint of old blood burst out, covering me from head to foot, and then fresh venous blood poured from the wound. The shell fragment had struck upward, tearing the subclavian vein, and as treatment the surgeon had debrided slightly at the side of the chest and corked the opening. There was no attempt at wide incision and packing down to the bleeding vessel. The patient was dead in less than fifteen seconds.

I had had a similar case of my own shortly before. The shrapnel had entered the back of the chest and torn the subscapular vein high up. I fumed as I made three enormous incisions trying to dissect out the bleeding vessel. Bleeding would stop with pressure and then blood pour all over me when I tried to clamp a hemostat on the right place. I packed him and sent him back to the rear to better men than I, with a prayer and a complete description of what I had done and failed to do. Major Freeman at the 20th General Hospital laughed when he saw my operative note and was still laughing two weeks later when he wrote me to say the patient had done well with no further operation, my pack having been removed slowly from day to day. But I know what Freeman would have said if I had just corked the wound and had not told him a major vessel was injured.

The excuse for the civilian hospital was that they had only half a dozen surgical instruments. Granted. But that is the very essence of my criticism. Half a dozen surgical instruments, two dozen bottles of medicines (half of them placebos), three or four L.M.P. degrees (licensed medical practitioner), or even an M.B., B.S. (bachelor of medicine, bachelor of surgery) do not make a hospital capable of caring for civilians wounded and sick in a war zone, even if they do constitute a fairly good dose of eyewash in the piping times of peace. If there hadn't been an instrument or a placebo or an L.M.P. degree around, the patients would have been brought to the Americans at once. What does the government intend to give Burma in the peace?

So we kept a few civilians in our wards, only those who would certainly die or need an amputation if we sent them out. I arbitrarily set the maximum number at fifteen so as not to interfere with the work for a total of five hundred beds for Chinese soldiers, which I knew would soon be filled and for whom I was requisitioning tarpaulins, cots, and blankets. But someone told General Willey that in order to care for those fifteen civilians, Seagrave was refusing to admit sick Chinese soldiers. That, if true, would have been a court-martial offense. General Willey very properly ordered me to get rid of all civilians at once.

We were deluged with natives needing treatment, many of whom had been treated without improvement at the civilian hospital. Portable surgical hospitals in the Mogaung, Kamaing, and Hopin areas continued to evacuate badly wounded civilians to us by train and plane for definitive treatment. How the civilians griped when we sent them away to the civilian hospital! Especially resentful were the Kachins. Most of their able men were in our army units helping us as Rangers and guerrillas as well as regular soldiers. Did that not entitle the sick and wounded of their race to our medical attention? It was especially embarrassing to me to have American soldiers pick up sick or hurt civilians in the street, many of them working as coolies for American units, and bring them to us, confident we would care for them, and then have to send them to the civilian hospital.

Furthermore, I couldn't rid myself of the idea that Stilwell had had some special reason for tolerating the existence of our "unorthodox, nameless, bastard" unit all those years—the desire to have someone to do unorthodox jobs in an unorthodox way to satisfy his sense of the fitness of things. His first assignment to us after our activation as the Seagrave Hospital Unit had been to care for civilian refugees in Assam in 1942. Then at Ramgarh we had wards for civilians. Then in the Naga Hills we had been ordered by General Boatner, as our third duty, to obtain the friendship of the natives through medicine.

When General Willey returned from his furlough I pointed out these things to him and General Cannon, and assured them we had never refused admittance to Chinese, even to Chinese goldbricks, on account of civilians. Permission was immediately granted for us to continue helping needy civilians on this basis.

With this permission we even did a couple of gynecological operations, one a large tumor of the uterus. And then Nurse Hkawn Tawng, one of our Burmese dancing girls, now eight and a half months pregnant, came to visit us and went to the movies with the crowd. On her way back she slipped and fell, went into labor, and we delivered another cute toy of a baby girl, while our enlisted men crowded around the doors of the operating room to catch the first glimpse of a baby being born.

The coolies who worked for us at the strip came over to work with us in town and we fixed them up in the old servants' quarters. At the strip the coolies soon learned that I spoke Burmese well. But I was too busy to waste time supervising them, so they sponged on us as they did on other American units and had sponged on the English for a century. On one of our busiest days setting up the Chinese hospital in town, I discovered that at eleven-thirty they were just eating breakfast and hadn't yet done a stroke of work. I stood them up with their Indo-Burmese boss in the center and gave them a ten-minute demonstration of bazaar Burmese which no white man is supposed ever to have heard, let alone have understood in its implications. I used the entire bazaar dictionary, except for one female term which I reserved as a token of my respect for women! The coolies stood there wide eyed and speechless until I was done, then forgot their breakfast and fell furiously to work. From then on we had no further trouble. We never had to urge the Burmese on. Outline the work to be done and they did it even though it meant working on for an hour or two after quitting time. On four occasions, when our work became lighter, I had to order them to stop working at five o'clock. They laughed, sang, joked. And when we were alerted for our next combat assignment and I hoped possibly the Kachin coolies might be persuaded to follow us, the Burmese came in a body and demanded to be taken along.

"Why do they want to stay with us?" I asked their spokesman, Dr. San Yee.

"They say this is the first time in their lives they have been treated white," he replied.

As our work began to fall into regular routines the amenities of the rear areas began to come into evidence. Ann Sheridan and other Hollywood personnel were coming to give us two shows, one at the Marauders in the afternoon and again at the strip in the evening. Special Service called me up soon after Ann's arrival and said she was coming to our hospital at eleven o'clock to be photographed with "Seagrave's Burmese Nurses." Would I please have the girls dressed in their best Burmese manner.

I knew the girls would be bored to tears—and they were. But after a lot of persuasion they fixed themselves up in their perfectly blended silk *longyis* and sheer jackets. Burmese girls love to dress up but not on command, and certainly not for other women. So while the ward work went to ruin, they sat for two hours with folded hands, waiting; but la Sheridan never came. I had planned to take half the girls to the afternoon show but was so full of adrenalin that I let them go alone.

They had no sooner set forth with all the transportation we had when the Special Service officer called up again. So sorry, Ann had been too busy to come but she would be brokenhearted if she had to leave C.-B.-I. without a picture of herself and the "Burma Surgeon." I would therefore go to the strip and meet the great lady when she visited the 44th Field Hospital there at four-thirty. I didn't dare say anything—out loud!

I located a jeep and drove back to the strip. Less than a month had passed since fighting had ceased but combat units and S.O.S. had changed the entire landscape. Bombed buildings had been torn down and rebuilt into huge tarpaulin-covered warehouses and barracks. Bomb and shell craters had been filled in, first with debris, then with earth, by bulldozers or by spade and shovel crews. Fire-blackened skeletons of native huts had been burned clean away. The railway was operating to Mogaung, with a jeep at each end of the string of handcars. Not even a fragrance of the Japs remained. Nature, too, had co-operated, for the shattered trees and bushes had grown new leaves to cover the scars of war. It was like spring. The airport was unrecognizable. Already it was one of the busiest fields in the world. I was proud of being an American and that Americans had thus rapidly repaired the damage they had unavoidably caused to this bit of Burma. Another two months and Myitkyina would be restored to a great deal of her original beauty.

Then a battery of cameras arrived, the signal for male temperatures in all the wards to rise to 106°. And finally Ann herself!

My thoughts are always incongruous. All I could do was stare amazed at America's latest hair-do. Then introductions began and I could think of nothing but what the feelings of the others in the Sheridan troupe must be. They were actually traveling incognitos—"also rans." There was as much ravishing beauty among them as Ann brought, but not a G.I. even glanced their way.

Instead of insisting on meeting the Burma Surgeon, Ann had never even heard of him. Why should she have? Film stars don't care about missionaries. But our theater photographers were determined.

"Miss Sheridan, shake hands with Colonel Seagrave again," they commanded.

Now who in blazes is Colonel Seagrave? thought Ann as she turned around to shake whatever paw might be extended.

"It's a shame you're forced to go through all this, Miss Sheridan," I commiserated.

"Oh, it is all part of the day's job," she shrugged.

"I'll be seeing you at the show tonight," I said as I turned away. But the jeep had other ideas. Just as we got back home it heaved a sigh of relief at having done its Boy Scout job for the day and went out of action.

I was pardonably skeptical when Special Service called me up a month later to say that an all-girl troupe of five American beauties would have dinner with our unit on Sunday at noon, after which one of the girls in American dancing costume wanted to be photographed with a Burmese nurse in Burmese court dress. The nurses were also skeptical. Hkawn Tawng was sick with a high fever but she was the only dancer we had and the only girl with a court costume. I told the girls about what was desired and left them to do as they saw fit. Being Sunday they would be dressed up anyway, in honor of the day. Hkawn Tawng began to overhaul her wardrobe.

But the five-girl troupe turned up one minute ahead of schedule. They took messkits and stood in the long chow line just like G.I.'s. They even helped themselves to Burmese food and, to my utter astonishment, ate it as if they enjoyed it. The previously disillusioned nurses stood on the sidelines diagnosing the American girls. Something was needed to break the ice. I went in to check with Hkawn Tawng as to which nurse was to wear her court costume for the picture.

"I'll wear it myself," she said. "It won't fit anyone else."

"But you still have a high fever."

"That doesn't matter. It will take only a minute and it's the least I can do for the army."

As I turned away my eye fell on Hkawn Tawng's baby and I had an inspiration. "Bring the baby out and walk around a bit," I said to the grandmother.

Soon the grandmother came out, a spotless four weeks' baby in her arms, dressed in a threadbare but clean little blanket. One of the American girls saw her and, letting out a whoop of delight, grabbed the tiny morsel and for an hour there was a snatching contest as to who should hold the baby. Then the disillusioned nurses melted and I heard them—for a wonder—saying nice things about the American girls in Burmese.

"They say you have adorable hair," I translated, sotto voce, to the fluffy blonde. "And you, according to them, have very perfect features and are, as the Burmese would say, very smooth." I turned to a third girl. "Being a mere male," I said, "I don't dare translate the very complimentary things they're saying about your figure!"

The leader of the group had by now found our little organ and sat down to it. But instead of producing the latest jive she picked up a hymnbook and in a beautifully cultivated voice began to sing and play the grand old hymns. Soon the nurses swarmed around her and joined in the singing, completely captivated.

Then Hkawn Tawng, supported by two nurses, and the American girl appeared in their respective dancing costumes and walked out to the bank of the Irrawaddi to have their pictures taken together.

The Burmese court dress consists of a bodice covered by a sheer gauze jacket that reaches just to the waist, ending in two little peaks that project slightly backward from ‘the side. The skirt is not a *longyi*, which is a perfect cylinder folded neatly about the body, but a *thamin*, a single sheet of gorgeous cloth that tucks in at the side and that in the days of the Burmese kings was split from hip to ankle, showing the entire thigh and leg as the lady walked or danced. To avoid too much exposure the Burmese court ladies and dancers developed the beautiful mincing step characteristic of Burmese dancing. The missionaries would probably throw a Christian girl out of church if she wore a true *thamin*, so Hkawn Tawng had pinned the open edges together to the knee, hiding her beautiful legs but at the same time making it impossible to move without the characteristic mincing step. She had used her make-up box well and you couldn't tell she was ill except for her heavy lids, and these also are a characteristic suggestive note of the Burmese dance. Aside from the fact that she nearly fainted when the cameraman delayed snapping the picture after ordering her to take a pose with one foot in the air, everything went well and we tucked the poor kid back into bed and said goodbye to our very considerate and tactful guests.

Incidentally I paid the ladies the compliment of calling off our Sunday-evening sing so all the nurses could go and see their show, which was delightful. Yet when we came home we passed thirty or forty vehicles leaving our messhall. The men from all over Myitkyina had come for our Sunday song service and though we were all away they had had the sing anyway.

If I had asked the U.S. Army for authorization for our Sunday-evening song service someone might conceivably have told me to be a Medical Corps officer and leave the chaplains to do the chaplains' work. I kept my mouth shut, had the services for the nurses but opened them to everyone. Sometimes we had only the nurses, sometimes a few enlisted men. At Myitkyina, on the river-bank, no one was present the first week but our own crowd. But we gathered in the operating room and sang in a real brick-walled room for the first time since Namkham. We had army hymn-books with notes. The acoustics were perfect and we really en-joyed ourselves. The next week two chaplains came; the week after, a squad of ground crew of the 10th Air Force. In a month the operating room was packed and men were standing around the doors. Then we burst out into the huge messhall, which we filled, and then, though the unit played hooky and went to the all-girl show, the men came anyway and filled the hall again. My friend Mr. Gustaf Sword, missionary to the Kachins in the Nam-kham area, told me that he had heard of our song services from enlisted men back in the States.

We were really getting little tastes of peace as we worked away at our five-hundred-bed hospital. After supper it was everyone's delight to go to the riverbank and sit, watching first the majestic, swiftly moving stream and then gazing off at the mountains that marked the border of China. Not many miles above Myitkyina the real Irrawaddi is formed by the junction of two great rivers which the Kachins have named the Mali Hka and the N'mai Hka. The great mountain mass between these two rivers is known as the Triangle and is inhabited by primitive Kachins who prac-ticed slavery and human sacrifice until very recently. Three huge peaks at the lower corner of the Triangle give Myitkyina its greatest beauty.

As the sun goes down at Myitkyina incredible thousands of lovely green parrots fly south over the river from their feeding grounds to their night's bivouac in the teak forest just below town. They come in flights of several thousand each, so close in their formation that they form a greenish black cloud, sometimes stretching half a mile across the river and beyond each bank. You can count perhaps a hundred flights of an evening. Occasionally something will upset the flight, which will then eddy and swirl like a cloud struck by a gust of wind. And always you hear the harsh notes of the beautiful birds calling to each other as they fly.

When the sun sets in Myitkyina you do not face west: that's too common. You face east and watch the suggestive, reflected tints on the China mountains and the broad river. Right across from us were native houses, untouched by war, pasture ground, and beautiful trees. From the highest point of that sunset-hued ridge you can see Tengchung to the east and, to the south, the tip of the ridge on which stands Sinlumkaba, summer resort for Bhamo District and for peace lovers from all over Burma. And, from Sinlumkaba, the hills around Namkham! Just two hops and a skip yet to go.

Even in the Hukawng we heard G.I.'s sing about the moon over Burma. Poor fellows, they didn't know it was just an imitation there. In Myitkyina we not only had the moon over real Burma, we had the *Thadingyut* moon over Burma. In the rainy season the Buddhists have a Lent just as Christians do in the spring. During Lent they strive to be especially good Buddhists and that means going to monastery schools on their Sabbaths and listening to the reading of the Pitakas, the Buddhist scriptures. On Sabbath nights the merit-seeking Shans sleep at the monastery. Their Lent, too, has an Easter—at the full of the *Thadingyut* moon which usually comes in October. To the Burmese and Shans, *Thadingyut* is the greatest feast of the year. At night hundreds of paper fire balloons are released, carrying light high up into the sky. Every good family lights all the candles they can afford around their own houses, carrying others to the pagodas and monasteries, for is not this the Feast of the Lights?

How I berated myself for not remembering that this moon was *Thadingyut*! I could have begged, borrowed, or stolen—or even bought, if necessary—tissue paper to make balloons (as I had made them for John and Sterling in Namkham) and made the first *Thadingyut* back in Burma memorable for our poor, hungry-hearted Buddhist nurses. But our three blue-blooded princesses,

Louise, Pearl, and Chit Sein, did not forget. Louise came to me at sunset.

"Daddy, tonight is *Thadingyut.*" She had to stop for five minutes while I cursed my memory. "Will you please let us go to the pagoda to place our candles? Captain Antonellis says he will drive us there in the jeep."

"Of course you can go," I said. Darn Antonellis anyway, I thought. He's always doing the right thing while I just go blundering along.

Much later that evening I turned out my light in my loneliness and went out to the veranda. There was the moon, high above the China hills, making a broad golden path across the Irrawaddi, and there, sitting on the bank of the river, their bodies sharply silhouetted against the perfect Burma landscape, were little groups of our personnel. Here an American boy and four nurses, there three girls and a couple of officers. Not a sound anywhere but you could feel them drinking in the beauty. Peace, peace again in Burma! The youngsters were out there enjoying it together. And I was all alone as usual. I went in, turned on all the lights, and set furiously to work.

Myitkyina was no longer a combat zone. It was a supply base. S.O.S. had taken it over—lock, stock, and barrel. And we were eating nothing but canned rations. Our food was worse even than it had been at the strip. The traditional fight between combat units and service units went on in the C.-B.-I. theater as it did all over the world. Already, with the coming of S.O.S., our happy-go-lucky red-tape-slashing days were over. You couldn't walk far without tiring your right arm answering salutes. Paper work haunted my sleep. But in Myitkyina I learned that S.O.S. always ate that way! They tied themselves tighter in their own red tape than they did the combat units and if there was any choice of foods, the delicacies went to the combat zone.

Although we knew that the battle had occurred at Myitkyina during the rice-planting season and therefore no rice had been planted, we certainly expected to be able to buy fresh meat and vegetables, chickens, eggs, and milk. As for vegetables, the natives weren't having any. The government was rationing the people like a paternal government should. To most, only rice and salt were given. To my way of thinking this should have been given to those who worked for it. Some were women and children who couldn't work for the army (but who could have made a great many truck gardens and planted a lot of late rice). Some were wealthy traders of Myitkyina who refused to demean themselves by working. These last I would have thrown into jail for refusing even the lowest coolie work, rather than feed them; or I would have put them to work at the point of the bayonet. For the others, the government could secure no seed—and Brayton Case was dead!

Brayton Case had almost single-handed fed the Chinese Fifth Army in the first campaign. He had walked out with us after General Stilwell. A typical missionary and unable to grasp in the slightest degree the psychology of Americans and English at war, Brayton had often made a nuisance of himself to British and Americans by worrying about people's morals and actions. American brass had even begged Stilwell to get rid of him. The British griped and gulped. But Stilwell's answer always was, "I need him when we get back to Burma." In Assam and in the Hukawng, Case made much ado about getting seed and having it planted by Chinese, Nagas, and Kachins in spite of the British Civil Affairs officers, whose nerves he frayed. Yet he made a wonderful success of the Hukawng, amazing to the Americans who saw signs of flourishing agricultural peace there only a few months after the war had passed on.

Yet Case was not in his element there. He was still working among foreigners, for the Kachins of the Hukawng do not speak Burmese. From Myitkyina and Mogaung south he would have been in his element. Nobody, not even the Burmese themselves, understood the psychology of the Burmese people half as well as Case. Born in Burma like myself, among the Burmese, he grew

up with them and worked for them and therefore spoke Burmese
even better than the Burmese, whereas I was born among the
Karens, spoke Karen as a boy, spoke Shan as a man, and learned
Burmese from necessity. If the Burmese Government had
shrugged and said, "There is no seed," Brayton would have found
it by the carload even if he had had to sweep it up personally from
the gutters of the bazaars and antagonize the government of
India into the bargain. He would have got priority of transport
for his seed to Myitkyina even if it had meant half a dozen American officers being sent back to the States in a mad frenzy. But
just as Mogaung and Myitkyina were falling to the Allies, a
ferryboat in which he was transporting some seed tipped suddenly
and precipitated him into the water, where his body, weighted
down with a heavy pack, sank like a stone and was never recovered.

Case not only greatly excelled me in speaking the Burmese
language in idiom but could beat me at my own game of getting
others to do my work for me. In fact, twice he tried to get me to
do his work for him. That was a mistake, for if anything I was
more interested in my work than he was in his. But he made a
good try and left me feeling that hot asbestos hands were reaching out to draw me into the pit for refusing him. When agricultural Burma lost Case, it lost the best friend it ever had and
automatically set back the restoration of Burma's full crops by
about two years.

S.O.S. wages were high—double prewar. I wonder the government didn't complain. Probably it did. There had been a great
deal in the press of India those years about the disruption of
economy caused by American G.I.'s and the prices they paid. I
personally regretted the enormous sums they paid for trash to
wily shysters who were already too rich. But high wages to men
who work hard should, for the sake of democracy and improvement in the standard of living for everyone that we talk so much
about, be allowed to disrupt a prewar economy a trifle. The nurses

of our unit had been drawing much higher salaries than before
the war and their standard of living had gone way up, but aside
from the inevitable couple of asinine fools, they banked their
money, in order, when peace came, to maintain the real improvement in their standard of living that they had obtained. Of course
they'd had a good bit of sensible advice!

I have always been irritated at the idea that the slightest mech-
anization of Burma will deprive the great coolie class of work. I
know a great many coolies with first-class minds who could soon
run the machines and improve the economic condition of the
country immensely. And with this improvement would come
increased buying power, improved standards of living, increased
demand, increased happiness everywhere. Let the coolie class die
out except for the half-wits for whom there will always be coolie
labor and let the rest of the country prosper in the way the inhab-
itants of one of the wealthiest countries in the world—in natural
resources—have a right to prosper. Don't forget that Burma has
the only real rubies in the world, the best teak and rice, the
second-best silver, oil, tungsten, tin, lead, jade, amber, rubber—
and was fast developing rich tung-oil estates before the Japs broke
loose.

For myself now there were deep drafts of peace. By the time
the hospital on the riverbank was a going concern, we had taken
on some twenty-five new girls and boys as probationers. If they
were to be worth much to us in Myitkyina, or beyond, they had
to know what it was all about—more than Naomi could teach
them in the operating room or Wasay and the head nurses could
teach them in the wards. So I began to give them classroom work
from ten to twelve every morning. The boys weeded themselves
out in a week, but that didn't matter since they were a small
minority, and in combat there is much an educated Burmese
boy can do that coolies cannot—or nurses, either. At the end of
another week I threw half a dozen girls out of the class, girls too
stupid to learn, letting them act as orderlies on the ward, where

they could ease the work of the graduate refugee nurses. The remainder were good or excellent.

If I had begun a regular course of training it would have been a year and a half before they would be worth much. I gave them instead a two months' bird's-eye view. First, three weeks of bandaging, bacteriology, and the parasitology so essential to surgery and to medical work among the Chinese, who are tanks for parasites. Then the twelve most common diseases of C.-B.-I., teaching only a bit of anatomy and physiology here and there so they could grasp the inklings of pathology. A day or two on the benefits of fever—a thought that never occurs to an oriental. Another day or two on the importance of charting. It was fun.

Probably the most fun in teaching consists in the teacher's study of his pupils, especially when they are Burmese girls, for the difference in race and sex adds spice to a difficult job. Nang Pri, who was a natural in practical surgery, never could answer the right question at the right time. Hkawn Raw, who had a false front in practical work, tried out a still falser front in the classroom and wondered why she couldn't kid the old man. Daisy and her younger sister Bessie both tripped over shadows when at work but never tripped over the trickiest questions in class. Julie was as sweet in class as out but took a few months to find out what it was all about.

As usual I taught in both English and Burmese. The star for several weeks was a very beautiful but very dark Kachin girl named Hkawn Rin who knew English almost better than Burmese. Her father had been an officer in the army and they hadn't heard of him since the first campaign. Then as I released the class one morning, she walked out of class and bumped squarely into her father who had just come down with General Haswell's troops from Sumprabum. That was the end of Hkawn Rin, whose father had a higher education in mind for her.

One of the girls was an Anglo-Burmese-Karen girl who appeared in the sort of short dress that the Anglo-Burmese think so very English. She was extremely awkward in these dresses and

appeared misshapen and devoid of beauty. She also seemed
either naked or about to be so at a second's notice. As an Anglo-
Burmese—with the accent on the Anglo—she was very dark and
not English at all. With her lack of clothing as an excuse I asked
Naomi to get her into Burmese clothes. Naomi gave her a couple
of *longyis*, which she consented to wear, but she couldn't get her
into Burmese clothes above the waist. Perhaps it was a good
thing for the peace of mankind that Naomi didn't succeed completely, for the *longyi* alone changed the ugly duckling into a
swan. As an Anglo-Burmese—with the accent on the Burmese—
the girl was an incredible beauty. You were struck at once by her
fairness and exquisite features. If she had worn the *longyi* properly, and with the Burmese bodice and sheer voile jacket, she
would have been completely irresistible.

Nobody in Burma can escape thinking of the problem of the
intermarriage of races. I have thought about it for years and my
ideas are somewhat as follows. The intermarriage of oriental
races immediately strikes you as being a very good thing, while
that of occidentals and orientals almost always seems to turn out
badly in the children, so much so that it is commonly said that
they inherit the worst characteristics of both races. Why should
this be so? I have seen misfit children of oriental combinations.
If a Chinese marries one of the races of Burma, in Burma, and
raises his children as Burmese, the combination is always a success. If, in Burma, he tries to raise his children as Chinese, the
combination is a failure. Indians who marry Burmese always
try to raise their children as Indians and so their children are always failures. Kachins and Shans occupy the same country; the
combination is successful whether the child is raised as a Kachin
or a Shan. In fact, these combinations, when the child is raised
according to the ideas of the prevalent race, tend to produce super
children. That is perhaps why combinations of Americans with
European races are so successful in America. They are raised as
Americans in American communities and are accepted—providing the combination is a combination of whites. Americans will

not accept color, so the combination of American with Negro does not work in America. But I would bet a hundred to one that it would work in Africa if the parents raised the child there as a Negro.

To me that is why the Anglo-Burmese does not succeed. The English will not accept color, yet the parents are determined to raise the child "English." I know an Anglo-Burmese woman who was charming as an Englishwoman, for she had had all her schooling in England. Yet she never lost her Anglo-Burmese accent which is too, too English to be true—as it always is. In determinedly trying to raise their child as English the parents show the community that they regard the English as the superior race. So the Burmese will have no more to do with the Anglo-Burmese than will the English whom they try to ape. The Anglo-Burmese is the original man without a country. It is all exemplified by our little Anglo-Burmese girl in Myitkyina. When she came in her "English" clothes, the nurses would have nothing to do with her and her airs. She put on a *longyi* and they began to accept her, even though the top half of her still tried valiantly to be English. If she had been willing to dress Burmese entirely they would have accepted her with open arms—as would every single American G.I. in the town. So perhaps it was just as well she determined to remain a hybrid and make extremely awkward her undeniable beauty.

Big Bawk had spent a postgraduate year with Captain Chesley in the laboratory at Ramgarh and, except with cultures, had become an extremely able laboratory technician. While my own knowledge of laboratory work was broader than hers, in the phases she had studied her knowledge was so much deeper that I never argued with her. In fact, I soon regarded her as infallible. We had the only microscope at the airfield during the entire battle for Myitkyina, and the decision as to whether an American soldier should be evacuated to base for malaria depended on the little

Dr. Seagrave in his Bamboo Basha

Burma Surgeon Returns

Kachin girl's diagnosis as to whether the malaria was malignant or benign.

At the riverbank the laboratory work for a five-hundred-bed hospital was extremely heavy so I set Little Bawk, who hadn't been well for months, to work in the laboratory with Big Bawk, where she could sit at her work. I put new girls on in rotation to help as bottle, tube, and slide washers and specimen collectors. One day Naomi appointed Hkawn Tawng's pint-sized twelve-year-old sister Roi Ji as bottle washer in her lab. Roi Ji ate it up. In five days she was using the microscope herself. In seven she was identifying malaria parasites in the blood, amoebae and ova in the stools, and then passing the microscope over to Big Bawk for final diagnosis.

Two weeks later Little Bawk called me to the lab.

"What's that red splotch in the center of the field?" she asked.

I looked. "They're not tubercle bacilli, if that's what you mean," I said, recognizing the Ziehl-Neelsen stain for sputum.

I went on with my work. Two hours later, while I was at rounds in my Chinese officers' wards, the laboratory bottle washer came to me.

"Daddy," she said, "Little Bawk wants you in the laboratory at once."

"Confound it, these girls order me around and I haven't any more sense than to obey," I grumbled, walking back to the lab.

"Take a look at that specimen," commanded Little Bawk.

I obeyed. "Beautiful! Beautiful! That's a lovely stain! Those are real tubercle bacilli. Loads and loads of them, aren't there? You're getting good, Little Monkey!"

Silence.

"That's her own sputum," said Big Bawk in an undertone that meant, "You unspeakable idiot!"

"Good Lord!" I looked around. Little Bawk had disappeared. I went around the corner to my room and found her crying. I put an arm around her.

"Little girl, forgive me. I never suspected it was your own sputum. I can't understand it. I've examined you very carefully three times since you coughed up that blood at the field and have never heard a râle. Please don't quit on me. I'll take you to the 44th Field Hospital and we'll get an X-ray picture of your chest."

I stayed awake hours that night cursing the spirit that made me drive people until they broke down and caught tuberculosis. Yet I could never control my disgust at people who wanted to win a war from an armchair. I always insisted on my officers, enlisted men, and Burmese personnel going to bed with malaria and dysentery but hadn't put myself in bed for two years with either one. But my body could take that kind of thing and these poor little bodies couldn't. And what chance had Little Bawk? Unlike Julia, from whom she had caught the disease, sleeping in the same bed at Ningam because there weren't enough blankets to go around, Bawk couldn't stay still. Intense by nature, she had an overwhelming dose of thyroid secretion. With a much quicker brain than mine—although she hadn't learned a fraction of what I'd been taught—she would never be able to stay still.

And the X-ray didn't help. There was a large band of active tuberculosis in her left lung, with much acute inflammation.

I went to Big Bawk.

"Little Bawk has got to stay in bed. I'm sorry. Choose the nurse who will be most useful to you in the laboratory and I'll give her to you; I don't care who she is," I said, expecting her to ask for Kyang Tswi or one of the other graduates who had worked with Captain Chesley.

"Give me Roi Ji," Big Bawk said without hesitation.

"You're kidding, aren't you?" I asked, stunned.

"No, indeed. I want Roi Ji."

So pint-sized twelve-year-old Roi Ji was installed as assistant technician in the laboratory, and, as bottle washer under her, I appointed half-pint Emmie.

Roi Ji felt her own importance now. Sitting in on a gossip fest of the graduate nurses she suddenly began to reminisce: "Once when I was young," she began, then stared when the older girls burst into gales of laughter.

Our stay at the riverside was not all peace. To start our troubles Major Dushkin was given a well-deserved lieutenant colonelcy and that, in our unit, is tantamount to transfer elsewhere. Then the American officers and men and the Burmese doctors and men were long overdue for furlough. While we were in the midst of increasing our ward space to the final high of five hundred and forty beds filled, a third of our male staff went off to Calcutta for two weeks. I had asked for a month in the States, not having been home for seven years, during which time my daughter Leslie had grown from a sixteen-year-old to a woman married to a naval ensign on duty on one of our big flattops. My son Weston had grown from a boy whose head reached my shoulder to a man whose shoulder my head would not reach and who was in the navy trying to qualify as a fighter pilot.

Don't let anyone talk to you about huge sacrifices made by foreign missionaries. They have the time of their lives. The only real sacrifice is that they can't watch their children grow up. I hadn't seen Tiny and the two little boys for two and a half years. I wasn't fed up with Burma. Far from it. But I could have enjoyed a few hours with the family, trying to remind them that I existed other than on paper, and censored paper at that. But I had reminded General Boatner that if the leave were granted at the wrong time I would be unable to leave.

"It's up to you whether you take your leave or not," he said.

For the six weeks after Myitkyina fell I could have been away and no one would have missed me. Then the first third of our male personnel returned and the second third was leaving when catastrophe hit us. We lost nine men and Captain Johnson on the rotation plan. Gurney, the only officer other than myself from whom the nurses would take orders, needed a vacation much more than I did. He had not only gone more months without one but had been on several flank moves through the mountains and had been ill several times. Besides, he had a date with a colonel of artillery at Imphal. Just before he was due to leave, my orders came through.

Gurney would gladly have given up his furlough in my favor but I would have none of it. He needed that vacation; and besides, not knowing Burmese, he couldn't teach the new girls. With only the rank of captain he couldn't manage the unruly Chinese officers' wards that he had had to turn over to me. Having lost half our American personnel, the staff running the five-hundred-bed hospital was almost completely Burmese.

I radioed back turning down my leave. You can't work for a man like Stilwell without realizing the job comes before the man.

When this became known the army from Ledo to Delhi to Karachi expressed itself roundly about that stupid Seagrave. I shrugged. I wasn't half so scared of the army as I was of what Tiny and the children would say. Tiny, expecting me back, had bought a used car and had a couple of spare five-gallon gas coupons. And they were having special musical concerts at nearby Los Angeles. . . .

One day as I strolled around butting into the wards of other officers, I saw a Chinese soldier with characteristic pimples on his face. I called the boys and had them put up a small tarp near the telegraph tower away from everyone else and transferred the smallpox patient there. None of the other officers had seen a case of smallpox. Then we had the whole area vaccinated. Only two other cases occurred.

Toi Roi asked me to look at a patient in her ward who was crying with a headache in spite of aspirin and codeine. I bent his head forward—or tried to—then sent him over to the operating room for a spinal puncture, which produced a milky fluid full of Gram-negative diplococci. In Burma, epidemic cerebrospinal meningitis is never really epidemic. The next two or three cases were picked up immediately.

But the high point came when Big Bawk walked into my room with a bottle full of dirty water containing white flecks. She laughed. "They say this is a specimen of stool from a new patient," she said contemptuously.

This time I was excited. "Put a specimen under the microscope for me to look at," I said, "then put cresol in that bottle and soak your hands in bichloride. Order the patient to be carried out to the smallpox ward at once."

I could find no cholera vibrios under the microscope but I phoned Colonel Dushkin to order cholera vaccinations immediately and went out to look at the patient. He was in a state of collapse. His eyes were deeply sunken. His forehead was moist but his body dry and cold and the skin of his palms wrinkled. His pulse was rapid and very small but not weak. He was incontinent. When he talked at all he complained of severe cramps around the umbilicus and of vomiting which had begun suddenly six hours earlier. I ordered a quart of glucose intravenously and massive doses of sulfaguanidine and sulfadiazine. We put a can of very weak permanganate solution beside him to drink. Two hours later, with collapse still more marked, I gave him a quart of plasma.

He was holding his own the next morning, though still in shock, incontinent, and unwilling to talk. We gave him the same glucose and plasma as the day before, and by the third day his body was reacting and warm and his eyes were beginning to come back out of the walls of his brain. The day we discharged him cured we received a radio message from the big laboratory in Chabua to which we had sent stool for culture: "Organism identified as malleomyces pseudomallei. Request further specimens of blood and stools and complete report of post-mortem examination."

I regretted, in my reply, that we could not give them the report on the autopsy as the patient had refused to die and had gone home! None of us had ever heard of malleomyces pseudomallei, but after much search Colonel Petersen discovered an article that stated that it caused a fatal disease with symptoms of cholera and that only two patients had ever been known to recover from it. This made three. There were no other cases.

We were having a game now with the divisional hospital of the Chinese 38th Division which had moved up the railway from Mogaung to join the new Chinese First Army under Lieutenant General Sun, while the 50th and 14th Chinese divisions moved to join the 22nd at Kamaing-Mogaung and form the new Sixth Army under General Liao. My old Tagap friend Colonel Lee was now a major general commanding the 38th Division. He had gained a reputation under Stilwell as one of China's great tacticians. The divisional hospital had equipment for a hundred and twenty beds but the officers had decided they needed a rest more than we, so they kept a maximum of sixty patients and sent the rest to us. A good many officers and men also decided they wanted a rest and some of these wanted the rest in Ledo. So they worked up what they felt were a lot of really good symptom-complexes and came to our hospital. In malaria country you can't prove a man a goldbrick in less than three days so we had to admit them. Then the officers demanded evacuation to the "real" hospitals in Ledo. I was in complete command of all air evacuation of Chinese and I wouldn't bite. I had worked with Chinese too long and I could take their gripes because I knew they liked me. When we had proved that the patients were goldbricking, we shipped them back to the divisional hospital, only to have the officers there send them back by return post with a brand new symptom-complex and we had to go through the same game again.

Whenever we got completely fed up we went out and had a baseball game, twenty-five on a side and with special rules:

1. Any man who knocks the ball into the nurses' home is out.
2. Any man who knocks the ball into the river—his whole side is out permanently and forever.
3. Women may run on the third strike if the ball is not caught. Men are out anyway.

4. Women may steal base. Men cannot run until the ball is hit. (That raises interesting complications.)

5. The first baseman must be a woman.

6. Shortstop must be a woman but she may be supported by half a dozen male shortstops.

7. Nobody is allowed to cheat more than once per game.

Colonel R. P. Williams, theater surgeon, whose special property we had always regarded ourselves, dropped in one day to chat. Our delight in his visit was dimmed by his information that Washington had ordered that we be anonymous no longer. We were to be activated as the 896th Clearing Company. It was too much trouble for Washington to remember, if we had no number, that equipment for an extra clearing company was always being needed in C.-B.-I.

"They will now have to promote me to the rank of major or captain!" I said.

"Oh, no! You will remain a lieutenant colonel and continue as before, with your civilian personnel. You will be assigned your full Table of Organization strength of thirteen officers and one hundred enlisted men but you won't actually get any more officers or men than you have now. Your additional officers and men will be put on detached service with other units who are short of personnel."

Strange are the ways of the army. Apparently, in spite of everything, we were to be the same "unorthodox, bastard" unit—but now with an illegitimate name as well. We would not only be assigned the old unorthodox jobs as whatever brand of hospital the tactical situation might demand, but now would have a new unorthodox job as a replacement pool for all the other units in the theater! The more I thought about it the more intriguing the thought became. Not by the widest stretch of the imagination could the "original" Seagrave Hospital Unit, as I always regarded the Burmese nurses and men, Captain Gurney and myself, be considered part of the 896th Clearing Company except for Gurney and myself. The Table of Organization of a clearing company calls for no nurses (certainly not for Burmese nurses) and for no civilians. No, we would be two units, the 896th Clearing Company with its dispersed American officers and men and the old Seagrave Unit. I would be the C.O. and Gurney the executive officer of both units, belonging to both.

I was sorry for the new 896th Clearing Company's Americans, for when a man is on detached service he can't be promoted. Promotions come only when on duty with the parent organization. For their sakes I would have to pray for the co-operation of Colonel Petersen in allowing me a free hand in shifting the men and officers around from duty with the parent organization to detached service elsewhere so that deserving personnel could be with me long enough to earn merited promotion.

I wondered about the old Seagrave Unit. Was this Washington's first hint that it was tired of Stilwell's old unorthodox, bastard unit and that soon there would be an order to disband it?

But I was sorriest for Gurney. If anyone in the U.S. Army deserved a majority Ted Gurney did. Now he would never be a major unless he left me or unless I conveniently stopped a Japanese bullet.

There was nothing to do but wait and watch developments.

There were evidences that the war might begin again. A liaison strip had been built between our house and the movie show. The little planes roared over us hundreds of times a day on various missions, missing our roof by inches. I was anxious to get started on the new campaign before the pilots decided to fly in the nurses' windows. For the third consecutive time, and this time seriously, I invited all my American and Chinese friends to Christmas dinner in our bungalow in Namkham.

9

Beginning of the End

Our second group of vacationing personnel was just returning to duty when Colonel Petersen flew in from base.

"The 38th Chinese Division will begin to drive south on October 16," he said. "You will furnish a surgical team with the first regiment. The 43rd Portable Surgical Hospital will follow the second regiment, and you will move as a clearing company with divisional headquarters. There is no heavy Japanese concentration reported north of the Taiping River at Myothit, although an occasional patrol has been reported as far north as Nalong. Your first semipermanent setup will probably be at Dumbaiyang, a day's journey north of Nalong. You will march, and Major Davison, chief medical liaison officer with the 38th Division, will furnish you with animal transport."

"What are we to do with this hospital?" I asked. "We have way over five hundred beds filled. Is the 48th Evacuation Hospital ready for Chinese patients? I have heard they are taking only Americans from S.O.S."

"They're not ready but I'm trying to rush them a bit with the idea of taking patients by Monday. Evacuate all patients that will take more than three weeks to get well to the 73rd Evacuation Hospital, those that will take two weeks to the 25th Field Hospital at Tingkawk, and try to get rid of the rest to the 38th Divisional Hospital, leaving a maximum of a hundred beds filled here. The 42nd Portable Surgical Hospital will move in and take over the hundred beds with your equipment."

Major Davison called up to say he would furnish twenty horses for the advance detachment, and since Gurney would not be back in time, Antonellis took command with Captain Fair and Lieutenant Breger, our dentist. They had a mixture of technicians

with them, American, Burmese, and Chinese. Everyone carried
a pack.

The men got off on schedule. Three nights later we received
a distress telephone call from the town of Kazu. It was Sergeant
Probst. The horse carrying the surgical instruments, sterile goods,
and plaster of Paris had stepped on a land mine and blown itself
up. The gauze and plaster flew into the trees and the surgical
instruments vanished over the horizon. None of our men was
hurt but the Chinese muleteer had lost an arm. Would we please
drop them substitutes for all but the arm at Kantaoyang the following day.

I telephoned Lieutenant Cook, Colonel Petersen's supply officer, who promised to take the instruments in a cub plane and
parachute them to Antonellis.

"What color parachute would your nurses like?" he asked.

"Red," I said, absent-mindedly. No one could promise to re-
place those instruments in C.-B.-I. Instruments were too scarce.
Some of those that had been blown away were my own and
Gurney's, from Namkham and Langhku.

Incidentally the nurses never saw the red parachute. The
Chinese apparently like red, too!

Try as we would, we couldn't force the number of patients
below four hundred. We could congratulate each other in the
morning as we put fifty or a hundred patients aboard planes for
Tingkawk and Shingbwiyang, but in the evening the railhead
would send us in an equivalent number. The hospitals in Mogaung and Kamaing were also alerted for action and were unloading their patients onto us. Getting a little more stern, we forced
the number down to three hundred, just as Colonel Petersen
drove in with real trouble.

"The 48th Evacuation Hospital isn't ready yet," he said, "and
the 38th Division has decided to send the divisional hospital
south ahead of you. They have a hundred and twenty patients to
evacuate tomorrow."

"Send them over," I said, as Major Stowe, the new command-

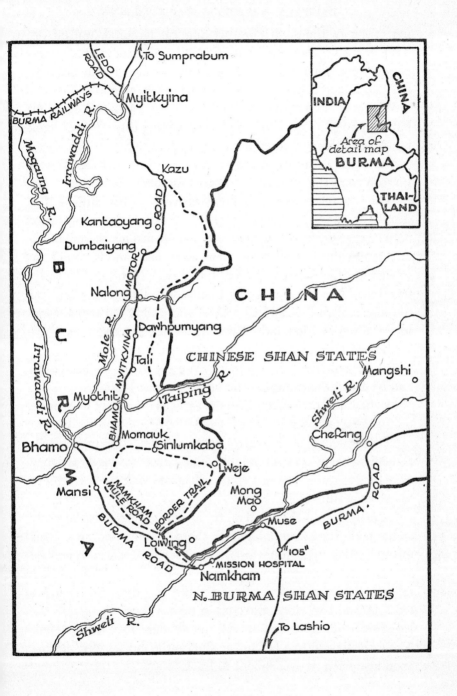

ing officer of the 42nd Portable Surgical Hospital, walked up. "We'll put up the ward tents that we pulled down today and admit them. Then we'll try to get the number of beds down to the two hundred Major Stowe says he can handle."

We took in the patients from the 38th Divisional Hospital but in spite of all effort during the remaining three days of work we still had three hundred beds to turn over to Stowe.

Many people dropped in to say goodbye those last few days. A surgeon from the 48th Evacuation Hospital spoke to me.

"Do you remember a Chinese casualty at the airfield that seemed to cause you some distress?" he asked. "Your operative note on that slip of toilet paper said you opened his abdomen and resected two feet of intestine, then, after anastomosis, found another three-foot stretch some distance away that you had to resect, too. Then you were going to close the abdomen, when you found a rent in the sigmoid and so you pulled the sigmoid out of a gridiron incision and stitched it outside the abdomen."

"Indeed I remember," I replied. "What did he do? Die?"

"Never turned a hair," he said. "We closed the artificial anus and he was running around the hospital when I left."

I sighed. I hoped all the Chinese casualties I'd have to operate on for the remainder of the war would have iron guts like that.

"Those toilet-paper operative notes of yours," the surgeon continued, "gave us a lot of trouble. The paper was so flimsy they were hard to read, but worst of all, our nurses stole the darn things to get your autograph!"

Colonel Hirschfield called up to say our vehicles must be ready at the main ferry at seven o'clock sharp the next morning. This meant getting up at four-thirty, even though Captain Whedbee and Lieutenant Carver, our old friends of the 13th Medical Battalion, offered to lend us three ambulances, three jeeps, and a truck. Afraid I wouldn't wake up in time, I asked the 42nd's enlisted man on night duty to call me at four-thirty without fail. Then we all went to a last movie show—the movies were getting good just when we were about to leave.

Three of the girls with spots of tuberculosis, Saw Yin, Julia, and Little Bawk, were left behind. They pouted when we left, although I promised to have them flown to our first semipermanent installation.

"Let it not be longer than five days," ordered Bawk.

The ferry was an amazing thing. Four large pontoon boats, each with its own outboard motor, were bridged together. All of our personnel except the enlisted men and the coolies were packed on board with a jeep and trailer and a lot of baggage. Then the outboard motors started with a roar and we were off to the east bank of the Irrawaddi for the first time in two and a half years. We had to go downstream to round Plum Island first and then beat our way up against the current on the other side. At the far landing was a Shan village. I sent the jeep on to Kazu full of officers and Burmese boys, the trailer piled with baggage, while we walked to the headman's house. This was the first normal-life village we'd seen in Burma.

The headman welcomed the "Burmese" nurses and even became friendly with me when he heard me talking to the girls in Burmese. I sat on a stool listening carefully for a word of Shan, for the people were talking to each other in Burmese, and many Shans in Burmese areas forget their own tongue. Then I heard a woman scold a child in Shan and I started chatting with the woman in their own language. How the jaws dropped! Many white people can speak Burmese quite well but the number in all Burma who can speak Shan intelligibly could probably be numbered on two hands. My wife was one of three white women whom I have heard speak Shan intelligibly. And yet Shan is so much more pleasant a language to speak than the more exact Burmese.

The nurses scattered through the village, meeting old friends and making new ones. Two of the girls stumbled on a native restaurant and brought me back a large dish of *hkow swai* (Shan noodles) and another of *wan toe poon* (pea jelly). Starved for good-tasting food, I gobbled them down with a prayer of thankfulness, enjoying even the hiccups that the hot chillies caused. Then Kyang Tswi whispered that I was invited to dinner at a nearby house. Real Burmese rice! I filled up again on their very good curry and hot salad. The first large meal I had eaten in months made me sleepy, and I was just dozing off on a wooden bench when I heard someone asking for the colonel. This was no time for visitors. I shut my eyes tight and they went away. When the arrival of the last of our equipment awoke me fifteen minutes later, one of the nurses informed me that I had missed a chicken curry dinner in another home because they hadn't wanted to wake me.

That afternoon we shuttled down to Kazu, the "end of the road," in the two jeeps and the weapons carrier. Captain Gurney had been assigned an old Japanese-Chinese camp on the bank of a deep swift river. There were a lot of flies and it was hot in the sun but it was interesting to sit and watch the Chinese being ferried across the river on single pontoons with outboard motors. The nurses spread banana leaves on the ground under their little bedrolls, the girls sleeping in twos again as they always did when we were short of transport. They insisted on making me a very narrow bed on "ten-in-one" ration boxes with a ground-sheet roof. Since I had "promised" the army there would be no rain until November 15, 1944, it would have been unwise to have a real roof!

The liaison officer of the 30th Chinese Division, which was in bivouac at Kazu, dropped in for a call, saying that he would arrange to put our jeeps across the river, since we could still use them another ten miles down the road to where fifty-five horses would meet us. That was good news. We were getting the breaks again.

Early the next morning, while a battalion of artillery was forcing its horses to swim the river, the local engineers began bridging two pontoons together for our jeeps. The Chinese mule skinners were having their troubles. Stark naked, they led the horses into the river until out of their depth, then prayed profanely that the beasts would continue over to the other side. At least a quarter of the animals decided that this bank was greener than the other and swam back again. Completely exhausted, two Chinese were saved from drowning only by the alertness of the American boys on the pontoons. By two in the afternoon our equipment and the artillery had completed the crossing. Then the pontoon boys took the nurses on a motorboat excursion up the river.

I should have gone on with the first jeeps to explore the "impassable" landslides that blocked the road where the British airborne Chindits had blown up a precipice to prevent Japanese reinforcements from reaching Myitkyina. If I had done so, I would have discovered that with fifteen borrowed pickaxes and as many shovels we could have made it passable for the jeeps within forty-eight hours, a trifling delay as compared to the time lost later. The jeeps could have been floated across the next big stream, bundled up in tarpaulins. But as we crossed to the south bank at Kazu, the captain of the animal transport assigned to us met me and arranged to pick up our supplies at the first landslide at seven the next morning. We had heard so many conflicting reports about the road that I sent Gurney ahead again to find a camp site, while I remained to see that all the nurses were herded onto the shuttling jeeps.

Since our fifty-five horses could move less than half our stuff, we left the rest with Sergeant Brough in camp in a glade and marched on to Kantaoyang, only to find that Antonellis and his detachment had pushed on to Dumbaiyang that very morning. Antonellis now had only three horses instead of sixteen so his equipment was left at Kantaoyang in the care of Lieutenant Breger and a Burmese boy. For bivouac we had been assigned the bald brow of a hill beside two new Chinese graves, and the merciless sun beat down on us. Cross at the heat and rather stiff from the first day's march, I found a tiny stream some distance away and sat in the shade of some bushes, determined to do nothing until the cool of the evening. When I walked back to camp Breger and the nurses had put up a lot of parachute tepees and were busily engaged sorting out mountain rations. Hkam Gaw rescued us from a supper of "health biscuits" by discovering a sack of Burmese rice abandoned in some nearby underbrush.

Major Davison was still in camp and pulled out a map to show me what was cooking. Advance Chinese units were halfway from Nalong to Myothit on the great Taiping River which empties into the Irrawaddi at Bhamo. They hadn't seen a Jap. The 113th Chinese Regiment was pushing on to Myothit. The 114th was following the "border trail" along the mountain ridge to prevent Japanese reinforcements from the Salween front coming over. The 112th Regiment was guarding the rear and right flank. We were to join the division's headquarters at Dumbaiyang next day but not set up a hospital, since the headquarters might move on immediately.

The new girls had made the march difficult the day before by their lack of discipline. Our unit was full of rugged individualists. Leaving Breger behind to lead on the Burmese coolies when they arrived with our power unit and heavy sterilizer, I formed the girls into line of march with myself in the middle of the line, where my alert eye could spot breach of discipline both front and rear. Chief Nurse Naomi set the pace, with E Kyaing and her clubfoot immediately behind her. The hottest hour of the day caught us crossing the shadeless Dumbaiyang plain. By the time we reached the river we collapsed in the shade of a tiny Chinese camp. Salt tablets and water treated with halazone tablets soon revived us, though I made a mental note to take a course of carbarsone, without waiting for the amoebae to develop, which halazone won't kill.

As we started on again we found Major Davison resting under a tree by the side of the road.

"So you decided to come on today, anyway," I said.

"Yes. We left at half-past ten," he replied, in a tone that reminded me we had started three hours earlier than he.

A few hundred yards farther on, Davison's party passed us at a trot, riding beautiful army-bred horses. No wonder they had caught up with us.

Davison was seated on a log at the entrance to our camp site.

"This is the man whom the entire Chinese Army calls *Lao E Guan*, the old doc," he said, introducing me to Lieutenant Colonel Pien, divisional surgeon.

"Heard about you in China months and months ago," Colonel Pien said warmly.

"You will move on with the division to its new headquarters on the south bank of the river at Nalong tomorrow," Davison said. He had been executive officer of a two-thousand-bed army general hospital in the States and loved moving medical pawns around the chessboard. "An airstrip for liaison planes is being built there," he continued, "but don't set up a real hospital. The 113th Regiment is almost at Myothit and hasn't yet found a Jap. There are a thousand Japs reported in Myothit area and another two thousand in Bhamo. Five thousand are said to be in Namkham."

"Yes, dug in on the mission hill and occupying my hospital," I interrupted, quoting grapevine information that had come to me.

"No one can understand why the Japanese have let us have all this gigantic area without a fight," Davison went on. "Kachins say the Japanese grand strategy is to suck us all into the Bhamo area and then wipe us out from the rear, but General Lee is guarding against this very thing by deploying the 112th Regiment on the right flank."

After we had all had a gorgeous bath in the cold stream, Colonel Burns, chief liaison officer, and Major Davison returned for a visit in the delightful parachute tent Antonellis and his boys had built for me.

"General Lee is unhappy that you are marching while he rides," they said. "He wants you to accept a riding horse for the trip to Nalong tomorrow."

"Thank the general," I said, "but ask him to excuse me from riding while my unit walks."

The next day's march was a mess. We had no sooner started when the battalion of artillery insisted on passing us. As soon as they got in front of us they stopped for a rest. It was positively nasty. I called the noon halt hours before noon and let the artillery get out of the way.

The Nalong plain was not nearly so hot and being a Shan plain (the name means "Great Rice Paddies") there were vegetable gardens and fruit trees growing everywhere.

"Why don't they let us choose our own site and then we could camp here and get a full stomach for once," grumbled one of the girls.

The site picked for us was an old monastery with a shrineful of Buddhas. Japanese had camped there and it was filthy and lousy with sandflies. There weren't enough shade trees for the men to hang up their jungle hammocks. Although we were next to the field where the liaison planes would be landing the next day, we were two miles from the dropping field and farther than that from divisional headquarters. Colonel Burns and Dr. Taubenfliegl rode off on horses to find us a better bivouac area.

From then on Taubenfliegl became a charter member of the 896th Clearing Company Reconnaissance Patrol. The site he chose was perfection—another monastery in a temporarily deserted Shan village with unlimited shade and surrounded by weedy vegetable gardens and fruit trees. The girls fitted into the monastery and one room of the nunnery, which we covered with a tarp, and I took another room in the same building. It wasn't the first time I'd spent a night in an abandoned nunnery. Gilbertson had a shack roofed with jungle-made clay tile where he could sort out our supplies. While the girls collected fruit and vegetables and chatted with the natives, who came out from the hiding places in the jungle when they saw Burmese nurses, the boys went to the dropping field and came back with—delightful surprise—sacks of Louisiana rice.

It was mostly the fault of our own unit that India furnished the Chinese Army such awful rice. Though Indian rice is no good in any case, we had been getting the best grade of milled, though not actually polished, rice until Major Grindlay began to see beriberi cases at Tagap and had one man die during an appendix operation from what Ba Saw diagnosed as "beriberi" heart. Losing a simple appendix case hit Grindlay in his tenderest spot. He demanded unpolished rice so loudly and repeatedly that India let us have it—with both barrels.

From then on we got nothing but the worst grade of Indian rice, rough brown stuff with the coarse hard shell scattered through it, dirty and full of little stones. Quartermaster at the base ration depots, not understanding that rice spoils easily after milling, dropped us sacks of rice from the top of the stacks until stocks were slightly depleshed, then followed with the lower sacks which by then were moldy, sour, and full of insects. Often the rice stank so while cooking that we could approach the chow line only by holding our noses. Now after a year, India's stock must have been low for they were dropping to Americans, at least, an occasional sack of Louisiana rice. How we gobbled it up! American rice is the cleanest in the world, though in taste it doesn't compare with Namkham Valley rice, which has by far the most delicious flavor of any in the world.

In peacetime I would have turned up my nose at boiled giant cucumbers, pumpkin, and squash. After two years of army rations they were delicious, especially when reinforced with tamarind, pomelo, fresh garlic and ginger, lots of chili peppers and a dash of Kachin "rotten beans" for seasoning. An hour's rest was required after such a meal.

The 38th Division pulled out and left us at Nalong. If we had to linger somewhere, that was the spot for me. Our horses went back for another load near Kazu. Our coolies caught up, staggering along under the weight of our power unit. Then orders came in by phone for us to push forward to Dawhpumyang with horses from the artillery battalion. The artillery promised us seventy

horses and turned up with fifty. There was a flurry as we abandoned cases of rations right and left—much to the delight of the
natives—and scattered bottles of medicine and pyrethrum (mosquito) bombs around for the nurses and myself to add to our
own packs.

We crossed a little ridge, rounded a corner, and there were the
Dawhpumyang rice paddies spread out below us. I stopped,
rubbed the cobwebs and sweat out of my eyes, and looked again.
It couldn't be. But there it was. The Dawhpumyang fields were
the beginning of the forest-floored Bhamo plain, and there, in
the distance, was the same blue ridge of mountains west of the
Irrawaddi at Bhamo upon which I had gazed so many hundreds
of times in the past twenty-two years. I pointed out the Bhamo
area to the nurses and they quickened their pace as if they intended
to sleep that night in Bhamo. The refugees were getting home to
their own mountains.

Major Davison was beside the road near some dilapidated
Kachin houses he had selected for our bivouac. "The 113th
Chinese Regiment has occupied Myothit and rubber boats are
being dropped to them tomorrow," he said. "The 114th has taken
the suspension bridge over the Taiping River on the border trail
and is pushing on to Sinlumkaba. Their last battalion leaves the
road ten miles south of here at Tali tomorrow morning to join
them there. Have a detachment with three officers ready to do a
double march tomorrow to catch up with them. They will have
twenty horses. You will go tomorrow to a tiny village called Numfang half a mile this side of Tali. You will have thirty-five horses.
No one can understand why the Japs don't try to stop us. General
Lee says he will be in Bhamo in a week."

I selected Captain Gurney, Dr. Taubenfliegl, and Dr. San Yee.
Since we had only five enlisted men available I included all my
good Burmese technicians and enough new Burmese boys to do
the dirty work. Boganaw went along as interpreter, for this was
Kachin country. Wong Jack went as cook.

"I hate to send you off on this flank, Doctor," I said to San Yee who always begged to stay with me, "but you may strike directly across the hills to Namkham and get there before us. Give your wife and child my love, if you do."

San Yee chuckled.

At Numfang there were three Kachin houses still standing. The nurses took over the biggest one, which, with extension of the floor space next day, gave them all room to sleep on the floor; the coolies took another and the Chinese detachment the third. For myself we put up a three-layer parachute tepee with a bamboo bed, while another was prepared for the three sick nurses who were flown in three days later.

With the 113th Chinese Regiment in control of the entire north bank of the Taiping River, it was decided to have the 112th join the 114th at Sinlumkaba and drive down on Bhamo from the east and south. The 43rd Portable Hospital's Kantaoyang detachment appeared with our horses just in time to take off in support of the 113th, but they had to borrow Captain Fair from us since they were short an officer.

The rest of us sat back to await developments. Interesting things occurred sufficiently frequently to keep us from too complete boredom. The 30th Chinese Division marched in and began to supply us with patients. There was a swarm of scrub typhus cases—the Shitsugamushi fever of Japan. This was unknown in Burma before the war but is one of the legacies to remain with Burma long after the Japanese themselves were driven out. Scrub typhus had caused more havoc among the Marauders before Myitkyina than had malaria.

One of the scrub-typhus patients died in our wards and the Chinese appeared with a Burmese wooden coffin, the first one we'd seen in years. As custom dictated, some Shan or Burmese grandee had purchased his own coffin years before his death in order to be certain there would be one on hand for his funeral. Now the Chinese had looted it for their dead comrade.

"*S'taing ga*," said the nurses. "If they're going to bury him in real style we will have to get busy!" and, lacking flowers, they gathered a lot of twigs and grass and made the hero a wreath.

A group of Kachins with baskets hanging from their foreheads walked by, and I called to the Kachin nurses to grab them and buy whatever vegetables they might have. As they were dickering, one of the men looked repeatedly at Nang Pri.

"Isn't your name Nang Pri?" he asked.

"Yes," she replied, smiling.

"You've certainly changed a great deal in three years. Do you know your father is living in our village on the mountain?"

Nang Pri started to cry. "May I go back with these people and visit my father for a couple of days?" she begged.

"Of course you can. How does your father happen to be in their village instead of at Sinlum?"

"He heard the Japanese were intending to arrest him as a spy so he ran away to China and didn't return until told the Chinese Army was pushing the Japs out."

Nang Pri returned three days later, wreathed in smiles and loaded down with ginger, mustard, fresh onions, garlic, and "rotten beans."

There was the sound of a gasoline engine one afternoon and a jeep drove in. Two Americans had floated it across the rivers at Dumbaiyang and Nalong, wrapped up in a tarpaulin. It was an omen that before long our own jeeps and other vehicles might catch up with us. Then Captain Whedbee and his clearing company marched in and we knew it was time for us to leave and catch up with the 38th Division. Orders arrived the next morning.

South of the Taiping the road was at first heavily graveled and then asphalted. We had been warned about mines and so weren't surprised when we saw near the road what looked like a Christmas tree. On one of the lower branches was a shirt, on another a pair of blood-stained trousers, on still others were a pair of socks, underwear, and one wrap-legging. They were the property of a former Chinese cavalryman whose horse had first proved that the road was mined. Beside the crater of the exploded mine Chinese engineers had dug up three others which they had piled beside the road. From there on we came to one mined area after another, the mines closer together the farther south we went, until in the most heavily mined area of them all we smelled the remnants of a water buffalo that had exploded half a dozen mines at once.

On a good many of the world's worst trails the nurses had frequently beat me into camp. But this asphalt road was too much for them to take. Unused to walking on hard roads, their arches gave way and I had rapidly to increase the rest periods to twenty minutes, then thirty minutes per hour. Finally some of them toddled away for ten minutes at a time, and some removed their G.I. shoes and went barefoot. At camp at the fifteenth-mile post they flopped on the floor of the house Major Davison had selected for their quarters. For the first time in three years of army marching they couldn't be enticed out for a bath.

Gurney and his men had completed their flank move to this same camp and were operating as we came in; but Momauk, the first large town near Bhamo, had just been captured and they moved on the next morning while we set up a clearing station and liaison planes flew into our back yard to evacuate patients.

Esther was preparing to give an anesthetic the next afternoon when she looked up and there was her brother standing in the gateway. It was perhaps just as well for me that I didn't see the actual meeting. By the time I came along Esther had calmed down a bit and told me, starry-eyed, that her father and mother, her elder doctor-brother Albert, and her adorable younger sister Pansy were alive and well and living only four miles away from us in a jungle village. The family had been planting their own rice and vegetables and, as confirmed vegetarians, had done rather well. Esther, who had missed her family desperately, went back to them that next day to help them through the period of reconstruction with the thousands of rupees she had saved for them from her salary.

As one girl after another found her people, the other girls from farther south began to smile and laugh from sheer good spirits,

accepting the omens as portending happy days in store for them
also.

The Kachin owner of the house in which we were living, an
old friend, dropped in one day properly to welcome us back to
Burma. Like everyone who had lived through the Japanese occupation he complained, first, that not one bit of cotton—woven,
unwoven, or raw—had been on the market since the English
left, second, that one person to each household was always away
on compulsory unpaid labor, and, third, that the Japanese had
driven off or shot all their buffaloes, cows, and chickens. Pigs, he
said, had been so contrary that the Japs had been unable to drive
them off. Since the owners were unable to feed them, the pigs had
become so wild that even the owners couldn't catch them or—
since the Japs had taken up all their guns—shoot them. If we
would shoot one of his own pigs for him we might shoot as many
as we wanted for ourselves.

We were more than agreeable to his proposal and, with the
householder as guide, got all the pork we could stow away at a
sitting.

The Chinese had now debouched on the entire Bhamo plain,
had wiped out company after company of Japanese, had cut the
Namkham and Sikaw motor roads, and had backed a thousand
Japanese into Bhamo town where they were completely encircled.
Gurney's detachment was five miles outside Bhamo town. We
in the main unit made one last march down the asphalt road
to Momauk town, arriving to the music of rifle fire as a company of Japanese was slowly being wiped out a quarter of a mile
away.

For our new location Major Davison had picked out the best
part of Momauk. A huge, well-built Buddhist monastery and its
outlying nunnery and resthouses gave us a perfect hospital setup,
while across the asphalt main road, two two-story wooden houses
gave us quarters for nurses. Our Chinese detachment and coolies
and sweepers appropriated two thatch houses. About ten days
later Colonel Burns, chief liaison officer, suddenly woke up and

complained to Major Davison that Seagrave had taken over the best part of the town.

"Doesn't he always?" chuckled Davison, who had at last obtained his dream: the perfect medical setup for a Chinese division. The 43rd Portable Surgical Hospital in two detachments, one with each of the two regiments on the Namkham Road, and Gurney's surgical detachment with the third regiment on the Momauk Road were less than two miles from the fighting front. Most of their casualties reached them by litter in less than an hour after being wounded. From the portables the casualties were being jeeped back on an asphalt road to our hospital. Just beyond our hospital the Chinese field hospital was taking all the medical work and much of the minor surgery. A quarter of a mile away hospital planes were taking on our evacuation patients for the short run to big institutions at Myitkyina. More than 50 per cent of the casualties never needed to be evacuated, and long before the fall of Bhamo two hundred casualties had been returned by us to the front—a whole company of troops. Davison had a right to be a bit smug.

One day, just after Captain Staples joined us, a Japanese sniper "burned" his neck with a rifle bullet. Staples and his men dropped in a ditch as a second bullet hit the earth at the edge of the ditch, spattering them with dust. I moved them back a mile. A few nights later the Japanese, fed up with the barrages of 155-, 105-, and 75-mm. howitzers that had been pounding them for two days from positions on three sides of Gurney, pulled up their remaining big guns to the very Chinese lines and threw fifty shells at point-blank range into Gurney's hospital area, hoping to destroy the amunition dump beside them. When Gurney and his men emerged above ground in the morning, their operating-room roof and their jungle hammocks and blankets were full of shellholes. I brought them back to our monastery, since patients could reach us within ten minutes of the time they had been reaching Gurney.

Our monastery was now really three hospitals. The upstairs floor was a field hospital, caring for patients who would take three weeks or more to get well. The larger area downstairs was a clearing station for patients who would be well in less than two weeks and for those who needed to be evacuated to the rear. The remainder of the downstairs was a portable surgical hospital operating on casualties direct from the front. The nunnery was a civilian hospital, filled with badly shattered natives, and the rest-house was an American hospital. Life was interesting.

And life was immeasurably interesting to the refugees. The day after we arrived, a well-dressed Shan woman hurried up and prostrated herself on the floor, much to my embarrassment. "My, but we're glad to have you back," she said. "We heard you were coming and I felt I must come right away to *wai* [a word that means something between to bow and to worship]. You may not remember me but you operated on me for uterine tumor four years ago."

Two bunches of bananas—the standard gift to important people—were laid on my table and the lady went off satisfied.

Then a group of Shans came in cautiously and fearfully, carrying a woman with a badly shattered thigh. What would these American doctors be like? When they saw Burmese nurses, they showed a bit more confidence. When Princess Louise started talking to them in Shan, they ceased trembling. When I opened up a barrage of Shan, they were at first speechless and then muttered to each other, wondering where I'd picked up their language. Hkam Gaw heard them and said, "Don't you recognize him? He's the Namkham doctor." They could hardly believe their ears, for though they had heard many tales of our hospital and though many of their people had been patients of ours, none of these men and women had actually seen me. From then on they were all smiles, confidently left the injured woman in our care and, next day, brought in three more civilian casualties and three baskets of fresh vegetables.

What with gifts of vegetables from former Namkham nurses and patients and their families and purchases from others who needed money, we never had a meal without at least one fresh vegetable, and for a period of two weeks I ate not one meal of rations except for the cereal and coffee at breakfast. As soon as Bulu, who had graduated from our training school in 1940, found we were in town she began bringing over four-course dinners every three days, cooking us special dishes that she knew, from her training years, I especially relished.

Bulu was the fourth of our old friends who was married, and all of them were eight months' pregnant. The story came out from different sources and tallied in the important details: The Japanese, a year before, had begun rounding up unmarried girls and carting them off to Bhamo where they were put on "duty" for a few months before being sent home. They didn't interfere with married girls. Promptly a large number of Christian Kachin girls; not wanting to be "employed," grabbed the nearest available male—though in at least two instances the man was thoroughly detested—and married him.

"Bulu," I said, "if you want me to deliver your first baby you'd better start taking quinine and castor oil and hire a jeep. We have no idea when Bhamo will fall and when it does we will move like a shot."

Bulu couldn't comprehend how little warning our group was often given or how fast we could move when orders came. Perhaps, too, she was a bit complacent about it. Suddenly late one night I was ordered to take a team and move early in the morning for the thirty-second mile on the Namkham Road. Whereupon Bulu immediately went into labor without the use of quinine, castor oil, or jeeps. Luckily I had left Ted Gurney behind to transfer our patients to the 13th Medical Battalion and Bulu was well cared for and a perfect delivery performed.

On Thanksgiving Day we did *not* have turkey. Bulu invited the older nurses and myself over to dinner at her house instead. She insisted our jeep could ford the stream and drive right to her house. My driver Taperek, however, thought he was driving an amphibious vehicle and didn't stop to look for a ford. Choosing the deepest part of the stream, he plunged right in to the top of the hood. Wet to the waist, we trudged the rest of the way.

Bulu's brother-in-law Zow Lawm was the former headmaster of the mission high school in Bhamo and had built a very nice house, with many old photographs of his schooldays tacked on the wall. Because of his great perspicacity and his determination not to give offense, the Japs had not destroyed his house, though a few months before, learning he had been giving information to the Allies, they had come to arrest him. Zow Lawm had run for the wild jungles and had only now dared to return home. We had a good view of his perspicacity and long suffering:

A 30th Division G-2 Chinese was in the house as we entered. He knew well who I was for he had been a patient of ours in Myitkyina and had created disturbances in our hospital at Tali. He was disgusted at our intrusion but went about his business. With a notebook and pencil he studied the old school pictures.

"Here, you, who is this?" he demanded, pointing to a girl in a picture dated at Mandalay in 1924.

The headmaster politely walked over and took a look and said, "Her name is Ma Hla Din."

"Where does she live?"

"She used to live in Monywa, west of Mandalay, twenty years ago."

"Where is she now?"

"I don't know."

"Why don't you know?"

"I haven't seen her since we were in school together."

"Is she alive?"

"I don't know."

The intelligence expert scribbled in his notebook and Zow Lawm returned to resume our interrupted conversation. In half a minute the expert jerked him over to another face in the picture, and the grilling went on. Zow Lawm remained patient as other group photos of 1924 and 1925 were scrutinized. Not once did he show exasperation. After forty-five minutes of continuous interruption the expert, in a gruff whisper, demanded, "I want whisky."

"We Christian Kachins do not drink and I have no alcohol in the house," Zow Lawm replied.

"Who is that man in that picture?" the expert demanded, repeating the performance for another five minutes—and then, "Give me whisky."

And so on endlessly until my patience was completely exhausted.

"See here," I said. "You're exceeding your authority in trying to scare this man into giving you whisky. You're not inquiring into anything that can possibly be of value. Those pictures were taken hundreds of miles away from here eighteen years before the war. You can read the dates on the pictures yourself and the names of the towns where the pictures were taken. You're not trying to get information. You're after whisky and I happen to know that these old friends of mine never drink. This is the headmaster of the Bhamo High School and he was Number Two on the Japanese list for execution for helping the Allies. Stop bothering him and us!"

"Who are you?" he growled in Chinese with a lot of filthy oaths, pretending he understood no Burmese though he had been talking continuously in Burmese for an hour.

"You know very well who I am," I said in my best Chinese. "I am Colonel Seagrave of the Seagrave Hospital Unit serving the 38th Division, the old doc of the Chinese armies. I can have you arrested for what you're doing now."

He burst into a terrific rage. What he didn't call me doesn't exist in the Chinese language.

I sat and stared at him.

He rushed to the door and screamed to someone outside. A Chinese tommy-gunner came rushing in. "Arrest that man and tie him up!" yelled the G-2 agent, pointing at me. The gunner, thinking of course he meant the native and not the American, seized Zow Lawm's arm roughly and ordered him forward. Zow Lawm went without resistance or protest.

"Not him! That American in the corner!" screamed the agent.

The soldier stopped nonplussed and eyed me to see if I were a safe American for him to deal with. Apparently I looked too old to be dangerous. To fortify himself he reached for the packet of American cigarettes on the table, took one, slapped the pack down, and started for me with his tommy gun poised.

"Get up!" he shouted at me in his most orthodox Chinese G.I. sergeant's voice. I sat and stared.

"Listen, big boy," I drawled. "I can have you shot for this. Let's us boys all go and have a talk with Generals Sun, Lee, and Tang and then we'll stand and watch you executed!"

"Get up!" he screamed, raising his tommy gun.

Now Little Bawk was getting worried. She spoke swiftly. "Do you know who he is? That American is the *yenjank* [commanding officer] of a great American hospital with the 38th Division. You're going to be in real trouble in a minute!"

At the dread word *yenjank* and the mention of the famous 38th Division, the sergeant faltered, looked at me in dismay, turned and ran for cover. The G-2 agent, now without protection himself, was at his wits' end how to depart gracefully and without loss of face. Zow Lawm and Bawk, anxious to get rid of his stench, quickly apologized for the "misunderstanding" caused by language difficulties and begged his indulgence.

"I did not know who Colonel Seagrave was," said the man I cured of malaria in Myitkyina two months before and who had been reminded of my identity in good Chinese minutes earlier. Then without his whisky, he backed bravely to the door and by morning was twenty miles away at Mansi.

I turned in a report through channels and three days later was informed that the G-2 agent had been apprehended at Mansi and shot. He must have been very gently shot, for a month later, with General Tang beside me, I saw him draw swiftly behind a tree where he had been abusing some Kachins, hoping the nurses and

I hadn't spotted him. Later I learned that he was going from one Shan village to another in the Namkham Valley, branding with hot irons any Shan who didn't have on his person as much money as the agent thought he ought to have. One of these Shans was a friend of mine, headman of Kong Wing village, who came to welcome me home. I saw his wounds. Three other Shans in the same village had also been branded.

After Thanksgiving the American infantry began to march past. As the boys caught glimpses of the nurses, choruses of whistles and catcalls rent the air. One group was given a breakfast halt right in front of us and dropped to the ground and started making coffee in their canteen cups over their canned heat. Pin-up girl Big Bawk stepped daintily across the road toward the hospital.

"Ann Atomy! *Hao-bu-hao!*" called an infantryman.

"That must be the Seagrave Unit," said another.

"Sure it is," said a third.

"What are they doing down here so close to the front?"

"They're always at the front. They operated on me in Myitkyina."

They thought I was out of hearing, as I sat wishing that our unit could be allowed to serve the American infantry. Just then Colonel Esterbrook stepped into the room.

"Colonel," he said, "I have a problem on my hands. We're ordered to march double stages around Bhamo and south and west toward Shwegu. We have no time to build liaison strips and no way to evacuate our road casualties. Is there any way you can help us?"

"The five-mile bridge and the eight-mile bridge on the Namkham Road have both been bombed by our air force," I replied. "I think I can ford the first stream and float a jeep across the second wrapped up in a tarp. If so, I can shuttle your casualties back here and fly them back to Myitkyina after a night's rest."

I set off with our coolies, intending to bridge the narrow deep channel across the first stream and look into the possibilities of the second. To my amazement Chinese engineers had already bridged the first with a part pontoon, part pier bridge constructed of captured Japanese pontoon boats and salvaged timbers from the outskirts of Bhamo, and were already halfway across the second. My only real opportunity to serve the Americans turned out to be too easy. Still it was fun and I made one ambulance trip myself, hoping the boys would get a kick out of having a lieutenant colonel for an ambulance driver.

After the infantry was out of the way the heavy guns began to roll by. It was the first time we'd seen our own 105's and 155's. Colonel Levell stopped in to pay his respects.

"Are you going to shell Bhamo?" I asked.

"Yes."

"Can we come down and watch you?"

"Sure. Come tomorrow at ten o'clock."

"Colonel," I went on, "I understand that in Namkham the air force has ruined only my operating room, but all native reports agree that the mission hill there is the center of the Japanese activities, not the town. In Namkham the Japs can't build their usual deep dugouts for they will strike water about six feet down. All their real defenses will be around the hospital."

"That is indicated by our intelligence reports," the colonel agreed.

"Sir," I said, "I feel the same way about that hospital of mine that a father feels about a dying son. He stands the son's death better if he can be present and helping. I am sure you will have to shell that hospital, but I wish you would promise me that when you do you will let me pull the first lanyard!"

"It's a promise."

The nurses and enlisted men who went with me to watch the barrage on Bhamo were properly impressed. The 114th Chinese Regiment under Colonels Chen and Peng had learned at last how to move in behind an advancing barrage and it was exciting to watch the officers in contact with headquarters and air observers giving orders and having the orders expertly obeyed. By afternoon the 114th Regiment had obtained their objective and captured their north end of the town. Now it was up to the 113th Regiment to take the rest of the town.

And then the tanks rolled by, lights and mediums. Colonel Brown, freshly discharged from the hospital, flew down and spent one night with me. Brown planned to attack Bhamo and show everyone how to fight.

Everyone felt Bhamo was in the bag, so Captains Antonellis and Fair and Dr. Ba Saw started off in the morning to begin a flanking move with the 112th Chinese Regiment on Namkham. Their vehicles had no sooner left when word came that the Japs had evacuated Bhamo. They must have heard Brown shouting the night before about what his tanks were going to do and just couldn't take it!

It was reported that two hundred Japs had escaped south along the riverbank, and Antonellis and his companions expected to run into an ambush at any moment during their first day. Colonel Brown was disgusted that his tanks hadn't had a chance to fight and sent several of the light tanks south in a futile effort to catch the enemy. The last effort on the part of the Japs before leaving had been to throw all their remaining 70-mm. shells at the 43rd Portable Surgical Hospital area.

The following day Major Davison informed me that he was going to visit the 43rd and congratulate them on their narrow escape, so I drove him down, hoping we could sneak into Bhamo by the back door and take a look at the wreckage of the large stone church I had built there. Two of the officers of the 43rd joined us. Stepping warily to avoid mines, we had only reached the south edge of the town when we saw my friend Colonel Peng also viewing the remains. Peng stopped his tour and insisted on escorting us all over, by paths that had been cleared of mines. There was nothing but destruction. The only building I saw in town that could be used for living purposes was the old Burmese Anglo-Vernacular School. I didn't see the north end. Shops where I had bought stores for years and the entire bazaar area, including the famous clock tower, the "Circuit House," Deputy Commissioner's and Civil Surgeon's houses, the Government Hospital—especially the hospital—were a complete loss.

Diagonally opposite from the hospital was my church. From the front no damage could be seen, save that the corrugated asbestos roof had been blown off. We entered and there was a huge oval hole in the rear wall where a 75-mm. gun had scored a direct hit. But my belief in cobblestone architecture was well justified: over the shellhole, the overhanging stone structure had not fallen and only part of one corner of the building nearby had been cracked. The pews had all been stolen but the complicated electric wiring remained, still usable after a bit of untangling. The mission could repair the building and make it as good as new with an expenditure of about a thousand dollars. Under my heavily reinforced concrete porte-cochere was written the reason for the shelling of the church: an arc cut an inch deep in the cement floor, on which the base of a Japanese 70 had rested. I went back to Momauk happy—and crazy to start for Namkham.

Home

ON THE evening of the day we inspected the remains of Bhamo the Civil Affairs officer gave a dinner to celebrate. As we were eating dessert Dr. Gurney came hurriedly in and informed me I was to telephone Colonel Van Natta, chief liaison officer of the Chinese First Army, at once. As I was reaching for the telephone Van Natta himself rushed in.

"The 30th Division is in trouble on the Namkham Road," he said. "They failed to patrol jungle paths in their rear and one battery of our 75's has been captured. There are so many casualties that their medical units are swamped. I want to borrow a clearing platoon of your unit until the situation clears up. You will leave as early as possible in the morning."

That sounded good. We would be forty miles closer home next day.

Taking Dr. San Yee and Dr. Mildred and the girls who had been through all the experiences in India and the Naga Hills, we set off in trucks and reported to 30th Division Headquarters at the thirty-second-mile post. The area allotted to us was the side of a hill, for the Namkham Road rises from Bhamo plain through steep mountains of very solid limestone. From the narrow ribbon of road the mountains drop away precipitously to the stream hundreds of feet below. There was room for one ward tent, an operating room with four tables, a shock tent, and then, for living quarters, parachute tepees scattered all over the hill.

Just below us was the 58th Portable Surgical Hospital and beyond them the 13th Medical Battalion's Clearing Platoon. I was distressed to have one of the medical officers of the latter come in almost immediately and complain about our choosing a site closer to the front than theirs. They had hoped, on the departure of the 58th next day on a flank move, to be doing all the surgical work.

"My dear boy," I said. "I didn't choose this site. I was ordered to set up here by your liaison officers. I have no intention of stealing your surgery. I don't care if I never see another casualty. I was ordered up here to help in any way possible because your medical system was screwed up and you were yelling for help. If any casualties are brought in here we will send them on to you. If you have more than you can handle, pick out the ones you want and send the nuisance cases back to us. We'll do your postoperative work."

Of course as soon as we arrived the emergency ceased to exist. The 112th Regiment of the 38th Division, which Antonellis was serving, threw in a roadblock behind the Japanese at the fifty-second mile and the Japanese pulled out from in front of the 30th Division. Our task in the Bhamo area had also been completed and the main body of the unit was ordered forward. But where were they to locate? There wasn't enough level ground around us at the thirty-second mile even for our personnel, let alone a field hospital. I gave in and ordered them to set up at Madanyang, a lovely position at the twentieth mile just before the road leaves the plain to start up the mountain.

For three long years I had been inviting everyone to Christmas dinner in Namkham, first in 1942, then in 1943, and now again in 1944. We were now only forty miles from our objective but still couldn't fulfill our Christmas obligations. It was irritating that not only were we not in Namkham for Christmas but had to be separated from each other. Our personnel liked to be together.

We could remedy the first defect somewhat. On the day before Christmas I called the nurses whose homes were in the Namkham area and we drove up to a point beyond Kaitik from which we could see, fifteen air miles away, the central portion of the Namkham Valley spread out before us. Namkham and the hospital area were hidden by the mountain from which Chinese mortars were still driving the last of the Japanese. While we were exploring for a better view a lone Japanese sniper, hidden in a brush a hundred yards away, tried ineffectively to pick us off.

At the thirty-second mile we found that the Kachins of the villages nearby had braved stray Japanese and the Chinese outposts to come down, welcome us back, and share Christmas with us. They had brought pigs, chickens, and eggs, and were already cooking the feast. Our stomachs full of fresh food, we had a short Christmas service together and then they went off home, their old-fashioned rifles and muzzle-loading shotguns ready for the Japanese.

We couldn't remedy the second defect completely, for Captain Antonellis' detachment was miles away over jungle paths. But it wasn't difficult to reach an agreement with the 13th Medical Battalion. They were anxious to let their men have Christmas Eve off duty so they could get tight, if they wanted to, and try to forget that they weren't having Christmas at home in the States. We wanted dinner with our main unit at Madanyang on Christmas Day. We therefore took all the medical responsibility for Christmas Eve, while the 13th assumed responsibility for Christmas Day.

While the 13th had their Christmas Eve party we built a huge bonfire and sat around it till midnight, singing carols and chatting. Many of the 13th's guests slipped out to join in our carol singing for half an hour or so. We were unhappy because we were still forty miles from Namkham at Christmas but there was a feeling of peace as we sang.

All was not peace, however, for we learned in the morning that three of the Japanese who had escaped from Bhamo, ragged, starving, and half frozen, had spent Christmas Eve in the Chinese camp and, oversleeping themselves on Christmas morning, were discovered and shot by the Chinese as they tried to escape.

We couldn't drive through Madanyang Christmas morning, for engineers of the tank battalion were blasting the granite-hard limestone cliffs at the sharp curves to make them passable for the tanks. But, by shuttling, we arrived in time for dinner. There was no fresh turkey but our boys had done their best with a bit of canned turkey and fresh venison, and a very good best it was.

We had few guests so the occasion was not as dignified as Christmas at Ningam in 1943. A tank sergeant produced wonderful guitar music and the rest of the program was placid and enjoyable. We hurried back at the conclusion of the program to another dinner with General Tang of the 30th Division.

There had been few casualties and we weren't busy. We had learned patience in our years of army service and we spent our time watching the engineers bulldoze and blast the road to twice the width of the original English road. Meanwhile officers of the Air Force, Tanks, Corps Artillery, First Army, kept dropping in continually with their maps to ask about the geography of the Namkham Valley, locations of fords and marshes, gravel banks and sand, and level plateau areas. Everyone was restlessly stamping around waiting for the 30th Division to take Namkham so they could get on with the war. The first through convoy for Kunming, China, was forming at Myitkyina.

But the 30th Division was bogged down. Impatiently the 112th Regiment of the 38th Division took matters into its own hands and walked into Loiwing, capturing the airplane factory site and landing field. Then it plunged on to the Mansawn ferry and back up the motor road toward the 30th. Still more impatiently, Colonel Levell of the heavy artillery begged Colonel Brown of the tanks to set his bulldozers to cutting a direct road down to Panghkam, near the Loiwing airplane factory, in order that the artillery and tanks could reach the plain ahead of the 30th Division and smooth things out so they could capture Namkham. Colonel Brown snapped at the suggestion and came to me with Colonel Sliney for help on a reconnaissance to locate the best short cut to the old mule road to Panghkam.

The nurses yelled *S'taing ga* after me as I set off with great dignity in a train of jeeps with a brigadier general in front and countless full colonels behind. We drove through to the fifty-second mile, where the Chinese told us we could go no farther as Japs were entrenched two hundred yards beyond. But that was far enough. We were at the entrance to the short cut and in sight of the hospital buildings at Namkham. Something had certainly happened. Even with binoculars, the outline of the buildings was indistinct, whereas the last time I had looked back from this spot, the naked eye could clearly see the red-roofed, pearly gray stone buildings, set like a jewel in the green of the foothills above Namkham, with the great twin seventy-five-hundred-foot mountains behind. Now the blur was so indistinct you could hardly be sure you were looking at the right spot.

While I gazed at the physical evidence of what was left of my lifelong dream, the tank officers explored and found a steep but steady descent by which they could reach the old mule trail, after a mile of bulldozing through the jungle. Colonel Brown decided this would be the route for his tanks and the artillery.

I was moody and silent on the return trip. My dreams for the Northern Shan States seemed pretty well shattered.

New Year's Day passed rather quietly. I sent the nurses down the hill to celebrate with the bigger group while I remained on duty. All returned after midnight except Big Bawk, who had come down with a severe chill and fever and had to be left behind. The next morning, as I was at my desk, I looked up and there was Big Bawk's father. I had never had much love for the gentleman. He was arrogant, loud-voiced, and much too full of phrases. He had been in hot water so frequently during the past years that I couldn't remember an occasion when he wasn't getting out of one mess or falling into another. Big Bawk inherited her sweetness and grace and in fact everything but her face from her dead mother. She and her father had been estranged for some time.

His second question nauseated me. "How much salary have you been paying Bawk these three years?"

His eyes glistened and his mouth drooled as I answered him. With a small part of Bawk's four thousand rupees as a dowry and the rest in his hands, he could marry her off at a very handsome profit to himself and live most excitingly and unethically for years to come.

My sympathy for Bawk increased. No wonder she'd been frantic through the years away from Burma. As anxious as everyone else to get back to her own country, she had no one left but this black sheep of a father. And on his first visit he was showing that what he was waiting for was not so much his daughter as her money.

I sent him down to Madanyang to see Bawk and they returned together.

"Daddy, I want to take a vacation at home. My father wants me to stop nursing, but I'm not ready to stop yet if you will let me continue working."

"Of course you can have your vacation. I promised you back at Ramgarh that as soon as you found your family you could take as long a vacation as you desired. How much money do you want to draw from the bank?"

"All!" interrupted the father.

"That wouldn't be wise, would it? The country is still unsettled and the Japanese are roaming these hills. You can't possibly need four thousand rupees, or even spend a thousand rupees, for months to come. I'll give you a thousand rupees only and then if anything happens to that you won't be destitute. The rest will be safe in the bank."

I could see Bawk's eyes shine with relief. Her father muttered something but he knew of old that I was a tougher man than he and that it was no use grumbling.

I sent for Bawk quietly when he was out of the way. "I knew more about your family affairs than I ever admitted to you, Bawk. You have a definite responsibility to your father but that is settled with this gift of a thousand rupees. He can't possibly need more than that except for wrong purposes. He is able bodied and strong and far too clever at getting along for his own good. You're more than twenty-one years old and your own mistress. If you let your father force you to stop nursing before you yourself de-

sire to stop—or force you to marry some fellow whom you have
no use for—I will never forgive you. Take two weeks' vacation
at home and if you aren't back on the motor road on the fifteenth
day I'll send two Marauders to your village to escort you. If your
father tries to lock you up, you can escape out of the back window
and these men will bring you safely to us."

The 30th Division Headquarters finally moved on from Kaitik
and the 38th Division settled there immediately. Major Davison
asked me how long it would take our entire unit, patients and all,
to move from our two locations to Kaitik. Predicating my reply
on the use of the level ground at the pass, I replied that we could
complete the move in twenty-four hours.

To my vexation the level area at Kaitik was still pre-empted by
30th Division Artillery who had no intention of moving. There
was nothing left but a Chinese cavalry camp on a hillside and
some rice paddies. It was a steep climb for the nurses to carry
their barracks bags, and men were scarce for they were driving
vehicles, loading and unloading, erecting ward tents and a
kitchen. The nurses, children, and I did our best to drag bedding
to the top of the hill but broke down and had to beg our coolies
to help us. Girls put up their own parachute tents. The ward
tents were placed in the rice paddies and patients were left on
their litters on the ground.

And then it rained. Water beat through the thin parachutes
and flowed in streams through the wards. Officers and men, nurses
and patients, all were sopping wet—in January, at an altitude of
four thousand feet, twenty air miles north of the Tropic of
Cancer. I had promised the army two to five days of rain each
month during the dry season. In November and December we
had had two days of overcast weather and a few drops of rain but
now in January we were having the real thing. Our move took
thirty-six hours instead of twenty-four.

But our troubles were still not over. Though it was raining the
38th Division Chinese Field Hospital, deciding they needed a
nice long rest, unloaded swarms of patients on us while we were

frantically trying to get our own patients out of the mud. If it hadn't been for the extraordinary efficiency of our enlisted men, acquired through long experience with difficult moves, our professional work would have broken down. Our three staff sergeants, Probst, Stolec, and Mortimeyer, especially distinguished themselves.

On the ninth of January, Lieutenant Rathje, our finance officer, had but one day to complete payment of the enlisted men with Antonellis, so we obtained permission to contact them. With Little Bawk, whose home was in the valley, and two of our former Marauders, we hopped into a jeep and set out to see how far Colonel Brown's dozers had succeeded in pushing their new short cut. They were already well down the mule trail and there were tracks of a jeep beyond the dozers. So we pushed on and, after almost running over a decayed Jap in a small stream, burst out onto the plain at Panghkam. We drove into the battalion command post and discovered one of the finest, most courteous young Chinese officers I'd ever had the good fortune to meet, a Major Shu. He furnished two guides to lead Lieutenant Rathje and the two Marauders up the jungle trail to Antonellis' hospital, while he led Bawk and me around the area, showing us the wrecks of the airplane factory and letting us use his binoculars.

This time it was possible to see quite clearly that the operating-room end of my stone hospital was in ruins. But the house Tiny and I had built seemed untouched. If only one of the buildings I had built remained unscathed it could become the nucleus for rebuilding the whole plant. But I crushed my hopes as they sprang again to life. The latest Chinese G-2 information reported six thousand Japanese still in Namkham. The 10th Air Force was not done with me yet—dive-bombing was going on at that very moment—and the heavy artillery had not yet begun to shell.

Major Shu was extremely kind. He served us tea, more tea, K-ration, and yet again tea. We had been chatting in what Chinese I knew, and in what English he knew. He wasn't aware of the fact that Bawk was most proficient in Mandarin, and she was greatly amused to hear him gripe in a charming voice to his lieutenant, "What am I going to do if these people don't leave soon? I haven't anything fit to give them for dinner. There is nothing but Spam and rice!"

Major Davison was excited when he learned on our return that we had actually driven to Loiwing and asked me to reconnoiter the location with him the next day.

"Major," I said, as we drove around the Panghkam area, "this is the place for a field hospital. There are no Japs between here and the river. The 30th Division has at last captured Manwing, where the motor road debouches on the plain south of us, and the 112th Chinese Regiment holds the flank on our north. You can see that there's no danger from the nonchalance of the Chinese soldiers, wandering without guns all over the plain in search of food. The only imaginable danger would be from shelling by 150-mm. guns."

"Yes, and they would be trained primarily on the Loiwing airfield to the north and the English fort to the south," the major replied. "Furthermore, you could hide a huge hospital in the area where Major Shu has his command post, if he moved out, and you could take shelter behind the high embankment of the irrigation ditch if the Japs started to shell you."

"The map doesn't show them all as motorable," I added, "but there are five motorable roads that come together at Panghkam over which casualties could be jeeped to us. There's the motor road through Loiwing to Wanting, a road from Panghkam to the Nawngtun ferry a mile north of Namkham, a road from Panghkam to the big ferry at Mansawn, and a road through Manwing to the big Shweli suspension bridge and a road through Manwing to the south flank at Mawswi. If Namkham turns into a big battle like Myitkyina this would be the ideal spot."

We were invited to have dinner with Major Shu and found his command post full of distinguished guests, Generals Sun, Lee, Tang and their staffs and a couple of photographers. General Sun had a huge map spread out on the table and asked me a question about geography. The candid cameramen and newsreel photographer set upon us, hammer and tongs, and it was amusing to see General Sun, docile for once, allowing himself to be pushed around here and there, posing with a former missionary. The general, on the insistence of the cameramen, welcomed me back to the Namkham Valley at least fifteen times that afternoon.

During dinner we had learned that the motor road was clear at last so we completed the round trip through Manwing and back by the Burma Road to Kaitik. Knowing Colonel Bob Thompson would approve anything he recommended, Davison gave me the "all clear" to begin moving to Panghkam the next day.

"It's almost twice as far as our last move and we have many more patients," I warned. "We may need three days to complete the move."

"Take as much time as you need," Davison said.

We made it in two days. Not only our old-timers but all our new personnel were crazy to see the valley the old man had thought worth spending his life in, and they worked with a will. They even failed to complain at having to tear up the Kaitik hospital before the finishing touches had been put on it and build a new one. And because we thought the conquest of Namkham would take at least a month, we made this the best tent hospital ever. Knowing it was around somewhere, I searched and found the cement floor of the shack where Al Anderson had set up his motor department when the airplane factory had been bombed out almost five years before. On this the Burmese boys put up an excellent operating room, while the coolies put up seven ward tents.

Ever since the day the chaplain of the 20th General had told me at the Pangsau Pass how glad he was to get out of Burma, I had heard Americans complain about Burma, its climate, its customs—everything but its people, whom Americans seemed to like instinctively. They had complained in the Hukawng, at Myitkyina, and at Bhamo. They didn't like the mountains between Bhamo and Namkham. Why good Americans should be forced to fight for a country like this was beyond their comprehension. But now all was changed. Everyone who took one look at the Namkham Valley gasped and took a deep breath of fresh air.

"Gee, Doc, this valley—it's beautiful! Beautiful! No wonder you want to get back!"

"And it's rich," I would reply. "Look at those thousands of stacks of rice waiting to be threshed. Yet the people haven't planted all their fields. The best rice in the world grows in this valley."

We heard there was a bazaar still operating in Panghkam, the first bazaar we'd seen in all stricken Burma. There were only a few stray Shan women and they were completely surrounded by Chinese eagerly bargaining for their food. It looked as if there would be none left for us.

"Hello, folks," I said in Shan. "It's good to see you again. I haven't seen you for three years."

They looked at me in bewilderment.

"Don't tell me I've changed as much as all that. I know my face is wrinkled and my hair is getting gray, but I'm the 'Doctor of Nawngsang Hill' all the same!"

"Our doctor, our doctor," said one old lady, grasping my hand. "Even your mustache has gone gray!"

When they calmed down a bit we began bargaining and then the Chinese were left out in the cold.

"How much is this bunch of mustard?" asked a nurse and a Chinese officer simultaneously.

"Five rupees," she said to the officer. And then, in an undertone to the nurse, "Take it for half a rupee but pay me after the Chinese leave." And so it was with other vegetables, fruits, and rice, real Namkham Valley rice! The Chinese went off in disgust.

Thereafter the bazaar sellers saved out stuff for us and brought it right to the hospital and we gorged three times a day and in between as well. One woman had a basket of vegetables for which she wanted fifteen rupees. While Bawk was getting the money it occurred to her the woman might like a handful of salt that was left over from the mess.

"Never mind the money," gurgled the woman happily as she reached eagerly for the salt. "Take them." She held out the basket of vegetables. Bawk took two bunches, a fair exchange for the salt.

"No, take them all, take them all! It has been years since we have had enough salt to eat."

Dr. San Yee walked by, spotted one of the women, and began talking eagerly. I heard the woman saying someone or other was dead but thought nothing of it. Many must have died while we were away. An hour later I saw San Yee on duty. His face was deeply lined and he looked years older.

"Who did the woman say was dead?" I asked, shuddering a little with apprehension.

"My wife, sir. She died five months ago of malaria because no one had any medicine for her. My son is still alive."

And five months ago we had been impatiently but comfortably settled in Myitkyina curing Chinese of malaria by the hundreds, while San Yee's wife sickened and died of neglect.

On January 14 I called Boganaw, the man whose family had been blown up into the telephone wires at Myitkyina.

"I have a feeling it won't be long now until we move into Namkham," I said. "For three long years I've been inviting everyone to a big feast when we get home and I don't want to be caught without food. How about taking a foraging party to N'Bapa and buying us some chickens, pigs, and eggs?"

Boganaw was delighted. He had many friends in N'Bapa.

On the afternoon of the fifteenth Colonel Van Natta walked in.

"How would you like to move?" he asked.

"Any time, any place," I replied, trying to look pleased but expecting him to give us another flank move. "Where are we going and when do we start?"

"How about moving to Namkham?" the colonel said, a twinkle in his eye. "The 30th Division walked in this morning!"

I was positively delirious and screamed out the news to the nurses.

That night General Sliney and Colonel Brown drove in to congratulate me.

"General Sun and Colonel Van Natta are going to escort you personally into Namkham tomorrow," Sliney said. "You are to be at Manwing headquarters at ten o'clock."

I couldn't sleep that night. We were at headquarters soon after nine-thirty but General Sun had already left. Colonel Van Natta told us that the time had been changed to nine-thirty and we would have to hurry to the suspension bridge area. In front of the Manwing bazaar Colonel Van Natta found some engineers who reported that there was no bridge across the Mawswihka and that there were huge bomb craters in the center of the road. Furthermore, their own dozers hadn't arrived. Van Natta told me to walk on beyond the Mawswihka to meet General Sun and he turned back to beg the use of Colonel Brown's dozers.

I found General Sun near what was left of the great suspension bridge. He had the two cameramen with him and they photographed our meeting.

"Where are the pontoon boats operating, sir?" I asked.

"There are no boats."

"We could cross by the Mansawn ferry."

"There might be snipers beyond."

So there had been no intention of walking into Namkham at all. Just picture taking! The conqueror of Namkham welcoming the Burma Surgeon home! I detest having my picture taken but it had long since been impressed on me that if the army thought they wanted pictures of you, you submitted. I would have gone anywhere to oblige General Sun and the photographers, without having a pretended trip to Namkham thrown at me.

On our way back we met General Sliney who hadn't been informed of the change in time and had sincerely desired to escort me into Namkham, since he was the only old-timer left besides myself who had walked out with Stilwell. He was out of humor at not being informed of the change, and when he discovered no actual crossing had been planned he became purple in the face and went on to the suspension bridge to cool off.

Staff Sergeants Probst and Stolec and Dr. San Yee were also in need of calming, so I suggested we explore the jeep road just to see if we could reach the ferry at Mansawn. As it turned out, on the way we passed within a hundred yards of a wandering Jap but we proved that jeeps could reach the river. Then we worked off the rest of our impatience with a game of baseball.

On the morning of January 17, 1945, I spent some time with air force engineers exploring the possibilities of a C-47 airstrip nearby. Just as I was returning to camp a jeep hurried up and an officer informed me that this time they were really intending to escort me to Nankham but that since they had to ride horses, they couldn't allow my personnel to follow me. I must be at the location of our 155-mm. guns in fifteen minutes. I decided to take Stolec, Probst, San Yee, and Ba Saw with me anyway and let them trail along on foot after the horses.

At the trysting place I found General Sun and his staff poring over maps and I noticed his finger tracing a path from the spot where we then were to the Mansawn ferry.

"You can drive a jeep to that ferry, sir," I said. "I drove there myself yesterday."

For a full fifteen minutes Sun lectured his staff because they hadn't known the road was jeepable. Then he ordered me to lead the train of jeeps.

We drove straight to the site of the big ferry and then noticed no one was following us. Probst went back to make inquiries and learned that some Chinese soldiers had led the general and his party off to a different, smaller ferry crossing. We hurried along but they were out of sight and it took us half an hour to find where they had crossed to a large island in the middle of the stream. We reached the other branch, however, before they finished crossing and the Chinese gave me priority. Newsreels cranked and the cameras clicked, as General Sun welcomed me to the valley all over again. Then, without waiting for the rest of my party, we walked out of the village and started across some paddies.

"This is the road to Namkham over here," I pointed.

"The general is going to Nawngkong first, to see General Tang," an aide explained.

"I'll wait by that big banian tree," I said.

"Don't move till I come back," the general said.

"Okay, sir."

We waited for an hour, then started toward Nawngkong to find out what had happened. On the edge of the village a cavalry-man met us and pointed to where the general's party had taken to horses and was heading across the paddies direct for Namkham. That released me from my promise to sit, and we marched down the road on the double-quick in an effort to catch up. San Yee and the rest of my party had taken an even more direct route to Namkham. Since his wife was dead San Yee was even more determined to see his son and he was letting no generals or lieutenant colonels force him to go slowly. All we saw of him was a small patch of dust. I was just as anxious as he to see what was left of my baby, the hospital I had built up in Namkham, but with all the brass hats, photographers, and correspondents around I had to bite my nails and do it in style and like it.

Namkham! There was nothing left of the poorer Chinese quarter of the town, although the wealthier Chinese traders' houses were still intact. Occasional houses had been destroyed by bombs but for the most part the dilapidated condition of the Namkham houses, as of those in all the villages of the valley, was due to the Shans themselves. Without being taught, they had learned dispersion. They knew that if they remained in the towns they would be bombed, so they pulled down the essential parts of their houses and moved out bag and baggage to the rice fields, where each built himself a tiny grass shack as far from his neighbor as he could get.

After we crossed the Namkhamhpong River the destruction caused by bombs began to appear. And then I noticed a peculiar thing. When the British first took over the Shan States sixty years before, Shans had ambushed and killed an English captain. As a reminder to the Shans that they must not do these things, the government buried the captain in the exact center of town beneath a huge banian tree and built a stone tomb over him, surrounding the grave with a wire fence fastened to concrete posts. A thousand-pound bomb had fallen right into the captain's tomb. Only the two concrete posts at the foot of the grave remained. Had the air force also destroyed Gordon Junior's grave? I was more anxious than ever to push on and see.

On the other side of the open area had been the great monastery of Namkham, the center of the town's Buddhism, a monastery so sacred that I had entered it only once in twenty years, and then with my shoes off out of respect for the religion of other people. It was in complete ruins, but out of the ruins still stood the great image of Gautama, the Buddha, almost untouched, the mosaic on the back of his throne still gorgeous in its beauty. Christians will read many meanings into the freak destructions of their churches in this war. Perhaps we will concede the Shans also the privilege of making something out of their great Buddha, sitting serene and unmoved amid the havoc of war.

Generals Sun, Tang, and Lee were inspecting the wreckage of the monastery. General Sliney and the staff were resting outside the abandoned shop where the nurses used to buy their silks and satins with money saved up from the pitiful stipends of sixty cents a month which was all I could afford to give them while they were in training. Probst, Stolec, and I, perforce, sat too. An hour passed and the generals reappeared. I had been sitting within a mile of the hospital for an hour, unable to go farther.

Now, surely, the wait was over. I stood up expectantly. But then General Sun sat down. Orderlies ran hither and yon, bringing tea, biscuits, and candy. I managed to choke one biscuit down. General Sliney watched me sympathetically. He was as eager as I to see what was left of my hospital.

At the end of the second hour General Sun decided he would push on. We passed by the all but ruined bazaar buildings; the Namkham bazaar had been the biggest and most colorful in the Federated Shan States. I had hoped the air force had had sense enough to destroy the awful post-office building but it was untouched, an ugly living monument to the unimaginative architectural ability of the Public Works Department. A battalion of Chinese were passing us now and they had impressed some natives into portering for them. I stopped. "Well, well, folks," I said in Shan, "how are you making it?"

They glanced at me, looked again, threw down their loads and grasped my hands. "Our doctor, our doctor, our doctor!" The newsreel camera began to grind.

General Sun turned to look, covered with smiles. "They recognize you, do they?"

"Shucks, they'd better! I've taken care of them since they were pups!"

As soon as I could tear myself away we marched on, waylaid frequently by other small groups. And then we were climbing the mission hill at last. At the foot of the hill was a sign in Japanese: "HEADQUARTERS, NAMKHAM GARRISON, IMPERIAL JAPANESE ARMY." In three years the Japs had not cut a weed. Branches of trees shattered by bombs were strewn across the road. We had to climb warily lest the Japs had laid booby traps. The center of the hospital gateway was occupied by the crater of a thousand-pound bomb. Other craters were everywhere. But the southwest corner of the hospital was intact. Again I was officially welcomed back to Namkham for the sake of the newsreel man, who posed

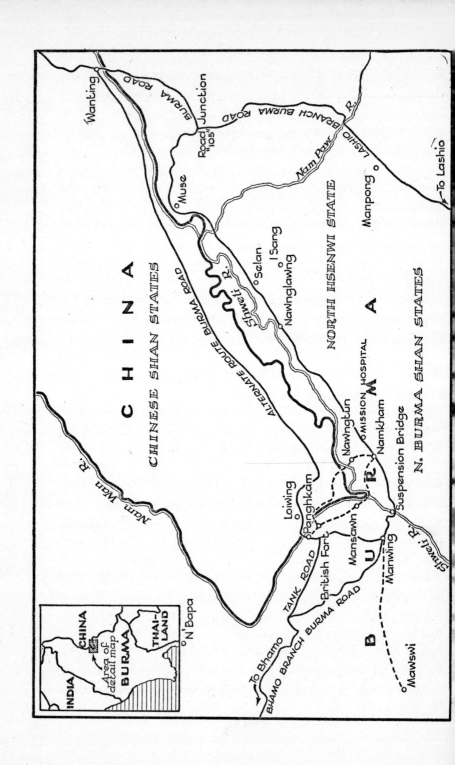

me several times in the way to demonstrate best the feelings he thought I had at the time. All I wanted was for them all to go away and leave me alone. At last the photographers were tired and the generals, exhausted, went away to rest. General Sliney, God bless him, deliberately chose a different route for his exploration and left me alone with Stolec.

A small feeling of satisfaction came strangely over me as I walked around. A thousand-pound bomb had struck within five feet of the wall of the men's wing, but all it had accomplished was the destruction of a three-foot pillar between two windows on the ground floor; the second story wasn't hurt. But the most extraordinary thing was that either God or the air force seemed to have decided that I was to practice no more gynecology or obstetrics, for the men's wards were all up except for the bathrooms and the women's wards were all down—except for the bathrooms. The maternity wards were completely destroyed but the children's ward and the ward for newborn infants were still there. My office and one private room were untouched except for bullet holes. The operating-room section and the women's wing were destroyed completely, but it had taken three direct hits and ten near misses to do it.

The iron roof had been torn almost completely off and what sheets of iron remained were full of countless holes from machine-gun strafing. Even the undamaged wards were deep in litter. Unwilling to sleep on teakwood floors, the Japs had built bamboo platforms a foot off the floor. In three years the place hadn't once been swept.

Out in the patio one of Tiny's red roses was bravely blooming as if to show the war was over at last.

I went over to the nurses' home. One of the front-door pillars had been smashed, the ballroom floor had collapsed, the roof was full of holes, and everywhere was Japanese filth; but otherwise the building was unharmed.

Then I started my search for Gordon Junior's grave. I feared the worst when I saw that the enemy had completely disposed of the banian tree beside him. It was incredible that the weeds could grow so high even in three years. Finally I found the grave, completely untouched. Roses were blooming in spite of the neglect, and beside the grave our poinsettias were in full flower. I felt much better.

Only one of the cottages which we used for private patients had been wrecked. The other cottages and the old dirty hospital building to which I had first come twenty-two years before and which I had often threatened to burn down were still there and immediately usable. The machine-gunners hadn't missed these roofs either; there wasn't a single roof on the entire mission hill that hadn't been riddled.

My other buildings were also usable. The damage to the stone church was slight, but the wallboards and the partitions of the house where Tiny and I had lived for eighteen years, and those of every other house in both compounds, had been torn off by the Japanese to build sheds and lean-to's.

On the Kachin compound was complete devastation. Only one small cottage and the schoolgirls' dormitory could ever be repaired. What our air force had not destroyed the enemy had.

Now that I'd inspected all the buildings of our working plant, I was free to visit the little cottage of stone Tiny and I had built for ourselves and used for two short years. The Japs had torn off all my copper screening from the doors, windows, front and back porches. They had torn off the paneled doors of our built-in closets. There was a hole in the dining-room floor. Not a stick of furniture anywhere. Then I opened the bathroom door. The Japanese had broken the toilet bowl loose from its moorings. The bathtub was gone. The washbowl had been torn out and was set into Tiny's neat closet on the back porch.

General Sliney obtained permission for me and my party to separate from the rest and go back to Panghkam alone. At the foot of the hill, in the ruins of the recently burned Christian Kachin homes, were the twisted iron of five of our iron beds and our bathtub, the enamel completely destroyed. I was told later that the Japanese had used them for the comfort of the Korean and Japanese prostitutes, whom in true Japanese style they had installed in Christian homes. The first Chinese shell thrown into the area, a phosphorus shell, had lit squarely in the area and burned both houses to the ground.

San Yee had been lost all this time. Ba Saw undertook to go find him in the rice fields to the southwest of Namkham where he had located his brother, cousins, and the son he had never seen. It took half an hour to pry San Yee loose from his son but when he came his eyes were shining and his face wreathed in smiles. "Such a nice big boy with bright red cheeks and so fat!" he chuckled. Ba Saw and the American boys were just as enthusiastic. San Yee had something to live for again.

The bamboo raft was just landing as we reached the river. A young Shan woman and a fair red-cheeked girl were aboard. The woman stared, threw down her baskets, jerked off her turban, and prostrated herself in front of me in the complete *wai*.

"*Goang Hpra, Goang Tra!* The grace of God and of the Law! It's our doctor! *Goang Hpra, Goang Tra! Goang Hpra, Goang Tra!*" and to my red-faced embarrassment she kept on *wai*ing me in spite of all I could do.

"Surely you know Dr. San Yee?" I asked, when I had calmed her down somewhat. She looked and then prostrated herself in front of him and went through the whole process again. Then suddenly she stopped and her face sobered.

"Your wife is dead!" she whispered.

"Yes, I know. But my son is alive!"

We crossed the ferry and it was darkening as we entered Mansawn. We took a different path from the one we had come over in the morning. A hundred yards ahead of us a Shan was climbing over a fence into his garden.

"Will this road lead us to the great monastery?" I called. He glanced at us as we approached but couldn't believe a man in uniform could be talking Shan so did not answer. I repeated my question twice before he realized I was talking to him, and then he answered yes. We were now only twenty yards away. Suddenly his eyes focused intently on me.

"Why, it's the doctor of Nawngsang Hill! It's been three years since you went away. Three years, hee, hee, hee! Three years, ho, ho, ho! Three years, ha, ha, ha!" he laughed hysterically and then his voice broke. He was still muttering "three years!" to himself, again and again, as we turned the corner and passed out of sight and hearing.

On our return the girls crowded around to hear the news.

"When are we going to move to Namkham?" they demanded, excitedly.

"Not until Major Davison says okay," I replied. "He knows how anxious you all are to go. It won't be long. But Dr. San Yee and ten coolies can certainly go over tomorrow and stay and clean up the nurses' home for you."

Dr. San Yee had just set out by the ferry route when Major Davison appeared.

"Let's go over and reconnoiter," he said.

"By the ferry?"

"No, the engineers have already thrown a pontoon bridge across. We can drive over."

We hurried. Davison hunted for booby traps and made inquiries about the disposition of troops. "I don't see why you can't come over right away," he said. "Your only danger will be from the Japanese 150-mm. rifle and you've been shelled before. Your whole hill is dotted with dugouts and trenches for you to jump into."

It was after twelve when we got back to camp.

"All the original unit nurses and Burmese boys will leave immediately for Namkham," I shouted. "Trucks back up to nurses' quarters immediately for baggage. Probst and Stolec and all Burmese coolies on board! Everyone else will follow tomorrow with the patients."

I was too excited to eat. The girls, convinced that Major Davison wouldn't hold them back, were already packed up and ready. Within half an hour we were away on the last lap. Then, for the first time in many weary months, the girls began to sing at the tops of their voices as we rode along.

I had thought I was excited but I was calmness itself compared to the nurses as they jumped out of the jeeps and ran into their home, tripping over the heaps and piles of junk the coolies had been clearing away. Each of them ran to the particular corner where her bed had been three years before and dumped her musette bag there, as one who would stake out a claim to a gold mine. Then they began to explore. They were delighted that the destruction wasn't more extensive. One girl found, in a bathroom, the first sheet of typewritten notes on anatomy I had been teaching her when we left Namkham for the Shan States front. Suddenly there was a burst of laughter from several of the nurses and they began to tease a companion who, running to a corner of the attic, had found there just what she hoped to find: a bundle of love letters from her sweetheart of three years before.

Then they ran out to the jeeps and brought the worn-out brooms we had looted months before in Momauk and set to work with a will. Soon they raised such clouds of dust that it was impossible to breathe. They tied handkerchiefs over their noses and continued to sweep but I ran out, to find that the coolies had stopped work to enjoy the delight of the nurses at their homecoming.

"Come on, let's go!" I shouted. "I promised we'd be ready for new admissions at noon tomorrow and we have three hundred old patients to bed down before then. Burmese boys, clean out the cottages! Half the coolies to the old wooden hospital! The rest, clean out what's left of the stone hospital wards! The nurses will cook our supper!"

Everyone became infected with my mad frenzy, and tons of Japanese dirt and trash began to fly out from the windows and doors. It wasn't safe to walk anywhere for fear of having a load land on one's head and shoulders. My old white-bearded Punjabi sweeper, who had adopted me in Myitkyina, had stowed away in one of the trucks and was standing by with a forlorn doglike expression on his face, fearful that I would make him work with the others rather than fix my own quarters for me.

"All right, Santa Claus!" I said. "Come along and I'll show you where I'm going to sleep."

Santa began to grin and trotted after me good-naturedly as I led him over to the stone cottage.

"I'm going to sleep here in the little front bedroom where my two sons used to sleep," I told him. "The other bedroom is to be for my guests."

His beard indicated that he was smiling from ear to ear. With a profound salaam he set to work and soon it wasn't safe to breathe in my house either.

Early Friday morning we set to work again keeping half a step ahead of the patients as they came over by the truckload. Heroically, the nurses bedded down patients on the wooden floors, saving the cots for wards with cement floors. Then they tagged the patients' foreheads with adhesive tape to correspond with their new positions, renumbered their temperature charts, and began dosing them with medicine and putting on fresh dressings. I must have walked ten miles that day without leaving our compounds, for the Shans had heard we were back and had turned out three hundred strong with dahs, shovels, and bamboo baskets.

"These people are from Manhong, Nawngsang, and Manhkam villages," said their respective headmen.

"Good! We need you!" I replied. "I will pay grownups one rupee per day and children proportionately."

"You won't pay us anything. You've been away three years and we had given up hope of your ever coming back. The Japs forced us to labor every day for nothing. Now for once we are going to do something just because we want to do it and not for money. Every village around Namkham is going to give you three days of free labor. There will be another group of villagers in tomorrow."

I felt like a candidate for president of the United States. All the Christians grasped my hands, while the Buddhists insisted on the complete *wai*. Then a group of girls ran up and I saw Hseng Hun, the Shan girl Tiny and I had put through the English high school. Excitedly I threw my arms around her and gave her a big squeeze while bystanders applauded and her mother stood by smiling delightedly.

"Are you married yet?" I asked.

"No," Hseng Hun replied demurely.

"What the Sam Hill do you think I put you through school for?" I demanded.

Paw Hpying Awn, the coolie I had trained to be a master mason and who had been the chief of those who built the hospitals, nurses' home, our cottage, and the church in Bhamo, pushed his way through the crowd, his eyes streaming with tears, his mouth set in a broad grin. I almost kissed him.

"I want you to work for me again. We must rebuild this hospital. Will you help me?"

"*Aw hka.* Yes, sir," was all the reply he could produce that day.

"I wish someone would tell Sein Hla Tha, the old headmaster, and Chief Nurse E Hla and the rest of my old staff that I'm home again," I said to everyone at large.

Koi's old father and mother came up and I drew them aside and asked Big Bill to give them two hundred rupees on account. Even a group of Shans who hadn't cared tuppence for me in the old days came to shake hands as if I were their long lost brother. I walked on, watching the villagers at work.

"That's he! That's our old doctor!" said a twelve-year-old to her younger sister.

"How he has aged!" exclaimed one after another of the old friends.

In the middle of the morning the new patients began to arrive to add to the melee, although I had set noon as the earliest permissible time. Dr. San Yee's brother Hsang Hsam, who had been prime minister of Hsenwi State, his cousin Hkun Hsam Myat, the lord mayor's son, and their cousin Hkun Myat Hsa, a barristerat-law, also called to pay their respects. They looked starved and haggard. The Japanese had been offended at their non-co-operation and had deposed them, forcing them to relinquish the title of *hkun* or prince and compelling them to start truck gardening. With them were San Yee's sister-in-law and son. No wonder everyone was delighted with the boy. The nurses began to strive for his affections. Looking at the beautiful girl who was his aunt, I began at last to place San Yee's charming wife whose name I had not previously recognized. He had really suffered a great loss.

I tried to organize the work of clearing away the rubble, saving up piles of stone and gravel for future use so that when bull-dozers came to fill in the bomb craters they wouldn't bury stone that we could use again. It was a nerve-racking ordeal. In the middle of giving instructions in Shan to the coolies, American officers would stroll up to congratulate me on my return. As I chatted hurriedly with them a nurse would break into the middle of a sentence with a demand in Burmese for instructions. Before long I couldn't be certain what language would pour out when I opened my mouth. I began to talk in Shan to nurses and in Bur-mese to Americans. Then the presents began to arrive. By Shan custom a present must be made in your home, the fruit, vege-table, or rice being laid on a table. But I had no table. Hour after hour I had to drop my work and walk to the kitchen, for-mally accept the gifts, and try to find some container to hold them.

Saturday morning the engineers drove in a dozer which I might use straight through the twenty-four hours. I didn't dare trust the bossing of the bulldozer crew to anyone else. Every minute of the day before, I had been planning just how the dozer could fill craters without pushing the remnants of the hospital down or burying precious materials that could be used in rebuilding. The dozer boys and I spent the day together. By the time they left, all the important craters around the big buildings had been filled and our roads cleared, widened, and in use again. The dozer was still filling craters farther away when I fell asleep.

Sunday morning Sein Hla Tha walked up.

"How did you learn I was back?" I asked.

"That mason, Paw Hpying Awn, ran all the way up the hill to tell me," he said. "We have been living in the woods behind Oilaw ever since the Japs came."

"How are Rosie and the children?"

"Rosie is well. She had a little son nine months ago but during the rainy season he suddenly died without anything seeming to be wrong with him."

There went another dream. After all my operations she had finally had a son, only to have him die before I could come back and take care of him.

"I heard about the boy's birth in Myitkyina. You left there the day before we captured the airfield."

"Yes, I was there. The Japanese forced me to act as interpreter and took me all the way to the Mogaung Valley. At one time I was only ten miles away from the American lines. They paid me eight annas Japanese money a day and my ration was rice and salt. The villagers received only rice. I was tired and sick but I couldn't get away from them to the Americans. Finally a Kachin showed me a jungle path the Japs didn't know about and I ran away and walked all the way back to Namkham. The Japanese threatened to burn down my house, as they threatened to burn down all the rice stacks in the fields, because the Shans heard the Americans were coming and refused to turn over any more rice. But they pulled out so suddenly, when they knew they were surrounded, that they didn't have time to carry out their threats."

"Have any of our people been shot by the Japs or raped?" I asked.

"I don't know of any shootings myself," he replied, "but an officer raped the beautiful Kachin lady teacher in Mr. Sword's school and she poisoned herself with opium the next morning."

"Is Little Bawk's father all right?"

"He was, the last I knew."

"Can you send a messenger to tell him she's back and wants to see him?"

"I'll send one in the morning."

"When are you coming back to stay?"

"Will they let us come back?"

"Certainly. You don't live on the main road. The villagers who live on the Burma Road can't come back yet, for some of their villages are being used by the army. But all of the Christians can come back and if anything is said I will tell them that I need you to work for me, and I do! I can't rebuild without all the workers who worked for me before and I need you teachers, Kachin as well as Shan, to act as foremen for me. I can't do all this myself; there's a war on!"

"What about the preachers and the schools?"

"As soon as the army gives me permission to bring back Dr. Ba Saw's wife and family from India, we're going to start a little school on our own. It will be done without government assistance. The nurses and I will pay the teachers' salaries out of our own pockets. Perhaps some of my officers and those of other American units will help. As for preachers, that will have to wait. That doesn't mean we're not going to have church services. Already officers of four different American units have come to me begging me to repair the church before I repair the hospital so they can have a nice place to worship. The army has repaired the church I built in Bhamo and is using it as a church for all denominations. That's what I'm going to do here. When the church is repaired chaplains of every denomination, including Catholics and Hebrews, will be invited to conduct services here. I couldn't do that in peacetime because the Baptists would have yelled. But this is war and I'm the boss of this hill!"

That night we had our sing in the stone cottage. Though the piano had been stolen, the nurses sat cross-legged on the floor as in the days of old and it was nice to have Sein Hla Tha's baritone voice with us.

The next day Ai Pan, the Shan pastor, his new daughter-in-law

Nurse Htawnt, and Hkam Gaw, who had taken care of John and Sterling, suddenly appeared. I threw an arm about each girl and squeezed, and I mean hard. Htawnt laughed and laughed and Hkam Gaw cried and cried. It was fifteen minutes before I could get loose and even then I couldn't stop Hkam Gaw's crying.

"We thought you were dead," she sobbed. "Three times the Japanese announced they had captured you. Once they said they had captured you and thirty Burmese nurses in the Hukawng Valley. Then they said they had captured you and five nurses and were taking you to Rangoon. The last time they just mentioned they had caught you and put you at forced coolie labor at Sagaing and I knew you couldn't stand that. It was only a few weeks ago that the airplanes dropped leaflets prepared by the O.W.I. saying that you and the nurses were all safe and already in the Bhamo area with the Chinese and American armies and we knew the Japanese had been lying."

"Come over to the house and I'll show you the family pictures," I said hurriedly, hoping to stop the sobs.

I drew out the pictures of Tiny, of Leslie and Weston, of John and Sterling. Hkam Gaw sat on the floor and spread the pictures out on my cot. When she came to Sterling's picture she pressed her face down on it and began sobbing again as if her heart would break. This was no good. I turned to Htawnt, a lovely Shan girl who, to my regret, had not gone out with us.

"Who told you you could go and get married?" I scolded fiercely.

Htawnt and her husband smiled. Nobody was scared of me any more.

"And how many offspring have you produced?" I demanded.

"One already and I am producing another at the moment."

"I'll say you are! I left you a young girl and here you are an old woman already!"

We continued to rail at each other until Hkam Gaw began to return to normal.

Things were happening every day and all day long. Ma Hkun,

the first girl trained by me to become head nurse at Namkham, came down from the mountains, children and all, and with her was Ma Nu. Seven months' pregnant she had walked twenty-five miles on mountain paths in one day just to welcome me home. Ma Nu, of Htawnt's class, was distinctly unhappy.

"You didn't come, and you didn't come," she complained. "My folks insisted on marrying me to a man I didn't want but I held off until I gave up hope of your ever returning. And now that you're back I'm pregnant and I can't start nursing with you again!" and Ma Nu also dissolved in tears.

My return was causing more tears than laughter.

"Listen, woman. We're going forward soon. Go on home and stay till the baby is born and then, when you hear we're back in Namkham, get a servant girl and come down and start nursing again."

"Will you take me?" she asked, astonished, her tears stopping and her eyes beginning to shine.

"Of course I will, you little fool! You're one of the best nurses we ever had."

Colonel Petersen flew down all the way from Myitkyina to congratulate me on my return. We were sitting on the front steps of the cottage chatting when around the corner appeared Ai Lun, my medical student, and—yes, there was E Hla! I ran past Ai Lun and threw my arms around her.

Colonel Petersen delicately withdrew and we all went in and jabbered for an hour.

"How many children do you have?" I demanded.

"Two of my own and the little orphan girl we adopted," E Hla replied.

"Are you coming back to work?"

"We came down to inquire if you wanted me."

"Silly girl, why didn't you bring the children and all your possessions down at once? You knew I'd want you."

"It will take a truck to bring us all down."

"You can have it. Where are my two Irish terriers with the pedigree from Ireland two pages long?"

"They took sick and died," she replied, looking away.

The next day at dinner Little Bawk was seething, as if she had something on her chest, so I took my messkit over to a corner to eat with her.

"E Hla says she lied to you yesterday about the two dogs because she thought you couldn't stand the truth. What actually happened was this. The Japanese were extremely provoked when they failed to capture you here. When they learned that Buddy and Podgy were your dogs they hung them up by the neck to a tree and split their bodies open while they were still alive."

I stopped eating.

In the evening E Hla brought her whole family to sit by the fire and talk. With her was Hkam Yee, one of the former teachers in our middle school who had served with our unit at the Shan States front and was in Selan when the Japanese came in.

"They caught Pastor Paw Hkam and his son and executed them in front of us all," he said. "The executioner's bullet broke Paw Hkam's hip and he fell to the ground. Then the executioner stepped up and slowly hacked off his head with a dull sword. When Paw Hkam was dead I heard the Japanese commander say they were going to execute all the people who had worked in your unit. They didn't know I was one of them. So I took off into the woods and warned all the others and we hid for months until there was a new commander."

People of all races had come to welcome me back. But it wouldn't be official without a British welcome. I was therefore delighted to see a jeep drive to the door and a British major general climb down—Major General Cavell, chief of all the anti-malarial work of India. He had come to Namkham once just before the fall of Burma, but I was at the front and we didn't meet. Now, hearing that I was at home again, he flew all the way down from Ledo just to extend a formal welcome. Cavell did me the honor to stay with me overnight and we had a long conversation, during which we talked about the future of Burma. I was surprised and delighted to find that he concurred in a good many of my ideas. This was all the more important to me because Cavell had once been invited to become inspector general of civil hospitals for Burma.

On Tuesday, the twenty-third, General Cannon came in to congratulate me.

"Well, Doc," he said, "what do you want to do now? Remain here in Namkham permanently?"

"Sir," I said, "we're in the army now. I have no choice as to what I will or will not do. But if I do have a choice I want to stay with combat until combat's mission in Burma has been completed. I was in combat with the Chinese troops in Burma before General Stilwell himself. The unit has been under combat ever since, although under loan to S.O.S. at Ramgarh. I would feel badly if we were transferred to S.O.S. before combat's mission is completed. After that, to be frank, I would like a station hospital assignment on the Burma Road with installations, say, at Namkham, Kutkai, Wanting, and even at Chefang and Mangshih which are Shan States in China. The engineers, S.O.S., and convoy drivers will need them. I'm conceited enough to feel we would do better at that assignment than any other American unit, for we know the languages and diseases of the country and would be happy as well. If our unit could combine such an assignment with a bit of U.N.R.R.A. medical reconstructive work for the people, we would be happiest of all."

"But if you remain with combat you will have to move forward," the general warned.

"I realize that, sir. But none of us expected to remain in Namkham permanently after our first arrival. We all expected to push on."

"Of course some of your personnel will have to remain here to guard the place and supervise the rebuilding. You must start rebuilding at once!"

"Sir, I accept that as an order. We have already begun to rebuild." I couldn't keep my delight from showing. I had thought I might have to beg for permission to rebuild. "But in order to rebuild in wartime we will need a lot of engineer supplies," I added.

"What engineer supplies will you need?" the general inquired, cagily.

"Cement and iron and stuff like that," I replied boldly.

"Certainly you will need cement. The engineers won't be able to give you much, of course, but they undoubtedly will give you some."

Was I getting the breaks again? An hour later I was sure I was. Lieutenant General Wheeler, formerly commanding S.O.S. in India and now on S.E.A.C. staff, also flew in to congratulate me. With him was Colonel Hirschfield of S.O.S.

"You're going to rebuild, aren't you?" the general asked.

I explained about General Cannon's remarks and my statement about cement.

"I told Colonel Hirschfield on the flight down that he must supply you with everything you need."

"That's an order, Colonel!" I said, turning to Hirschfield.

Colonel Greene of the engineers looked over the buildings. "Doc," he said, "why did you study medicine?"

A note came from Boganaw saying he had secured twenty-six pigs, a cow, and a hundred and fifty chickens and would be on the road on Wednesday. I promptly sent out invitations to everybody from General Sultan down to come to a feast and entertainment on Thursday afternoon to celebrate our homecoming. Then I scouted around for Chinese, Shan, and Burmese cooks so everyone would find some dish to his taste. The American boys cooked steaks and creamed potatoes and made delicious pies.

And then, just as everyone was frantically preparing for the great evening, an avalanche of newsreel cameras, with sound and radio-recording apparatus, and sixty correspondents fell upon us. We had planned Burmese and Chinese dances in which the nurses were to take part and all our Karen personnel were singing ancient Karen songs. The newsreel men wouldn't be able to photograph these at night so we had to stop everything at two o'clock and put on an extra show for them. Repeat after repeat was necessary until everyone was satisfied. People were beginning to eat before we were done.

I had expected some three hundred Shan guests, a hundred and fifty Kachins and, if lucky, about three hundred Americans. As it turned out we fed sixteen hundred people—or tried to. Many went away empty or half-filled. The Shans had for days been welcoming us with open arms, and according to Shan custom this was my special dinner to them. The Kachins, once a year, put on a great dance called a *manau* which combines sex, religion, and war. The Japanese were so afraid of them, however, that they forbade the Kachins to hold a *manau* and it had been three years since the last one. The Kachins were uncertain what the Chinese and Americans would do to them if they had the big dance and were intending to postpone it further when they heard I had come home. That gave them an idea. If they had the *manau* under my auspices, they were sure nobody would interfere. I regarded it as a great compliment to their knowledge of my tolerance that they were so certain I would permit this heathen ceremony on Christian ground; but I was appalled when I saw some three hundred and sixty Kachins come in from the mountains to the west and another hundred and fifty from the mountains to the east where the Japanese patrols were still operating.

The greatest compliment of the day, however, was the arrival of whole villages of Palongs, timid Buddhist mountaineers. To have the Palongs pass through the Chinese lines in order to welcome us home was a compliment indeed. I posed for a photo·

graph with the Senior Buddhist Abbot of the Namkham Valley.

But the guests of honor—the American officers, Chinese officers of field rank, and the sixty correspondents who were following the first convoy through to China—were late. General Sun
at the last moment had invited them all to a party celebrating the
arrival of the convoy. To make matters worse, there were, as the
news broadcasters admitted, still two Japanese snipers with rifles
on the road. What the broadcasters neglected to state was that
the snipers' rifles were 150-mm. rifles! So the generals were fighting a war and Sun's party also was late. I gave up hopes of their
coming at all, and since I already had two brigadier generals,
Sliney of the artillery and Pick who built the Ledo Road, I decided to start dinner with the twenty guests who had arrived. We
had no sooner sat down when the others poured in, General
Cannon with them. Still we were minus the three chief Chinese
generals, Sun, Lee, and Tang.

I suggested the usual toasts: to the Chinese First Army, con-
querors of Namkham; to the artillery, the best part of the Chinese
Army; to the liaison officers; to the tanks; to the engineers who
built the Road; to the pipeline; to S.O.S.; to the convoy; to Generals Sultan and Stilwell. But I brought the house down with
my last toast: "To the 10th Air Force and their precision bombing of the Namkham hospital!" Everyone shouted *"Kambei!*
Bottoms up!"

The only place big enough for the entertainment was the upstairs floor of the nurses' home. When Colonel Greene saw the
number of people crowding upstairs he began to feel for a moment that perhaps I was right for having studied medicine instead of engineering, but after careful examination of the gigantic
timbers on which the upper floor rested he walked right up with
the rest of the crowd.

Having welcomed the U.S. Army to that first Christmas in
Burma at Ningam, I now welcomed the army to Namkham and
told the guests I hoped that I was the only American soldier to
return home and find everything he owned destroyed by his own

air force! We had prepared some authentic items. The Karen singing—all the girls in adorable Karen costumes—was the real thing and very beautiful with its close harmony. Nurses put on a parody of a Chinese dance, dressed in modern Chinese clothes which they had made from torn silk parachutes. Princess Louise and M.T. Lu did solo Burmese dances and M.T. Lu a duo dance with a Burmese boy. This dancing, too, was authentic. Two pretty Kachin nurses sang a duet. They were suffering from stage fright but their gorgeous Kachin clothes, heavy with silver plaques, and their beautiful faces made them an immense success. The prime minister had secured expert Shan male dancers who put on a series of skillful sword dances with two swords, which made the front-line spectators wish they'd taken standing room in the back after all. The rest of the program was just for fun. But the crowd had to go outside for the last number, the most authentic of all: the great Kachin *manau* dance with two hundred dancers.

The Kachins had fenced off a large area of the football ground. In the center were two *nat* poles, reminiscent of the totem poles of the American Indians. All the men were armed with drawn swords and with rifles or muzzle-loading shotguns on their backs. All, men and women, were a bit tight. Two chiefs, who outranked all others, had on high feathered headdresses and led the dance. Between the *nat* poles were the musicians playing on native pipes, gongs, cymbals, and drums. The music was weirdly exciting, with a powerful rhythm. In long rows they danced back and forth, sometimes like a snake dance. To an unsophisticated observer the steps were all the same, but I had seen *manaus* done for fun before and had heard stories of the unfettered *manaus* in the animist areas. Whether these Kachins would go to the usual extremes or tone the dance down because they were on Christian land I could not know.

Flashlight bulbs were exploding and radio-recording men were at work in the midst of the dancers, who tolerated them unconcernedly, grateful for the protection the U.S. Army gave them. But five or six correspondents, who had been tight and noisy all evening, decided they would show the Kachins how their *manau* looked to a foreigner and, jumping into the enclosure, began to interfere with the dance. I lost no time in gruffly ordering them out of the ring and insisting that the sober correspondents keep them out! It would seem that correspondents aren't accustomed to reading any but their own writings, for these men should have known that a Kachin in a trance is nothing to be played with; these two hundred Kachins were in a religious, sexual, alcoholic war trance, the first they had indulged in after three years of abstinence.

But I had to leave early. A Chungking Radio broadcaster, who was too much of a rugged individualist to record while others were recording, had insisted on a midnight séance and I had to order the tired girls and boys out again. By the time he was done with me I was stammering like a Sunday-school child reciting his first poem.

That afternoon word came that Little Bawk's father, hearing she was safe, had started down the mountain from his home in I Sang village to greet her, only to be refused passage by Chinese outposts. It was unreasonable of me to be irritated, for there was a war on and the Chinese, never omniscient, couldn't know that this man had been a constant thorn in the flesh of the Japanese. But after all the girls had gone through for the Chinese Army, I felt they ought to have recognized the father of a girl who had nursed so many of them. Major Lee ran at my call and wrote out a beautiful Chinese pass for my signature. The Kachin chief of Oilaw produced two guides. My two Marauders jumped to their guns and set off with Bawk to fetch her father down the hill in style.

Just as we sat down to the great dinner an excited voice screamed for me. "Daddy, Daddy, Father is here!"

Maru Gam is the only Kachin I've ever known with the spunk to stand up to an American missionary and tell him just what he thinks of him. Older than I and the father of twelve, he looked about thirty-five. He walked up to me with friendly dignity.

There was no gushing about how glad he was to see me back. For the moment, at least, he didn't give a hoot about my return. The person he was rejoiced to see was his daughter Maru Bawk, Little Bawk, and he didn't care who knew it.

The difference between the fathers of the two Bawks was very apparent. Not once did Maru Gam ask either Bawk or me how much salary I had been paying her or how much money she had in the bank. On the contrary.

"Daughter," he said, "you've been away from home a long time. You must be badly in need of spending money. Here's twenty rupees for a start."

Embarrassedly Bawk told him she didn't need it. She'd been saving up money for him!

Not once did he ask her to give up nursing. Not once did he complain about his treatment at the hands of the Japs, though for several months they had been so eager to catch him that he had had to sneak out of the village at night and march a hundred miles across the mountains to hide, east of the Salween River, until the hue and cry died down.

I told him about Bawk's tuberculosis but he had no recriminations to offer for the woeful way I had overworked the girls. He asked what Bawk wanted to do and when she said that after two weeks at home she was going to push forward with the unit, he was well satisfied. I warned him that Bawk couldn't walk to their village on the mountaintop and he agreed to return home the next morning and send a horse for her on Saturday.

The next day Colonel Brown's tanks cleared the road junction at the 105th-mile post of the two large-barreled "snipers." When I drove Bawk down the road the next morning the great convoy was forming, ready to start for Kunming. Bawk's horse was waiting for her at Nawnglawng, a mile beyond the lead truck. I decided to do the thing in style. Ever since the fall of Burma in 1942 we had been serving the troops who were fighting to get convoys into China and now the first one was going through. General Sliney, the only other officer besides myself still left of those who had walked out with Stilwell, was just starting back for the States. Stilwell himself was gone. I had welcomed the army into Burma. Who was better entitled to bid them Godspeed on their way to China? I turned the jeep off the road, backed it to right angles, stood up on the hood, and took the salute. Generals, colonels, majors, sergeants, and even buck privates entered into the spirit of the occasion and gave me "Eyes Right!" and stiff, precise salutes, though they had broad grins on their faces at the presumption of that queer bird, the Burma Surgeon.

Tonight, as I write, the convoy is safely in Kunming. It is lonely without Uncle Joe here to celebrate with us. All the hospital wreckage has been cleared and everything looks as if a new building was in process of construction. Ah Kway, my old Chinese carpenter, is making new furniture out of the wrecked lumber. Soon he will start on new doors and windows. My American boys have fixed up the collapsed floors and are now jacking up roof trusses. The engineers are working with us and giving us salvaged equipment. The Shan men and women are down in the bed of the Namsari collecting new stone and gravel. A party is at work collecting limestone and firewood near the limekilns. Our hospital is running over five hundred beds. We are alerted to send a hundred-and-fifty-bed field hospital unit to Manpong down the Burma Road toward Lashio. Some officer once said that Seagrave's war would end at Namkham and that no one would be able to force him to leave, so I'm going to command that advance echelon myself with Drs. Ba Saw and Mildred Pan Hla. Just for spite I'm going to be the first member of our unit to leave.

For my personal war with the Japanese is not over. Kyang Tswi and Esther are at home with their parents. Big Bawk and Little Bawk, Kaw Naw, Ma Grawng, and "Chubby" Malang Kaw have had vacations with theirs. Tugboat Annie almost reached home but was turned back by Japanese patrols. But Julia, Naomi, Wasay, Saw Yin, Ruby, Emily, Chit Sein, Nang Aung, Pearl, Louise, and "Jackie" E Kyaing live far to the south. It will be months before these last of the refugees can return to their homes. They are happy here at Namkham in their adopted home, as I am. But not until they can see their people and then decide whether or not to continue nursing will my personal fight with the Japanese be over.

And after the war? With the clearing of the Japs from our territory the Kachin Christians held a great convention to which I was invited as guest speaker. I informed them of Britain's recently announced plan to give Burma complete self-government as soon as the havoc of war was cleared away and the country restored to a semblance of a peacetime basis. I reminded them that the real Burmese people greatly outnumbered the sum total of all the other peoples of Burma—the "tribes" as we call them: Kachins, Karens, Nagas, Lahus, Chins, and Taungthus; outnumbered them even if we included the Shans with the tribes. I reminded them that almost all the Christians of Burma were in this minority of the tribes; that not only had the Christians not yet discovered a common ground for co-operation with the Buddhist majority but that the native Baptists had never even come to regard the Methodists, Episcopalians, and Presbyterians as Christians like themselves.

"What will happen to you," I asked, "if, when Burma is given her independence, you have not resolved these differences between races and between faiths as these nurses of ours have resolved them? Oh, I realize it's the tribes of Burma that produce the real fighters and not the Burmese themselves. So what? Civil war? And do you think you will win without weapons? If other countries make weapons available it will be to the Burmese, the majority rulers of the country. No, it will be massacre, and already the census shows that you Kachins are dying out at the rate of 1 per cent per year from disease. There is only one hope for you if you wish your race, your Christianity, and your democratic spirit to live in Burma after the British withdraw. You must realize that your differences of race and faith are of little importance and that only one thing matters: that you are all citizens of Burma whether Kachin or Shan, Karen or Burmese, Christian or Buddhist. The nurses in our unit have proved it can be done. And in every way you must co-operate in our medical program for Burma."

I sat down feeling that I had surpassed myself and given a rather good speech. How would these people react to my advice? It was only a few minutes till I found out, for as we waited for dinner the Christian Kachin leader Ebbyn led me aside.

"Is it true," he asked me, much worried, "that there is a Catholic priest at work in the Myitkyina and Bhamo areas?"

"You mean Father Stewart? Yes, indeed. He stayed in Burma throughout the Japanese occupation and put us Baptists to shame. He has been a source of endless comfort to the people in all their troubles. He is a great man."

"Well, then," said Ebbyn, "we Christians must get a hustle on or he will be converting some of the Kachins to Catholicism."

"Aren't the Catholics Christians?" I asked.

"Well," he hesitated, "Catholics don't practice everything the Bible says."

"Do we Baptists? Listen, Ebbyn, when you get home you take your Bible and a pencil. If you're busy, never mind the Old Testament. And leave out all the Epistles if you must. But just read the four Gospels through carefully once more and underline everything Jesus taught that Baptists don't always practice. Be honest about it and if when you're done your Bible isn't rather badly marked up, I'll be greatly mistaken."

Ebbyn wouldn't eat dinner with me after that caustic remark.

And as soon as I had gone the executive committee of the Kachin Christians met to discuss the measures to be adopted to prevent the dying out of their race. I couldn't believe my ears when told that they had voted unanimously as follows: That if any Christian Kachin man desired to marry a girl of any other race whether Christian or not he should be permitted to do so, for the girl would become a Kachin. But if any Christian Kachin girl were to marry a man of any other race, even if that man were a Christian, she should be excommunicated from the church!

In spite of all the good the missionaries had done for the country they had failed to teach the people that they were all Burmese and that people of other denominations were Christians like themselves. The job I had had before the war was too small. I had trained nurses only, and though the girls had astonished not only me but a good part of the world by surmounting their racial and creedal differences for the good of their country and had shown a spirit of selfless, untiring, and loving service to the sick and wounded of all races, what good would that do if the men and the doctors had not grown in the same way at the same time?

Last night I lay awake hours remembering my old ruined dreams. Perhaps they were gone forever. But I could still dream of rebuilding so that my successor would start his work with a beautiful, modern hospital and not with a mass of rubble. And perhaps something still more wonderful might prove possible—a hospital of a thousand beds instead of three hundred; a hospital where young medical students could come for internship and surgical training, where the men of Burma would catch the spirit that seemed so beautiful to me in the girls of our unit; not a Baptist hospital alone but a Christian hospital; a hospital that would appeal to Americans whether church members or not; a hospital above denomination where Buddhists and animists could come and receive loving care when sick and learn that peace comes only to men of good will.

It was a beautiful dream—and outside the stars were shining.

Books That Live

The Norton imprint on a
book means that in the
publisher's estimation it
is a book not for a single
season but for the years.

W · W · NORTON & CO · INC.